PAKISTAN: A MULLAH–MILITARY ENTERPRISE UNLIMITED

PAKISTAN: A MULLAH-MILITARY ENTERPRISE UNLIMITED.

P. C. JOSHI

KALPAZ

Pakistan: A Mullah-Military Enterprise Unlimited

ISBN: 978-81-7835-929-8

Published in 2013 in India by
Kalpaz Publications
C-30, Satyawati Nagar,
Delhi-110052
E-mail: kalpaz@hotmail.com
Phone : 9212729499

Lasser Type Setting : Quick Media, Delhi
Printed at : Chawla Offset Printers, Delhi

Dedicated to the memory of
Late Shri Purnanand Sanwal
and
his daughter
Late Smt. Ganga Joshi
of
Anand Niwas, Nainital
Who put me on the path of progress way
back in 1958 and their debt I can not repay.

Contents

Preface

Many standard works on Pakistan by reputed writers that deal work all the topics in an 'exhaustive manner' are available in abundance but a book describing all the salient development of Pakistan 'at a glance' right form the day the idea of its inception was mooted till Gen. (Retd.) Pervez Musharraf resigned from Presidency, perhaps, was found wanting. The book "Pakistan-Mullah Military Enterprise Unlimited" narrating all such events in brevity with dates etc. in condensed form is ventured to meet such a requirement. In that sense it is a complete study of Pakistan.

Infiltration of religious extremists and other Islamic militants into India to fight proxy war in Kashmir, inciting locals/muslims to rise against the lawful governments in north eastern states and other places in India, pushing in drug and sending fake currency notes through Indo-Pak border or by Couriers via Nepal and Bangladesh, carrying out subversion sabotage and false propoganda crying violation of human rights by India are a few steps, clendestine activities apart, that ISI has been carrying out with impunity with a view to 'break India form within' as suggested by the former ISI chief Lt. Gen Asad Durrani and by way of inflicting a 'thousand cuts'. Immediate concerted action both defensive as well as offensive by India is the urgent requirement before it is too late. Late it already is.

There are certainly considerable number of people in Pakistan who desire excellent relations with India. But either they have no say or at times they get 'ISI's 'hospitality' as happened with Najm Sethi of the Friday Times, Lahore. Even if the democratic civilian' government desires balanced relations with India, the question is whether Pakistan Army and its ISI would at all allow it. They have to obey the dictates of Army so far as matters relating to India are concerned.

Gen. (Retd.) Pervez Musharraf had stated on April 12, 1999 that 'the low intensity conflict with India would continue even if the Kashmir problem is resolved." ISI on its part time and again has been punctuating India through its outsourced Taliban or militant Islamic outfits in doing some mischief or the other like bombing Indian Mission in Kabul on July 7, 2008, holding a meeting in Nepal on July 13, 2005 with LeT, JeM, SIMI and D. Company representatives of militant groups in North East to create disturbances and Communal violence, with the aim of cutting the strategic chickhens neck. Even President Barack Obama in an interview to Fox News in September 2008 said "we are providing them (Pakistan) military aid with having enough strings attached. They are not using it to defend Pakistan, they are preparing for a war against India."

While writing this book, special care has been taken not to transgress into the arena 'prohibitive' by concerned authorities under any Act or rules framed there under. Even moral and ethical considerations have been taken care of to avoid any controversial mention of any event though in the words of Shri Satinder Lambah former High Commissioner of India to Pakistan "Pakistani diplomats in India are hosted and Indian diplomats in Pakistan are roasted."

P. C. Joshi

Acknowledgement

My special thanks to Shri E.N. Rammohan IPS (Retd), former Director General BSF for his kind and timely succour for going through this book and making necessary suggestions and observations.

I also owe special thanks to my daughter-in-law Superna and my relative Shri Hari K. Mathur for helping me with all the required material from various websites.

My son Hari and his wife superna, second son Ravi and his wife Reema (Mona) and my daughter Mrs. Reema (Renu) Joshi and her husband Rakesh never let me feel any paucity of funds for buying latest books for references. Without financial support from Hari and Ravi, it would have been difficult to refer to the latest books on the subject. To all of them my deepest gratitude.

I am also grateful to SHRI K.L. MURADIA, Shri B. Jha and Shri V.P. Mahajan for bringing books for me from America and Canada.

Author

Rulers of Pakistan

Governor Generals

1.	Qaide Azam Muhammad Ali Jinnah	–	Aug. 15, 1947 to Sept. 11, 1948
2.	Khwaja Nazimuddin	–	Sept. 14, 1948 – Oct. 16, 1951
3.	Malik Ghulam Muhammad	–	Oct. 17, 1951 to Oct. 5, 1955
4.	Maj. Gen. Iskander Mirza	–	Oct. 6, 1955 to March 22, 1956

Presidents of Pakistan

1.	Maj. Gen. Iskandar Mirza	–	March 23, 1956 to Oct. 27, 1958
2.	Field Marshal Muhammad Ayub Khan	–	Oct. 27, 1958 to March 25, 1969
3.	Gen. Yahya Khan	–	March 25, 1969 to Dec. 20, 1971
4.	Z.A. Bhutto	–	Dec. 20, 1971 to Aug. 13, 1973
5.	Chaudhary Fazal Elahi	–	Aug. 14, 1973 to Sept. 16, 1978
6.	Gen. Zia-ul-Haq	–	Sept. 16, 1978 to Aug. 17, 1988
7.	Ghulam Ishaq Khan	–	(*i*) Aug. 17 to Dec. 13, 1988. (*ii*) Dec. 13, 1988 to July 18, 1993.
8.	Wasim Sajjad	–	July 18, 1993 to Nov. 13, 1993.

9. Farooq Leghari – Nov. 14, 1993 to Dec. 2, 1997
10. Rafiq Tarar – Jan. 1, 1998 to June 20, 2001
11. Gen. Pervez Musharraf – (*i*) June 20, 2001 – Nov. 29, 2007 (*ii*) Nov. 29, 2007 to Aug. 18, 2008.
12. Muhammad Mian Soomro – Aug. 18, 2008 to Sept. 9, 2008 (Acting)
13. Asif Ali Zardari – Sept. 9, 2008 continues.

Prime Ministers of Pakistan

1. Liaqat Ali Khan – Aug. 15, 1947 to Oct. 16, 1951.
2. Khawaja Nazimuddin – Oct. 17, 1951 to April 17, 1953
3. Muhammad Ali Bogra – April 17, 1953 to Aug. 11, 1955
4. Chaudhury Muhammad Ali – Aug. 11, 1955 to Sept. 12, 1956
5. H.S. Suhrawardi – Sept. 12, 1956 to Oct. 18, 1957
6. I.I. Chundrigar – Oct 18, 1957 to Dec. 16, 1957
7. Malik Feroz Khan – Dec. 16, 1957 to Oct. 7, 1958
8. Gen. Muhammad Ayub Khan – Oct. 24, 1958 to Oct. 27, 1958
9. Noorul Amin – Dec. 7, 1971 to Dec. 20, 1971
10. Z A Bhutto – Aug. 14, 1973 to July 4, 1977
11. Muhammad Khan Junego – March 23, 1985 to May 29, 1988.

12. Benazir Bhutto – Dec 2. 1988 to Aug. 6, 1990
13. Ghulam Mustafa Jatoi – Aug. 6, 1990 to Nov. 6, 1990.
14. Nawaz Sharif (*i*) Nov. 6, 1990 to April 18, 1993.
    (*ii*) May 26, 1993 to July 18, 1993.
15. Balkh Sher Mazari – April 18, 1993 to May 26, 1993.
16. Moeen Qureshi – July 18, 1993 to Oct. 19, 1993.
17. Benazir Bhutto – Oct 19, 1993 to Nov 4, 1996.
18. Malik Meraj Khalid – Nov. 5, 1996 to Feb. 17, 1997.
19. Nawaz Sharif – Feb. 17, 1997 to Oct. 12, 1999.
20. Zafrullah Khan Jamali – Nov. 23, 2002 to June 26, 2004.
21. Chaudhary Shujat Hussain – June 30, 2004 to Aug. 27, 2004.
22. Shaukat Aziz – Aug. 27, 2004 to Nov. 15, 2007.
23. Mohammadmian Soomro – Nov. 16, 2007 to March 24, 2008.
24. Yusuf Raza Gilani – March 25, 2008 continues.

Chief Martial Law Administrators

1. Field Marshal Muhammad Ayub Khan – Oct. 7, 1958 to June, 8, 1962.
2. Gen. Agha Muhammad Yahya Khan – March 25, 1969 to Dec. 20, 1971.
3. Z.A. Bhutto – Dec. 20, 1971 to April 21,

		1972
4. Gen. Zia-ul-Haq	–	July 5, 1977 to Dec. 30, 1985.

Chiefs of Pakistan Army

1. Gen. Sir Frank Messervy	–	Aug. 14 1947 to Feb. 15, 1948.
2. Gen. Sir Douglas Gracy	–	Feb. 15, 1948 to Jan. 16 1951.
3. Field Marshal Ayub Khan	–	Jan. 17, 1951 to Oct. 27, 1958.
4. Gen. Mohd Musa	–	Oct. 27, 1958 to Sept. 17, 1966.
5. Gen. Yahya Khan	–	Sept. 18, 1966 to Dec. 19, 1971.
6. Lt. Gen Gul Hasan	–	Dec. 20, 1971 to March 2, 1972.
7. Gen. Tikka Khan	–	March 3, 1972 to Feb. 28, 1976.
8. Gen. Mohd Zia ul Haq	–	March 1, 1976 to Aug. 17, 1988.
9. Gen. Mirza Aslam Beg	–	Aug. 17, 1988 to Aug. 15, 1991.
10. Gen. Asif Nawaz	–	Aug. 17, 1991 to Jan. 8, 1993.
11. Gen. Abdul Waheed Kakar	–	Jan. 12, 1993 to Jan. 11, 1996.
12. Gen. Jehangir Karamat	–	Jan 12, 1996 to Oct. 7, 1998
13. Gen. Pervez Musharraf	–	Oct. 7, 1988 to Nov. 28, 2007.
14. Gen. Ashfaq Parvez Kayani	–	Nov. 29, 2007 continues.

ISI Chiefs (Since 1965)

1. Brig. Riyaz Hussain Khan	–	(1965–66) He was DG ISI on Jan. 10, 1966 when Tashkent Declaration was signed.
2. Brig. Mohammad	–	Served under Gen. Ayub

Hayat		Khan regime
3. Maj. Gen. Akbar Khan	–	under the regime of Gen Ayub and Gen. Yahya Khan.
4. Lt. Gen. Ghulam Jilani Khan	–	1970–1977 under Gen Yahya, ZA Bhutto & Zia-ul-Haq.
5. Maj. Gen. Riaz Mohammad Khan	–	(July 1977 to June 1979) He died of heart attack.
6. Lt. Gen. Akhtar Abdul Rehman	–	June 1979 to March 1987.
7. Lt. Gen. Hamid Gul	–	March, 1987–April 10, 1989
8. Lt. Gen. (Retd.) Shamsher Rehman Kallu	–	May 24, 1989 to Aug. 1990.
9. Lt. Gen. Asad Durrani	–	Aug. 1990 to March 1992.
10. Lt. Gen. Javed Nasir	–	March 1992 to May 1993.
11. Lt. Gen. Javed Ashraf Qazi	–	May 1993 to Aug. 1995.
12. Maj. Gen. Nasim Rana	–	Aug. 5, 1995 Oct. 12, 1998.
13. Lt. Gen. Khawaja Ziauddin Abbasi	–	Oct. 12, 1998 to Oct. 12, 1999.
14. Lt. Gen. Jamshed Gulzar	–	Acting chief form Oct. 12, to Oct. 20, 1999.
15. Lt. Gen. Mahmood Ahmed	–	Oct 20, 1999 to Oct. 7, 2001.
16. Lt. Gen. Ehsan-ul-Haq	–	Oct. 7, 2001 to Oct. 2, 2004.
17. Lt. Gen. Ashfaq Kayani	–	Oct. 3, 2004 to 21 Sept. 2007.
18. Lt. Gen. Nadeem Taj	–	21 Sept. 2007 to Sept. 29, 2008
19. Lt. Gen. Ahmed Shuja Pasha	–	Sept. 29, 2008 to Continues.
20. Lt. Gen. Zahir	–	ul-islam-March 19, 2012

Milestones

Aug. 14,	1947 :	Pakistan came into existence at midnight
Oct. 24,	1947 :	State of Azad Kashmir comprising areas of Poonch, Muzaffarabad came into being under sardar Muhammad Ibrahim.
Oct. 26,	1947 :	Pakistan invades Kashmir. War lasts until Jan. 1949. Hostility broke out an Oct. 22, 1947 itself.
Sept. 11,	1948 :	Qaid-e-Azam Mohammad Ali Jinah expires in Karachi.
Jan. 1,	1949 :	Un Security Council orders ceasfire in Kashmir.
Oct. 16,	1951 :	P.M. Liaqat Ali Khan shot dead in Rawalpindi.
Sept. 8,	1954 :	Pakistan Joined SEATO
Feb. 24,	1955 :	Pakistan signs Bagdad pact (later became CENTO).
Mar. 23,	1956 :	Pakistan became Republic. Adopts name of Islamic Republic of Pakistan. First Constitution passed. Maj. Gen Iskendar Mirza becomes first President.
Oct. 7,	1958 :	Governor General Iskandar Mirza enforces 1st Martial Law. Ayub Khan becomes Chief Martial Law Administrator.
Oct. 24,	1958 :	Ayub Khan becomes Prime Minister.
May 1,	1959 :	System of 'Basis Democracies' introduced which was adopted on June 12–13, 1959. Capital shifted to Islamabad from Karachi.
Sept. 19,	1960 :	Indus Treaty signed at Karachi between Nehru, Ayub and Mr. I liff, vice President of world Bank.

Mar. 1,	1962 :	New Constitution enacted. Martial law lifted on June 8.
April 28,	1962 :	Election for new National Assembly held under Basic Democracy System.
Feb. 24,	1963 :	Border Agreement with China.
Sept.6–22,	1965 :	17 days Full scale Indo-Pak war over Kashmir.
Dec. 22,	1965 :	Pakistans first atomic reactor inaugrated.
Jan. 10,	1966 :	Taskent Declaration signed. Forces of both the countries to be withdrawn to pre-Aug 5, 1965 position.
Nov.	1967 :	PPP formed.
Mar. 25,	1969 :	Ayub Khan resigns. Hands over power to Gen. Yahya Khan who promptly imposed Martial law.
	1970 :	1st general elections of the country on the basis of 'one man one vote'.
Dec. 3–17,	1971 :	Third full scale war between Pakistan and India. Dhaka fell and Pakistan dismembered. Bengladesh comes into existence.
Dec. 20,	1971 :	Gen. Yahya hands over power to Z.A. Bhutto.
April 20	1972 :	Martial Law lifted. Intrim constitution enforced.
June 18,	1972 :	G.M. Syed of Jeeya Sind Mahaz demands Provincial Atonomy.
July 2,	1972 :	Simla Agreement signed between India and Pakistan.
April 10,	1973 :	Parliament passes new constitution unanimously which came into force w.e.f. Aug. 14, 73.
April 28,	1973 :	Prisoners of 1971 War.
Aug. 14,	1973 :	Z.A. Bhutto took over as Prime Minister

		and Chaudhry Fazal Elahi as President of Pakistan.
Jan. 1, 1974	:	All Banks nationalised.
July 5, 1977	:	Gen. Zia-ul-Haq clamps down the 3rd Martial Law after seizing power. Bhutto arrested.
June 11, 1978	:	All Pakistan Muhajir Students Organisation formed
April 4, 1979	:	Z.A. Bhutto hanged till death.
Nov. 17, 1979	:	Elections postponed further. Gen. Zia announced process of Islamization and enforcement of various Hudood Laws.
Dec. 27, 1979	:	Soviets invade Afghanistan. US President Jimmy carter announced $ 400 million economic assistance to Pakistan.
Jan. 18, 1980	:	Gen. Zia described $ 400 million offer of aid to fight the soviets in Afghanistan by way of 'Jehad' as 'PEANUTS'. President Ronald Regan later on raised it to $ 3.2 billion.
Jan. 20, 1980	:	Islamaization of economic system of promulgating 'Zakat' and 'Zxshr' ordinances. Influx of Afghan refugees into Pakistan started consequent upon the soviet entry into Afghanistan.
March 1981	:	A Provisional Constitutional Order replaced 1973 Constitution to a large extent declaring Martial law as above the Judiciary.
Mar. 2, 1982	:	PIA plane hijacked to Kabul.
July 1, 1983	:	6th Five year plan launched. Movement for Restoration of Democracy (MRD) started against the Zia government.

		Gen. Zia introduced Majlis-e-Shura in place of Parliament amending the 1973 constitution.
May 1984	:	Mohajir Qaumi Movement emerged, out of All Pakistan Muhajir students Organisation formed on June 11, 1978.
Feb. 25, 1985	:	Non–Party elections held. Mohammad Khan Junejo oppointed Prime Minister.
Nov. 19, 1985	:	8th amendment to the Constitution passed giving Gen. Zia sweeping powers.
Dec. 30, 1985	:	Martial Law lifted.
Sept. 15, 1986	:	Pact for nuclear cooperation with China.
Feb. 2, 1987	:	Gen. Zia visits India to watch India-Pakistan cricket match.
April 10, 1988	:	Ojheri Ammunition Depot explosion.
Aug. 17, 1988	:	Gen Zia alongwith 29 other perishes in a plane C–130 crash in Bahawalpur.
Nov. 16, 1988	:	Benazir Bhutto and her party PPP win 39% of votes in general election.
Dec. 1, 1988	:	President Ghulam Ishaq Khan nominates Ms. Benazir as PM.
Dec. 13, 1988	:	Zia Confident Ghulam Ishaq Khan sworn in as President. On Dec. 12 he was elected President for 5 years.
Mar. 13, 1990	:	Benazir declares "Pakistan would fight "a thousand years' to free Kashmir.
Aug. 6, 1990	:	National Assembly dissolved. Benazir Bhutto sacked on charges of corruption. Ghulam Mustafa Jatoi, a Sindhi politician appointed caretaker PM.
Aug. 24, 1990	:	General elections held for 217 NA seats (207 for muslims and 10 for non-muslims). IJI and PPP were in the field.

Nov. 6, 1990	:	Nawaz Sharif elected Prime Minister.
Jan. 8, 1993	:	Gen. Asif Nawaz Janjua COAS dies all of a sudden in Army House in Rawalpindi.
Jan. 12, 1993	:	Gen. Abdul Waheed Kakar appointed new chief of Army staff.
April 18, 1993	:	Nawaz Sharifs government dismissed by Ghulam Ishaaq Khan. Balkh Sher Mazari appointed Caretaker P.M. Supreme court restored Nawaz government in May 93.
July 16, 1993	:	Banazir Bhutto called for long March on Islamabad.
July 18, 1993	:	President Ghulam Ishaq Khan and Prime Minister Nawaz Sharif simultaneously stepped down. Moeen Quereshi took over as Caretaker Prime Minister Wasim Sajjad as Acting President.
Oct. 6, 1993	:	Election held for 207 NA seats.
Oct. 19, 1993	:	Benazir became PM for the second time.
Nov. 13, 1993	:	Farooq Leghari elected President.
June 5, 1994	:	Nawaz Sharif asks President Leghari to explain involvement in Mehran Gate Scandal. accuses government of corruption and urges President Leghari to resign.
Sept. 20, 1996	:	Mir Murtaza Bhutto along with 7 Companions killed in Karachi.
Sept. 27, 1996	:	Kabul city fell to Pak created and aided Taliban
Nov. 5, 1996	:	Farooq Leghari dismisses Benazir government for humiliating Judges Corruption and economic mismanagement.

Jan.	7,	1997 :	Creation of 10–member Council for Defence & National Security (CDNS) took off.
Feb.	3,	1997 :	General elections held. PML–N wins by landslide margin. The nation goes to the polls 4th time in 10 years.
Feb.	5,	1997 :	PM elect Nawaz seeks closer ties with India.
Mar.	3,	1997 :	US identifies Pakistan as a major money laundering country.
Mar.	28,	1997 :	Peace talks at Foreign Secretary level between India and Pakistan resumed.
June	16,	1997 :	Writ filed in the Supreme Court for closure of ISI's political cell.
Dec.	2,	1997 :	President Farooq Leghari resigns.
May	28,	1998 :	Pakistan Conducts 5 nuclear tests in Chagai Range.
Jan.		1999 :	Pakistan intrudes into Kargil.
May		1999 :	India discovers incursions by Pakistan Army into Kargil and Drass area. Counter–measures takne by India in June–July 1999.
July	4,	1999 :	P.M. Nawaz Sharif rushes to Washington to meet President Clinton to seek his help to end fighting in Kargil.
Oct.	12,	1999 :	Gen. Pervez Musharraf takes over the country in a military coup. Nawaz Sharif overthrown and arrested.
Jan.	12,	2002 :	Musharraf said "Kashmir runs in our blood. No Pakistani Can afford to sever links with Kashmir... we will continue to extend our moral, political and diplomatic support to Kashmiris. We will never budge from our principle stand on Kashmir. Kashmir has to be resolved

through dialogue in accordance with the wishes of the people of Pakistan and in accordance with UN resolution."

Jan. 23, 2002 : Wall Street Journal's South Asia Bureau Chief Daniel Pearl kidnapped in Karachi and later murdered by his captors (For further references kindly see at page 148,–151, 163,–64 , 168–69)

Recent Blasts in Pakistan

2005

Mar. 20, : A bomb went off in a shrine in Gandhawa (220 miles east of Quetta) in which 44 persons killed and many injured.

2006

Mar. 2, : A suicide attack outside US Consulate in Lahore killed a diplomat and four others.

Nov, 8, : In Diplomat, a man wearing explosives attacked troops killing 42 soldiers, 20 injured.

2007

July 4, : six soldiers and two children killed in NWFP by a suicide bomber. In the same province elsewhere a roadside bomb aimed at Police killed 4 civilians.

July 8, : 3 Chinese workers were killed and 1 Chinese worker wounded in Peshawar by unidentified gunmen. 1 policeman was killed in a blast in NWFP.

July 14, : A suicide car-bomber attacked military convoy, killed 24 soldiers of para military forces and wouned 29 in North Waziristan.

July 15, : In a suicide bomb attack in Swat 16 people, most of them paramilitary soldiers, were killed. A suicide bomber targated a police recruiting centre in Dera Ismail Khan in NWFP killing 29.

July 17, : A suicide bomber killed 16 people outside a Court in Islamabad where suspended chief justice Mr. Iftikhar Chaudhary was scheduled to speak. In North Waziristan also a suicide bomber killed 4 person including 3 soldiers.

July 18, : Militants in North Waziristan attacked a security forces convoy and killed 17 soldiers.

July 19, : In 3 separate attacks in a single day in Hub, Hangus and Kohat at least 52 people killed.

July 27, : A suicide bomber attacked a restaurant in Lal Masjid complex in Islamabad. 13 people, most of them policemen, were killed.

Aug. 13, : On the eve of 60th Independence Day, a roadside bomb killed 4 persons in northwest Pakistan.

Sept. 1, : 3 para military soldiers and 2 children killed in Northwest Bajaur.

Sept. 4, : In Rawalpindi near GHQ 25 ISI personned killed by two suicide bombers when 2 bombs hit army bus.

Sept. 11, : A suicide bomber blew himself up inside a mini bus as Police try to arrest him killing 17 people in Dera Ismail Khan.

Sept. 13, : 20 Commandos tasked to track Osama bin Laden's network were killed by a suicide bomber in an Army Canteen near Islamabad.

Oct 1, : A suicide bomber disguised in a Burqa struck at a police checkpost in north western Pakistan killing at least 16 people.

Oct. 18, : One suicide attack and another small blast that targeted former PM Benazir Bhutto killed atleast 139 people in Karachi in a rally in her honour. She had returned to Karachi after 8 years self-exile.

Oct. 25, : A blast rips through a security forces vehicle of an army convoy in Swat Valley where by 30 people were killed which included 17 soldiers.

Nov. 24, : On the eve of the return of Nawaz Sharif form exile, 2 suicide attacks against security forces in Rawalpindi took place in which 35 persons were killed. An explosive-laden car rammed a ministry of Defence bus taking personnel to work while another bomber blew up his car at a checkpoint outside Army Headquarters.

Dec. 17, : 10 military recruits in north-western town of Kohat killed by suicide bomber.

Dec. 21, : A suicide bomber killed at least 41 persons in a mosque in North-west Pakistan during Eid prayers.

Dec. 27, : Benazir Bhutto was killed in a gun and bomb attack after a rally in Rawalpindi. 16 others were also killed in the deadly attack blast.

2008

Jan. 7, : Al–Qaeda linked militants in nort-hwest Pakistan attacked government sponsored peace movement and kill 8 persons.

Jan. 10, : A suicide bomber walked upto policemen stationed outside the Lahore High Court and set off explosives. 24 including 17 policement and 3 peroess by killed. 80 others injured.

Jan. 14, : 9 people killed in a bomb attack in Karachi.

Jan. 17, : A teen ager blew himself up in a shiite Muslim prayer Hall in Peshawar. Atleast 9 people were killed and 25 wounded.

Feb. 25, : 25 wounded suicide bomber killed 8 people including Lt. Gen. Mushtaq Baig in Rawalpindi.

Feb. 29, : Suicide bomber struck at funeral of a slain policeman in Swat Valley killing 40 persons.

Mar. 4, : 2 suicide bombers blew themselves in Naval

War College, Lahore. 8 persons killed and 24 injured.

Mar. 11, : Federal investigation Agency (FIA) building in Lahore attacked and destroyed by a suicide bomber. Another blast occured near Zardaris house in Lahore. In both the incidents 30 persons including 24 cops were killed and 200 injured.

June 2, : A suicide bomber blew up a car outside Danish Embasy in Islamabad killing 6 persons.

Aug. 13, : 9 persons killed and more than 35 injured in a suicide blast in Lahore targeting policemen on Guard duty on the eve of Independence Day. 2 policemen and a women were among the dead.

Aug. 19, : A bomb explodes in Dera Ismail Khan killing 23 people.

Aug. 21, : Outside the Weapons Factory of the Main Defence Industry Complex in Wah, two suicide bombers blew themselves up kill 67 and wounding 100 persons.

Sept. 6, : A suicide car bombing billed at least 35 people and wounded 80 at a police checkpost in Peshawar.

Sept. 20, : A Suicide Truck bomber attack Marriott Hotel in Islamabad killing 60 people and wonding 270. The hotel where mostly foreigners used to stay was completely burnt.

Oct. 7, : One person killed and 3 injured in 3 small bomb explosions in a juice shop in Garahi Shahu near Lahore. An unknown group called Tehreek-ul-Haya (Movement for Decency) claimed responsibility since the shop was considered as 'dating point' for lovers.

2009

Feb. 5, : In Dera Ghazi Khan, at least 24 people killed

in a shia mosque in suicide bombing.

Feb. 20, : In Dera Ismail Khan, suicide bomber killed 27 people and injured 65 in an attack on a funeral procession of a shia person killed a day earlier.

Mar. 3, : Sri Lankan cricket team that had gone to Lahore to play was attacked while on way to stadium by bus. 6 team members were injured when they were fired at. 7 police personnel guarding the team were killed. 12 terrorists attacked the cricket team near the Gaddafi Stadium. The Bus driver, Meher Mohammad Khalil who saved the team from a barrage of bullets and grenades, was invited to Sri Lanka on April 6, 2009 with his wife by the Sri Lankan government to spend a week in Luxary. Sri Lankan cricket board showered Sri Lankan Rupees one million on the braveheart Khalil.

Mar. 16, : A suicide attack occured side a restaurant and Taxi stand near crowded inter-city Bus stop in Pir Wadhai Chowk in Rawalpindi. The head of the suspected suicide bomber was found at the site. 14 people were killed and 18 others wounded.

Mar. 23, : In the Sitara market of Islamabad a suicide bomber blew himself up at the entrance of Police Special Branch building killing one Policeman who was on Guard duty and injuring 5 others. The suicide bomber was trying to enter the building.

Mar. 27, : 50 persons killed in a mosque in northern-eastern town of Jamrud when a suicide bomber blew off the mosque.

Mar. 30, : Police training academy was attacked which is located on the outskirts of Lahore i.e. at Manawan. 4 terrorists were killed and 3 captured. 8 cadets were killed wounding scores of others. Operation last for about 8 hour begining for 7.20 a.m.

April 4, : A suicide bomber blew himself up inside a base of para military troops Frontier Constabulury camp in Jinah Super market in Islamabad in which eight troops were killed and several injured. It was followed by Gun fire also.

April 4, : A suicide bomber attempted to target a security forces convoy that was going form Bannu to Miran Shah in North Waziristan The bomber detonated his explosive laden car when the security forces opened fire at him. 17 persons including 5 children were killed and 30 injured.

April 5, : A crouded Shia mosque in Chakwal (Punjab) was attacked by a teeenage suicide bomber About 30 people of the religious gathering were killed. Fedayeen al-Islam claimed the responsibility for the Shia-mosque attack. 200 injured.

April 15, : An explosive laden vehicle was rammed into a policy/security checkpost in Tangi area of Charsadda district in NWFP. 16 people including 10 policement killed

April 16, : Militants blew up a women in the office of an NGO and a cable TV network in NWFP. Taliban termed the attack as a compaign against 'vulgarity and obscenity.'

April 18, : A suicide attacker detonated a car bomb into a police checkpost killing 23 people most of them security personnel in Doaba, a town in restive Hangu tribal district.

A total of 1395 people have been killed in 1942 terrorist strikes during the last 15 months in Pakistan which includes seven terrorists in Islamabad in which 87 people were killed since January 2008 to March 2009.

April 25, : A bomb disguised as a toy exploded outside a primary girls school in Luqman Banda village of Dir district in NWFP. 13 children most of them girls killed. 40 houndred.

April 26, : An explosion in a vehile killed 6 people in North Waziristan. Injured children were treated in Miran Shah hospital.

May 11, : A suicide bomber killed 10 people at a security post including two para-military soliders in the outskirts of Peshawar city.

May 16, : In Peshawar, a car bomb ripped through a street killing people.

May 22, : Five persons killed, 20 injured in a powerful car bomb blast that targeted a Cinema Hall in Peshawar

May 27, : Tehrik-e-Taliban Punjab claimed responsibility for two suicide bombing of a Lahore Police Buliding killing 24 people. It was ISI buliding. Lohore blast was done to avenge SWAT operation.

May 28, : Three bombs exploded in Peshawar killing 5 people and injuring over 70, A suicide bomber rammed a car parked with explosives to a police checkpoint on Peshawars outskirts. In yet another attack, 13 people wer wounded when a terrorist exploded an auto rikshaw near a police point in Dera Ismail Khan.

June 1, : Four persons were killed and 13 others injured when a bomb exploded at a crowded bus stand in Kohat town.

June 4, : Militants shot 5 policemen and a soldier after targeting a convoy with a roadside bomb in Mardan first.

June 5, : A suicide bomber struck Friday – prayers at a crowded Mosque in Hayagai Sherqi in Dir area (NWFP). 40 persons were killed.

June 6, : A suicide bomber blew himself up at the office of a Police Emergency Response unit (Rescue Unit 15) in G–8 sector of Islamabad injuring 4.

June 9, : In a massive explosion, a suicide bomber attacked Pearl Continental Hotel in Peshawar city killing 23 people including two UN officials and injuring over 50.

June 11, : (*i*) Bomb in train toilet killed one and injured 35. The train was tracking form Karachi to Quetta

(*ii*) A Taliban suicide attacher carried a deadliest attack at a police checkpost near Pearl Continental Hotel in Peshawar killing two police constables and blowing himself up and injuring 14 perons.

June 12, : Taliban killed Dr. Sarfaraz Naeemi, an anti Taliban cleric, Principle of Jamia. Naeemia seminary in Lahore. In another attack, a vehicle full of explosives hit an army mosque in Nowshera leaves 6 people dead and more than 90 injured.

June 14, : A suicide bomb killed 8 people in a busy pir market in Dera Ismail Khan.

June 26, : (*i*) A suicide bomber forced his way into pok and killed two soliders, injured 3. It was first such attack in Pok.

(*ii*) In Peshawar, militants bombed a girls Primary School using 40 kg of explosives.

(*iii*) In South Waziristan, 4 soldiers were killed and 18 injured in remote controlled bomb attack on a Convoy.

June 30, : In first ever incident of suicide bombing in kalat area (Baluchistan). a hotel was targeted 5 killed and 11 injured

July 2, : A motor cycle born suicide bomber ramed his bike against a bus belonging to Heavy Mechanical Complex, a military weapons manufacturing facility at Chur Chowk Junction in Rawalpindi killing himself and 6 others and injuring 36. Amir Mir Journalist said the bus was carrying ISI personnel.

July 13, : In a massive blast in the house of a clerik in a village on the outskirts of Mian Channu near Multan, 11 people killed and 100 injured destroying 25 houses in its immediate vicinity. Explosive Cache seemed to have been stored in the house which ignited. Police foend four(4) Jackets used by suicide bomber and six(6) Rocket Launchers in the rubble.

Aug. 10, : (*i*) A roadside bombing in Matani, Peshawar.

(*ii*) Interior Minister Rehman Malik said that Pak security forces foiled a plan to attack the HQ of country's Spy Agency and the Parliament House.

Aug. 15, : A suicide car bomber struck into an Army Checkpost near Khwazakhel in which 6 persons including 5 soliders were killed and 4 injured.

Aug. 17, : A bomb planted in a pick up exploded at a Petrol Pump in Shabqadr in Charsadda area. 7 people including 3 children killed and 15 injured. Qari Shakeel, Commander Tehrik-e-Taliban Pakistan claimed responsibility for the deadly explosion.

Aug. 27, : A suicide bomber struck at a checkpost in Khyber region near Torkham border in Pakistan's tribal belt. 22 persons mostly security personnel killed. Pak Taliban claimed responsibility stating that it was the first retaliation for thier leader Baitullah Mehsud's death on August 5, 2009.

Aug. 30, : A suicide bomber blew himself up at a police training station ground in Mingora town. 14 police trainee killed and 22 injured.

Dec. 4, 2009 Hashim Masood (19) the only son of Lt. Gen. Masood Alam, Corps Commander Peshawar was killed in a blast in Mosque.

Total deaths in terrorist attacks since 2003 :

2003 189

2004 863

2005 648

2006 1471

2007 3599

2008 6715 – of the 965 people killed by human bombs in the year 2008, the number of civilian Casualities stood at 651, security personnel at 159, 155 policemen.

2009

2010 – 52 suicide attacks. 1224 people killed.

2011 – (till May 2011) 21 attacks 377 killed.

Terrorist Attacks Against Police

2005	113
2007	1820

Total death toll for policemen in this period rose form 9 to 575.

Fact File

1. Geographically located between latitudes of 23°30′ and 36°45′ north and between the longtitudes of 61° and 75°31′ east. It land area in 778,720 Sq. Km. Pakistan Shares 595 km long border with china in the north, 2,252 km long border (Durand Line) with Afghanistan in the North-west, 805 Km long boundary with Iran in South-west and 1,610 km long border with India in the East: The southern border of Pakistan Consists of 700 Kilometers Coastline which run along the Arabian sea form the border of Iran in the west to Rann of Kutch in the east.
2. Population : In August 1947 it was 32.5 million. But now it is 172,800,048 with a growth of 1.9%. Population consists of Punjabi 44.65%, Pakhtoom 15.42% Sindhi 14.1%. Sairaki 8.38% Baluchis 3.57% and others 6.28%. Muslim who migrated form India and are called Mohajirs are 7.57%. Pakistans census of 1998 showed 2443614 Hindus, simply under 2%. Hindus in Pakistan are allolted separate electroate. Prominent people amongst Hindus mainly based in Sindh province, particularly in Karachi are Ex chief Justice Rana Bhagwan Das. Fámous Crictker Danish Kaneria and Fashion designer Deepak Perwani also have their place. One Sikh gentleman has also been inducted into Pakistan Army as a commissioned officer. Muslims stand devided among Shias and Sunnies. Shias consists of 20% and Sunnis 79% Christian and Hindus together consist of 5%.
3. Languages : Urdu is official language. Punjabi is spoken by 48%, sindhi by 12%, Sairaki by 10% and Pashto by 8% and Balochi by 3%.

4. National Holiday is on March 23 known as Republic Day. It was an March 23 1940 a resolution at Lahore was passed to create Pakistan.

5. CONSTITUTION : Pakistans Constitution saw many ups and downs. On April 12, 1973 it was passed but on July 5, 1977 it was suspended. On December 30, 1985 it was restored only to be suspended again on October 15, 1999 by Gen. Musharraf who imposed Army Rule in Pakistan. The Constitution was restored in stages in 2002 and amended on December 31, 2003. It was once again suspended on November 3, 2007 when Gen Musharraf slapped Emergency in the country. It was restored on December 15, 2007 mainly under pressure from the united states of Amierca.

6. GDP : is $ 160.9 billion (official Exchange Rate). GDP (Purchasing Power Parity) US $ 451.2 billion 2007 was 3% of the GDP.

Unemployment Rate	7.4%
Public debt	49.8% of GDP
External debt	US $ 43.23 billion till 2008
Inflation	24.4% in 2008
Literacy rale	42% for female and 67% for male.

7. **NATIONAL ANTHEM : Poet Hafeez Jullundhari wrote the words. Ghulam Ali chagla set the Pakistan National Anthem to music. He has been honoured 4 years after his death and 43 years after his official regonition of his composition.**

8. **Pakistans Common Borders with Neighbours**

Pak – Afghan border (Durand Line)	2,252 Km
Pak – Iran border	805 Km.
Pak – India border	1,610 Km.
Pak – China border	595 Km.

8. **Administrative Group :**

DMC – District Management group

SG – Secretariat Group

PSP – Police Service of Pakistan

OMG – Officers Managment Group

Pakistans Civil Awards :

(i) Nishan–e–Pakistan (Highest Civil Award)
(ii) Nishan–i–Imtiaz
(iii) Hilal–i–Shujaat
(iv) Sitara–i–Imtiaz
(v) Sitara–i–Quaid–e–Azam
(vi) Tamga–i–Shujat
(vii) Tamga-i-Imtiaz

Military Awards :

(i) Nishan–i–Haider (NH) (Highest Military Award)
(ii) Hilal–i–Jurat (HJ)
(iii) Sitara–i–Jurat (SJ)
(iv) Tampha–i–Jurat (TJ)
(v) Sitara–i–Basalat (SB)
(vi) Tamgha–i–Basalat (TB)
(vii) Tamgha–i–Khidmat (TK)

Pakistan Army :

6, 20, 000 on active duty

11 corps. 7th largest Army in the world.

Army owns 11.58 acres of land and assets

worth $ 20 billion. Runs a number of business.

Present day Pak based Transnational Terrorist Outfits

1. Hiz-ul-Mujahideen
2. Harkat-ul-Ansar (non Harkat-ul-Mujahideen)
3. Lashkar-e-Tayyeba or Taiba or Toiba (LeT)

4. Jaish-e-Mohammad
5. Al Badr
6. Lashkar-e-Jabbar
7. Jamait-ul-Mujahideen
8. Harkat-ul-Jehad-al-Islami
9. Muttahida Jehad Council
10. Tehrik-ul-Mujahideen
11. Ikhwan-ul-Mujahideen
12. Islamic students League
13. Tehrik-e-Hurriat-e-Kashmir
14. Tehrik-e-Nifaz-e-Fiqar Zaffaria
15. Al Mustafa Liberation Fighters
16. Tehrik-e-Jehad-e-Islami
17. Muslim Mujahideen
18. Al Mujahid Force
19. Tehrik-e-Jihad
20. Al Barq
21. Tamir-e-Nau
22. Al Qaida
23. Afghan and Pakistan Taliban (Tehrik Taliban Pakistan)
24. Sectarian groups
    (*i*) Sipah-e-Sahaba (for sunnis)
    (*ii*) Tehrik-e-Jafria (For Shias)

Pakistani Terrorists Detained at Gitmo after 9/11

At Cuba's Guantanamo Bay prison, 67 Pakistan's terrorists were detained by the USA following 9/11 attacks on USA. The prison is managed by CIA. List of most wanted 40 persons Indians as well as Pakistanis (The Times of India, December, 13, 2008) given to Pakistan by India demanding their handing over[x]

'Khalistani' militant groups

1. Gajinder Singh Khalsa (Dal Khalsa. Involved in hijacking of Indian Airlines aircrafts in 1981)
2. Lakhbir Sing (ISYF – Rocle group)
3. Paramjit Singh (Khalistan Commando Force)
4. Ranjit Singh a.k.a Neeta
5. Wadhwa Singh (Babbar Khalsa Internatinal (BKI)–

IC – 14 Hijacking

1. Althar Ibrahim (Pak national)
2. Azhar Yusuf & Mohammed Salik (Pak national)
3. Zahir Ibrahim Mistri (Pak national)
4. Syeed Shahid Akhtar (Indian)
5. Shakir Mohammed @ Sarkar (Pak national)–
6. Abdul Rauf (Pak national)

Parliament House Attack in 2001

Maula Masood Azhar – JeM Chief (Pak national)

Terrorists Involved in J & K Military

1. Mohammed Yusuf Shah a.k.a Salauddin, Pak national – Supreme Commander of Hizab-ul-Mujahideen
2. Amanullah Khan (Pak national) JKLF
3. Feroz Abdul (Pak national)
4. Zakiur Rehman Lakvi (Pak national) involved in Mumbai terror attack (Nov. 26–29, 2008)
5. Amir Raz Khan–(Pak national)–Ahmedabad Serial blasts 2008.

Five Hijackers of IC 814 on December 24, 1999

1. Ibrahim Athar alian chief (brother of Masood Azhar)
2. Sunny Ahmad Qazi alias Burger
3. Shahid Sayeed Akhtar alias Moti or Doctor
4. Zahoor Ibrahim Mistri alias Bhola

5. Shakir alias Shankar alias R.G. Verma all of them are still at large

Co-conspirators

1. Abdul Rauf (Maulana Masood Azhar's brother)
2. Yusuf Azhar (Masood Azhar's brother-in-law)-still absconding. All these 7 persons are Pakistani nationals.

Three Terrorists Who were Freed on December 31, 1999 of IC-184 with 179 Passengers. Total 192 people.

1. Maulana Masood Azhar s/o Allah Baksh Sabir (He founded Jaish-e-Mohammad)
2. Omar Sheikh or Omar Sayeed Sheikh (He is in jail in Karachi for murder of wall street journalist Daniel Pearl)
3. Mustaq Ahmed Zargar (He is from Al-umer Mujahideen)

Three Conspirators of IC–184 Incident

1. Abdul Latif of Mumbai
2. Dalip Kumar Bhujail of Kalimpong
3. Yusuf Nepali from Nepal

   (They had arranged fake passports for hijackers, for their stay and arms etc) since they were only support players, they were sentenced on Feb 5, 2008. seven years RI and fine of Rs 10,000 were charged under sections. Latif was sentenced to Life.

   307 IPC — attempt to murder
   363 IPC — Kidnapping and abduction, 5 year prison lern
   342 IPC — Wrongful confinements.

6. Mohammed Abdul Sahid @ Bilal (Pak national HUJI Commander
7. Azam Cheema (Pak national)
8. Rahil Sheikh

D-Company + 1993 Mumbai blasts + smuggling of Arms and Ammunition, Counterferit Currency, Human Trafficking

1. Dawood Ibrahim

2. Ibrahim (Tigar) Memon
3. Ayub Memon
4. Anis Memon
5. Sheikh Shakeel @ Chota Shakeel
6. Anwar Ahmed Haji
7. Mohammed Ahmed Dosa
8. Ishaq Hussain @ Ali Moosa
9. Sagir Sabir Ali Sheikh
10. Aftab Batk (Pakistans national)
11. Javed Patel @ Tailor
12. Karimulla Habib Sheikh
13. Salim Abdul Ghani Gazi
14. Riyaz Abu Bakar
15. Munaf Abdul Majid
16. Mohammed Tanvir
17. Khan Bashir Ahmed Ainul
18. Yakub Khan
19. Mohammed Shafi.
20. Irfan Ahmed.

Planes Hijacked to Pakistan from India

Sept. 29, 1971 : Srinagar bound Indian Air lines Plane diverted to Islamabad by Kashmiri militants.

Sept. 29, 1981 : Delhi–Srinagar 1A flight diverted to Lahore by Sikh militants.

Sept. 13, 1984 : Srinagar–Delhi flight of Indian Air lines taken to Lahore by Sikh militants.

Dec. 24, 1999 : IC–184 form Kathmandu diverted to Lahore and ultimately landed at Kandhar.

1
A Glance at The Creation of Pakistan and Growth of IB and ISI

India's struggle for independence, mostly led by Hindus, in a way began in 1920s. In thirtees All India Muslim League, which was organised mainly by 1930s Muslim from UP (then known as United provinces) saw an opportunity in 1906 in Dhaka and towed with the idea of having a separate muslim homeland. Major part in the formation of All India Muslim League was played by muslim from Muhammadan Anglo-Oriental College, Aligarh founded by Syed Ahmad Khan in 1875. A Muslim poet Iqbal originated the idea of Darul Islam and emphasised such a need for an independent home state (Dar-ul-Islam) for Muslims. Chowdhary Rehmat Ali who was till then staying in England named such a Muslim independent and separate homeland as Pakistan in 1933 and founded an organisation named as Pakistan National Movement. Nawabzada Liaqat Ali Khan, a leader of Muslim League, assigned the task of taking up welfare of Muslims in the sub-continent to Mohammad Ali Jinnah, who had already joined muslim league in 1913 itself and had returned to India in 1935 form England. The activities of Indian National Congress for independence were seen by Muslim League as against muslim and an idea which gained immediate currency was spread. And the idea so spread was Islam was in danger. In fact the Indian National Congress was considered as a party of Hindus and fear psychosis of "Congress-Raj" which indirectly meant 'Hindu Raj' in the estimation of Muslims, gripped their minds. The decades of thirtees and forties were full of activities by leaders of congress as well as that of Muslim League which ultimately led the Muslim League to hold a convention in Lahore on March 23, 1940 where a resolution was moved by A.K.M. Fazlul Haq, a Bengali muslim which was passed to form/demand a muslim state or muslim majority areas. Unity of muslim was their main plank in putting forward this demand. When some of the Muslims did not support the demand for partition Muslim League gave a slogan" Muslim hai to Muslim League main Aaa" (If you are a Muslim, join the Muslim League). In remembrance of this convention of March 23, Pakistan celebrates it National Day of March 23 each year. By November Lahore Convention came to a more concrete shape when Sir Abdullah Haroon Committee demanded a muslim state in the north-western portion of India and the other one in the north-east which was also a muslim majority area. All through Jinaah and his corhorts remained apprehensive of Hindu dominance. The two nation theory which propounds that muslims and hindus could not co-exist was a product of such an apprehension based on history and culture of both the religion. The times of early forties were such that the British rulers were already overworked and vexed because of world war-II. Congress was demanding immediate withdrawal of Britishers from India passing resolution of July 14, 1942. Quit India movement gathered momentum on ultimately facing British Parliament to approve India Independence Act on July 1, 1947 which led to the creation of separate muslim homeland called Pakistan on Aug. 14, 1947 and made rest of the India and independent nation granting freedom on Aug 15. India was partitioned or Communal lines. Thousands and Thousands of muslims mainly form UP migrated to Pakistan. Justice Mohammad Carim, Chagla has opined in his autobiography "Roses in December" that but for the demand of Uttar Pradesh muslims, there would have been no Pakistan. It was Sadly followed with more than one million people butchered on both sides of nearly demarcated borders and ten million people migrated, from India to Pakistan and vice versa. Country's division also saw birfurcation of national assets, Civil Services and Intelligence gathering machinery which was Intelligence Bureau at that time. M.A. Jinnah stated that muslims left behind in India and vice versa i.e. hindus left behind in Pakistan would be treated as "Reciprocal Hostages". But this idea is totally negated now. ISI, IB and MI besides other small and local agencies Even Mohajirs i.e. those who migrated to Pakistan in 1947 and who were responsible for creating Pakistan are viewed with suspension. In all enquiries against a person there is a column stating "Is he/she a Mohajir?" Indian muslim girls seem to be very happy and eager to marry Pakistani muslim groom but once they do that, they are not treated in a dignified way in their places of marriages. Most of them long to return to their parents back in India. While seeking visa to return to India they narrate very bitter and sad tales of their experiences. Believe it or not, they are treated like "use and throw." Hindus living in Sindh remain under constant fear. Either they are compelled to convert to Islam or their daughters under threat are kidnapped and muslims forcibly marry them. In most of the case no police action in taken by Muslim police or even the Hindu parents are killed by the muslim who forcibly marries their daughters. Most of the Hindus want to migrate to India but cannot do so because of constraints at the policy level of the governments. Their plight is horrible.

The country called Pakistan is, indeed a beautiful place, its capital Islamabad superb and idylic. Pakistani are a wonderful people, very hospitable, courteous, industrious, vivacious and deeply religious which has now turned into fundamentalism and intolerance. In good olden times the area now known as Pakistan was inhabited and blessed by holy saints, hermits and many pious souls. Lord Ram's son Luv and Kush were there. Mahabharats Gandhari belonged to that area i.e. Gandhar which was a flourishing culture under Kushan Kings, Gautam Buddha, Emperor Ashok, Guru Nanak Dev ji and even many muslim saints had bestowed the area. Lord Shiva had its temple in Katasraj. The great economist and politician Chanakya was born in Chiniot. Taxila was a celebrated seat of learning. Mohan Jo Daro was a symbol of a highly developed civilization. Pakistan's survival today, inspite of so many odds and their adverse thinking and attitude towards India, can certainly be attributed to the fact all these godly people, saints and scholars had once blessed the area, some after-effects are still continuing. But the impact of their blessings now seem to be obliterating gradually and slowly and the country now faces serious multifarious problem. The founder of Pakistan Mohammed Ali Jinnah wanted to build Pakistan a secular state with a muslim identity where there could be tolerance for religious minorities, a civil code and secular educational system. Jinnah said "I would rather be protector general of the rights of the Hindu minority in Pakistan than the governor-general of Pakistan. You will find in the course of time Hindus would cease to be Hindu and Muslims would cease to be muslims, not in the religious sense, because that is the personal faith of each individual but in the political sanse, as citizens of the state...." Pakistanis have put sincere efforts of prove Jinnah 'Otherwise' in this regards.

No sooner Pakistan came into existence in August, 1947 it had one point programme-take Kashmir by hook or crook and continue hatred against India and hindus. The initial impression that the Congress was a hindu organisation has been wiped out of their minds. Instead of setting down in a newly created nation and looking after muslim who had migrated from India into, Pakistan, the Pakistan Army and authorities made 'Kabayalis' (tribals) to attack Kashmir in October, 1947, it self, just after two months of its inception with a view to annex Kashmir with Pakistan. Ghulam Ishaq Khan, who later on rose to become president of the country happened to be in Srinagar town in August 14, 1947 i.e. the day of its creation. He was accompanied by Roedad Khan who later on Joined civil services of Pakistan in 1949. While driving through Srinagar, Ghulam Ishaq Khan would ask his driver to slow down the car every now and then and address the nearest Kashmiri and ask him to say "Pakistan Zindabad" and pay him a rupee. Such was the obsession for Kashmir, Mohammad Ali Jinnah had himself ordered attack on Srinagar Kashmir on October 27, 1947 and by midnight of October 29, Pak raiders under the Command of Akbar Khan who was known as 'Gen. Tariq' were just 4 miles from Srinagar. Incidently, Akbar Khan who was promoted Major General in December 1950 and who had derived the nickname of 'Gen. Tariq' from muslim conqueror of spain Tariq Bin Ziyad, was involved in Rawalpindi Conspiracy cases, which was first coup attempt by Army in Pakistan. He was imprisoned for 14 years but released in 1956. Thereafter he wrote a 30-page article on 'How to liberate Kashmir' directives of which are being implemented by Pak Army even today while directing militants into Kashmir to carry on proxy war in J&K. Huge chunks of land were occupied by raiders which in now known as Pak occupied Kashmir (POK). Inter Services Intelligence (ISI) was created in 1948 to gather strategic intelligence from these area. Intelligence Bureau (IB) which already existed at the time of partition since IB was also devided and a portion of it came to Pakistan, was not considered sufficient for this purpose though a very competent officer Mr A B Awan headed it at that time. Since the attack on Kashmir was conducted by Army. It assumed full powers and till date it continues to be fully powerful in Pakistan.

Mr. M.A. Jinnah died of Tuberculosis on September 10, 1948 and struggle to attain leadership of the country began between feudals and the Army. The first Prime Minister of the country Liaqat Ali Khan was assassinated in Rawalpindi on October 16, 1951 by a Pastoon separatist. Some say that he was assassinated because he was working on a framework of favourable solution regarding settlement of the Kashmir issue while certain hidden forces were against this[1]. Country was beseized with refugee problem of tremendous magnitude. Indeed, it was a tumultur ous period for the nacent country.Gen. Mohammad Ayub Khan was made Chief Commander of Pakistan Army on Jan. 17, 1951 with the recommendations from the Governor General, Mr Iskander

Mirza and Begum Liaqat Ali Khan replacing Sir Douglas Gracy. His appointment was not liked by a few senior Army officers which resulted in Rawalpindi or Attock conspiracy case. These upheavals made Ms. Fatima Jinnah say in Karachi on June 28, 1958 (Id day) that the progress of Pakistan towards a fully democratic state has been dogged by the elements and the forces who neither participated in the struggle for Pakistan nor had any faith in the idealism which inspired that struggle. By a tragic combination of circumstances, the country's destiny fell into the hands of elements who have done their worst to stifle people's urge for progress and brought the country down to its present state of misery and frustration. This sorry plight has been the direct result of the scramble for pelf and power, ignoring all vital national interests and all principles of ethical and political rectitude.

Civilian government of Malik Feroz Khan Noon was dismissed by Governor General Iskandar Mirza on Oct. 7, 1958 and he abrogated the constitution, enforced martial law making Gen. Ayub Khan as Chief Martial Law Administrator banning all political parties. On Oct. 8 Gen. Ayub issued a series of regulation imposing death penalty for certain offences and rigorous imprisonment ranging from seven to fourteen years for certain other type of offences.

Special Military Courts and summary military courts have been set up to try and punish persons contravening the regulations. Feroz Khan Noon and other members of his dismissed Cabinet were virtually put under House Arrest in Karachi since martial law was imposed. Noon and his colleagues were prevented from contacting each other or members of public. President Iskandar Mirza was heavily guarded.[3] Gen. Ayub himself disclosed (Karachi, Oct. 9, 1958) that he had told the President (Mirza) before the abrogation of the Constitution that if he failed to act "to bring about a change" in Pakistan, the Army would force a change.[4] On October 24, 1958 Gen. Ayub became Prime Minister and on Feb. 17, 1960 he emerged as first elected President. Iskandar Mirza was unceremoniously dismissed and exiled to London on Oct. 27, never to return to Pakistan. Nehru termed this development as establishment of dictational rule in a member country of the Common wealth for the first time. The editorial of the Hindu newspaper on November 22, 1958 had stated "the very fact of massive military aid to Pakistan (by America) has created in that country a vested interest for the Army and undermined any opposition political party which ventured to criticise the foreign policy of the Government." The editorial assessment of 1958 hold good even today in the year 2008. Under Gen. Ayub at least seven person remained as Prime Minister. He befriended many heads of state and developed friendly relations with the United States of America and visited Washington in Sept./Oct. 1953 to meet John Foster Dulles, the Secretary of state and his military advisor Admiral Arthur W. Rdford to strike a deal with US to become its eastern anchor in an Asian Allance Structure but demanded right price for it. He told to US officials "our army can be your army if your want"... Thereafter he met President John F. Kennedy in July 1961, Joined SEATO in 1954 and Bagdad Pact in 1955 (it later on become CENTO in 1958). His main emphasis in developing ties with USA was to modernise Pak military with US arms and ammunition and demand economic aid for Pakistan. On March 5, 1959 Pakistan and USA signed a bilateral defence Agreement at Ankara providing for "appropriate action, including use of armed forces" by US to assist Pakistan against" aggression.[4A] In April 1965 he tried to bestfriend Russia and met Kosygin and others in Moscow on April 3, he also visited China on March 4, 1965 and met Chairman Mao-Tse-Tung and Liu Sho chi with a view to develop friendship between Pakistan and China. On June 2, 1965 Prime Minister of People's Republic of China Chow-En-Lai paid a return visit to Rawalpindi and met Gen. Ayub Khan. He is also credited with building a new capital Islamabad for Pakistan. the remained neutral when China invaded India in 1962 though it could be largely attributed to the American pressure exorted President John Kennedy. But full scale Indo– Pak war of 1965 over Kashmir, after Paunching 'Op Gibraltor' on Aug. 8, 1965 which miserably failed, was implemented from Sept. 6, to 22, During the war lresident Field Marshal Ayub Khan had undertaken a secret trip to China to discuss war situation personally with the Chinese leadership. Incidently, whenever Pakistan entered into a war with India. Its leadership always dashed to Bejing for consultations. Ayub visited Taskent on Jan. 3, 1966 where he signed Tashkent Declaration on Jan. 10 to end the war started by Pakistan. Gen. Ayub is also credited with concluding Indus Water Treaty with India which provided 80% water to Pakistan and 20% went to India. The treaty war signed at Karachi on September 10, 1960 between him, Jawahar Lal Nehru and World Bank Vice President Iliff. The following day Nehru was received by President Ayub Khan at Murree.

Gen. Ayub's rule was full of problems for him. There was no Constitution of Pakistan. The first Constituent Assembly known as Basic Principles Committee could not give a Constitution and it was dissolved on Oct. 24, 1954 giving birth to a new Constituent Assembly in June 1955 which did produce a Constitution for Pakistan and which was promulgated on March 23, 1956. The Constituent Assembly adopted the name of Islamic Republic of Pakistan. However, the Constitution stood abrogated by Iskander Mirza on Oct 7, 1958. Then problems were faced by Ayub in Kalat and had to order arrest of Khan of Kalat in Oct. 1958 and seized his estate. Ayub faced bickerings from political as well military officers. There were problems in erstwhile East Pakistan. He allowed American U-2 spy plane's flight from Peshawar base for which he got a good rebuke from USSR. Ayub had somehow an inkilkling that during 1962 Indo-China war, America chose to side with India and perhaps this was one of the reasons why Pakistan befriended China. Pakistan even illegally gifted 5180 Sq km. of Indian territory in Saksgam valley of Pok in March 1963 simply to please china. China continues physical occupation of 38,000 Sq miles of territory in Aksai chin plateau in Ladakh. He was instrumental in the formation of Pakistan Atomic Energy Commission (PAEC) in

1957 and formed Pakistan Institute of nuclear science and technology (PINSTECH), Karachi Nuclear Power Plant (KANUPP) some 18 miles away from Karachi trying to make Pakistan self dependent on nuclear energy sector.

One of the blunders Gen Ayub made was that in the year 1968 he issued an ordinance that empowered the government to withdraw the degree of any student which resulted in mass student uprising, participated and actively supported by peasants and workers giving it a colour of leftist uprising. This movement was exploited by Z.A. Bhutto who had already formed a political party by name of Pakistan People's Party (PPP) in Nov. 1967.

On Nov. 11, 1968 and Hashim had attempted assassination of Gen. Ayub in Peshawar with the idea of removing him altogether so that Bhutto could take over. Great as Gen. Ayub was, he was worried lest people harm Hashim who was overpowered by a pensioner 'Subedar'. Gen. Ayub feared another attempt on him arranged by Z.A. Bhutto himself since Bhutto had started hating him and wanted him to be removed from the scene once for all. Gen. Ayub was a kind hearted man, honest, decent, dignified, cultured straight forward and very gentle. He forgave even those who were responsible to bring his downfall. He and his family members never accepted any costly gifts which they could not reciprocate.

Yet Students, Workers and peasants revolt against Gen. Ayub and a wave of riots all over against the military dictator forced him to make unceremonial exit in 1969 passing the mentle to Gen. Yahya Khan in March 25, 1969. Z. A. Bhutto, to a large extent, was responsible for his ouster.

Gen. Ayub ordered formation of a covert action division within ISI in 1950 after creating ISI itself in 1948 to investigate and assist Indian insurgents from India's North-East i.e. Nagaland and then Mizoram. The same division of ISI later on was engaged to assist Sikh Home Rule Movement led by Sardar Charan Singh Panchi in London which ultimately resulted in demanding 'Khalistan'. Gen. Ayub also started making use of ISI in internal and domestic affairs of Pakistan since he was besieged with various multifarious problem. ISI was not able to provide accurate and timely intelligence to Gen. Ayub during 1965 Indo-Pak war though it was very active during 1964 Presidential elections. Gen. Ayub scolded the then DG ISI on Sept. 7, 1965 for his failure to locate India's 1st Armoured Division.[5] He even setup a Committee headed by Gen. Yahya Khan to examine the working of ISI/IB/MI etc. and make them more professional. Of Course, Gen Ayub had one of the excellent Spy masters in AB Awan as Director Intelligence Bureau Ayub's Kashmir attacks and Indo-Pak war of 1965 made IB/ISI personnel more aggressive and hateful towards India and Indians. As Pakistan kept on drowning deeper in political, economic and military chaos and upheavals, its intelligence gathering machinery kept on becoming powerful stronger, sharper and independent ultimately adopting a posture of a state within a state. Pakistans themselves fear ISI/IB/MI etc. today constantly. Events during Gen Ayub's period expanded intelligence agencies base and area of their operations, activities and domain giving them absolute authority and immunity. Propoganda machinary was also geared up. They say one muslim soldier could carry out fight with five (5) Hindus-thus making a target of Hindus and encouraging them to fight Hindus. The confidence inculcated into them by Pakistan Army or ISI or even Islamic militants forget the final outcome of 1971 war where 93,000 soldiers of Pakistan Army surrendered to India. It was greatness of Indian government and its Army that all PoWs were treated well. But Pakistan forgets such things. Their memory is short in this regard.

The 'Basic Democracy' system of government comed and applied by Gen. Ayub was inappropriate under the prevailing circumstances in Pakistan and as such it could not last long.

REFERENCE

1. The Herald, Karachi June 2002 Page 19 article-Media by Shiraj Raj.
2. Id day message by Ms. Fatima Jinnah—The Hindu at July 1, 1958.
3. The Hindu Oct. 10, 1958.
4. The Hindu October 11, 1958.

4. (A) The Hindu March 6, 1959.

5. Zulfi Bhutto of Pakistan : His Life and Times—Wolperts 1993.

2
General Agha Mohammad Yahya Khan's Period

General A.M. Yahya Khan's regime was comparatively a short one ending on Dec. 20, 1971 consequent upon the surrender of Pakistan Army in East Pakistan on Dec. 16 and breaking away that part of the country. Gen Yahya desired that the integrity of Pakistan and glory of Islam maintained at all costs by all Pakistanis. He imposed martial law on March 26 dissolved National and Provincial Assemblies. He announced first national general election scheduled to be held on Oct. 5 1970 (which were held on Dec. 17, 1970) on the basis of one-man-one-vote. PPP swept the victory in West Pakistan whereas Awami League routed all political outfits in East Pakistan. Gen. Yahya had designated Sheikh Mujib as Prime Minister. As Muslim League had done to the Indian National Congress of undivided India, demanding a separate homeland for muslims, exactly same was done by Awami League which was founded by H.S. Suhrawardy and led by Sheikh Mujibur-Rehman when it demanded a loose Confederation between the two wings of Pakistan. On Feb. 13, 1971 Gen. Yahya gave a call to hold the National Assembly session in Dhaka on March 3 which was opposed tooth and nail by Z.A. Bhutto. Reeling under immense pressure, Yahya relented and on March 1, he announced the postponement of the Assembly session. Sheikh Mujib and his Awami League members were not allowed to form the government. Instead, Pakistan military attacked Awami League members on March 25, arrested Sheikh Mujib-ur-Rehman and Dr. Kamal Hussain, thus started conducting misguided operations. From this point began the chain of events that brought the downfall of Gen. Yahya and dismemberment of Pakistan giving birth to a new country which came to be known as Bangladesh. Z.A. Bhutto encouraged and supported the Army's action and resultantly Gen. Yahya's short lived milatary rule saw the 3rd full scale war (Dec. 3-17, 1971) with India over East Pakistan ending in fall of Dhaka, surrender of 93,000 Pakistan soldiers to Indian Army who were taken as PoWs. Almost 3 millions Bengali's were killed by Pak Army. The first attack was made by Pakistan Air Force on Indian position on Dec. 3. Yahya was dubbed as butcher of East Pakistan and was forced to hand over power to Zulfiqar Ali Bhutto on Dec. 20 who became Chief Martial Law Administrator of the remaining part of the country i.e. West Pakistan. Much of the blame for the tragedy can be attributed to the adament nature of Z. A. Bhutto. Pakistan broke into two pieces in 1971 simply because the Army (forced by Z. A. Bhutto) did not want the Awami League which had won Dec. 1970 general election to rule the Country. A correct analysis of dissection of events by posterity would not blame Gen. Yahya for this break up.

Gen. Yahya Khan is credited for developing close relations with the United States of America. US President Richard Nixan visited Pakistan five times during his regime to rebuild America's relations with Pakistan. He was instrumental in arranging Dr. Hennery Kissingers disguised and clandestine visit to china on July 9, 1971 to July 11, 1971 leading to Nixon's visit to that country in Feb. 1972. China had also kept Kissinger's visit secret untill he left back for Islamabad.

During Gen. Yahya's rule ISI mostly remained busy in obtaining domestic intelligence of political nature and kept a tab an Indias moves in Bangladesh. Nothing substantial was achieved by them accept that the intelligence personnel become more anti-Indian because of the ultimate break up of their country. They became more and more involved in collecting domestic intelligence. Incidently, Gen. Yahya himself distrusted ISI chief. Bangladesh war generated more hate against India and Indians since in their thinking it was India who caused division of their 'mulk' and the main task of IB/ ISI/IB was to counter and mitigate the Indian influence in the then East Pakistan.

Gen. Yahya had created a National Security Cell (NSC) to mullify the variance of intelligence reports received by various agencies. Since their reports different from each other, NSC was tasked to receive intelligence reports from these agencies, then prepare a composit picture before presenting it to the President.

Gen. Yahya was a kind hearted and straight forward person respecting sentiments and rights of all persons. He used to give lavish gifts from his own pocket only. He was interested in 'Ghazals' particularly sung by Noor Jehan. Interested and shortsighted people spread all sorts of cheap rumours against him. He was a victim of intrigues played by interested persons. He was not a politician but people played politics with him. He was, like Gen. Ayub Khan, great at heart and forgave every one who conspired against him and misled him. This greatness was imbibed on him by virtue of his birth in a family of Kizalbash residing in Peshawar. A happy-go-lucky man, he cared for his words and prestige. Mr. Roedad Khan writes about him 'Yahya was a good man but hardly a good President. His dominant quality was his authenticity and transparency. He wore no mask and was totally devoid of hypocrisy. In financial matters, Yahya was scrupulously honest and died almost a pauper.[7] After giving up the power, he was put to confinement and even his pension was forfeited.

*Pakistan – A dream gone sour – by Roedad Khan Page 166.

3

Zulfiqar Ali Bhutto's Era

Zulfiqar Ali Bhutto, Raja of Larkana and a feudal lord from Sindh, a declared 5th son of Gen. Ayub Khan, father of Pakistani atomic bomb programme was included in the Cabinet of Ayub Khan on Oct. 28, 1958. On a sudden demise of PM Mohammad Ali Bogra in 1963, Z.A. Bhutto was made Foreign Minister. He came in clash with Ayub Khan on the question of Tashkent declaration brokered by Aleksei Kosygin of USSR between Pakistan and India after the 17-days Indo-Pak war of 1965 that began on Sept. 6, Unhappy, Bhutto left the Cabinet and formed Pakistan People's Party in 1967 with politicians from both the wings of Pakistan. He exploited mass movement of students in 1968 which was also participated by peasants and workers giving an indication of a leftist movement which, in fact, it was not and emerged as a leader using communist jargons like egalitarianism, exploitation etc.

Talking for masses he nurtured a soft corner for feudal lords since he himself was one of this flock.

Gen. Ayub who was in the habit of writing daily diaries noted in his diary on May 23, 1967 that Z.A. Bhutto had Offered to be a US Spy.[1] When east Pakistan was trying to secede, Bhutto supported Gen. Yahya Khan in the secession putting stiff resistance to all reconciliatory measures taken by Gen. Yahya Khan. In fact, Gen. Yahya Khan was agreeable to all the demands put up by Awami League and Sheikh Mujib but unfortunately and incidently, in the end as destiny would have it, agreed "Bhutto's dictates who had given a slogan to East Pakistan Idhar hum, udhar tum." On Dec. 20, 1971 Z. A.

Bhutto was flown into Rawalpindi from Rome where he took over from Gen. Yahya Khan and became President and first Civilian Chief Martial Law Administrator. When the constitution of Pakistan was adopted on April 10, 1973, he become Prime Minister on Aug. 14, 1973 and gave catchy slogans to Pakistans in March' 71. like 'Roti, Kapra aur Makan' But all this was drama and simply to befool the country men. Z.A. Bhutto had conspired alongwith Air Marshal Abdul Rahim Khan and Lt. Gen. Gul Hassan during East Pakistan crisis when they were sent by Gen. Yahya Khan to china in mid-November 1971 to ascertain the extent China would support Pakistan in case of full war with India. The idea of sending Air Marshal Rahim Khan and Gen. Gul Hassan was to make sure that Bhutto conveys the exact version back to Gen. Yahya of Chinese advise regarding their help in case of war with India. China did not favour that Pak should go to war with India and advised provisional political measures to gain time. But Bhutto reported back painting entirely a different picture-that of a very positive response. All the three members posed to appear very enthusiastic and pleased. Their attempt should be to convince Yahya of an overwhelming Chinese support in lase of was and that the chinese had promised to immediately supply almost all the military hardware requested during the visit, that the Chinese 'crack' troops possessed the capability to cross the snowbound Himalyas[2] Sure of Chinese support, Gen. Yahya ordered crackdown on East Pakistan and declared war on India. Had Z.A. Bhutto not been playing the mischief of telling blatent lies to Gen. Yahya history perhaps would have been different of Indo-Pak relations. No chinese support was to come and Yahya thinking that the chinese have converged of their support through him, went to war resulting in dismemberment of the country and ultimately facilitated his own ouster which in fact, was the game plan of Z.A. Bhutto with the help of Air Marshal Rahim Khan and Gen. Gul Hassan. After the war was over, Bhutto signed Simla Accord on July 2, 1972 with Mrs. Indira Gandhi. Continuing the facts of the game played by Z. A. Bhutto, both Rahim Khan and Gul Hassan felt elevated and started calling themselves "King makers" which was not liked by Bhutto once he became Prime Minister. Bhutto played with them also by way of removing them from their positions so swiftly and secretively that they could have no inkling of impending catastrophy which was to befall on them. When they heard it on March 3, 1972 that they have been replaced by Gen. Tikka Khan as the new Chief of Army Staff and Air Marshal Zafar Chowdhury as Chief of Air staff respectively, they became stunned. However later on Bhutto, in a way, rehabilitated Air Marshal (Retd.) Rahim Khan by appointing him as Ambassador of Pakistan to Spain. Gen. Gul Hassan commanded respect in Army. Yet, to every body's surprise, Army did not come out openly in revolt because of their defeat in East Pakistan but in their heart of hearts they were itching to take revenge for maligning the Army and humiliating their chiefs by Civilians. Army never forgave Z. A. Bhutto. Lt. Gen. Gul Hassan, the last Commander-in-Chief of Pakistan Army died on Oct. 9, 1999 at Command Military Hospital, Rawalpindi. On his death, the only article of value turned out to be his Margalla Suzuki Motorcar and nothing else. No house, No plot, No land. He had placed Rs 2,200/= with his driver for his shroud and burial expenses.[3] Such a great man honest to the hilt. A Commander-in-Chief of Pakistan Army from Dec. 20, 1971 to March 2, 1972 and no Bank balance, no House and no plot even! can we learn something from him?

ISI Chief Lt. Gen. Ghulam Jilani Khan had impressed upon Z.A. Bhutto to appoint Gen. Zia-ul-Haq as chief of Army staff though a superior officer had once described Zia-ul-Haq as being unfit to be a military officer.[4] Zia was a devout muslim, a religion who gave a slogan of 'Iman' Taqwa and *'Jihad fisabil Allah'* (Faith, piety and Jehad for the sake of god) and propogated Islam. He introduced common prayers and religious education in army during his rule. Z. A. Bhutto as Prime Minister himself had encouraged religious fundamentalism and appointed a Minister to look after religious affairs of the country.

ISI Chief Jilani prompted Bhutto to hold National and Provincial Assemblies election as his personal prestige was sky-rocketing and suggested March 7, 1977 as the date for holding such an election. Massive rigging and aftermath religious demonstrations by political parties particularly by Nine-Parties group Pakistan National Alliance (PNA) and demand for Nizam-e-Mustafa etc. compelled Bhutto to seek Army's help in controlling such demonstration. Army's thinking was that the continued and prolong exposure of Army to quell civilian uprising would make senior Army Commanders to loose strip on soldiers and decided to topple Z. A. Bhutto and took over from him on July 5, 1977. On July 3 itself DIB Rao, Abdul Rashid and Gen. K.M. Arif had met Z.A. Bhutto and hinted a possible military take over. The 9-Parties opposition group of PNA was formed in Jan 1977 to oppose PPP.

On July 5, 1977 Gen. Zia-ul-Haq seiged power from Bhutto who was hanged on April 4, 1979 for abetling the murder of Nawab Muhammad Ahmad Khan, father of Ahmed Raza Kasuri, a PPP MNA who had become a dissident and arch opponent of Z.A. Bhutto. The tarset of Federal Security Force (FSF) was Ahmed Raza Kasuri but accidently his father Nawab Muhammad Ahmed Khan got killed on Nov. 10/11, 1974 by unknown killers in Lahore.

In 1965 the then British High Commissioner in Pakistan reported to London in an official dispatch that "Bhutto would destroy himself - - - - and was born to be hanged"[5]. Incidently, Bhutto himself had selected Gen. Zia-ul-Haq for the post of chief of Army staff on March 1, 1976 superseding six more competent Army Generals.

Z.A. Bhutto had enlarged the scope and role of ISI and formed internal security wing in 1975 after legalising ISI's involvement in domestic survellance and collection of intelligence against his political opponents. He created a separate corps of intelligence in Pak Army under the Command of a Lt. General which came to be known as crops of intelligence or ISI Directorate. He also planned to have all Army officers screened by the Police and intelligence etc. which was disliked and rejected by senior Army officers like Gen. Gul Hassan Khan. Bhutto also encouraged its intelligence apparatus to operate against Indians at various levels. He put Pakistan on the nuclear map and encouraged Dr. A.Q. Khan to make Pakistan a nuclear power. Main aim of which was to use it against India. He called it a 'Islamic Bomb'. In Aug. 1973 he created an Afghan cell in the foreign office. It was he who created Federal Investigation Agency. (F/A) His main thrust was "Islam is the solution and Islamic bomb is the means". He made Islam state religion for the first time in Pakistan to investigate corruption. He also created Federal Security Force (FSF).

On home front he had become almost a 'Dictator' and ruled with iron hand. He suppressed insurgency in Baluchistan ruthlessly. Baluchis have confronted the government on five occassions so for. In 1975 the elected government of the National Awami Party in Baluchistan was dissolved by the centre and the Sardars resisted Bhutto's proclamation against sardari system pravelent in that province. They took up arms in 1973 against Federal Forces resulting in the death of 5,300 Balochis and 3,300 Pakistanis soldiers of Pak Army. Even today they resent construction of Gwadar Port, demand removal of army cantonments from Kohlu, Dera Bugti and Gwadar and also demand with drawal of Frontier Constabulary from Baluchistan. On Oct. 24, 2008 PPP Co-chairperson Asif Ali Zardari offered apology on behalf of all Pakistanis to the people of Balochistan for all the oppression, Federal government did on them. Mr. Salig Hassan has predicted break up of Pakistan into three (3) states-Baluchistan, Pashtoonistan and Punjab and Sindh merging with Baluchistan.[6]

During the later years of his rule, Bhutto had become

very arrogant, thinking too much of himself and looking down on others, Quite intolerant of any opposition. It was this behaviour of his that brought disaster for him. Army was against him since he questioned their capacity for fighting army, intelligence and security agencies were also against him. In trying to create a base for himself, he devasted the national economy, encouraged and aggravated sectarian rifts etc. He was a split personality. He declared himself Martial Law Administrator, where as Pak Army morale was at zero level because of their defeat in 1971 Indo-Pak war. He dissolved the provincial government which were democratically elected simply because he could not tolerate these Assemblies with his opponents in them as members. On Jan. 1, 1974 he ventured to nationalise all Banks.

Towards India, Z.A. Bhutto always advocated a hardline and adopted confrontational policies and attitude. He was prepared to carry on a thousand year war against India.

During January/February 1974 which was a difficult year for Z.A. Bhutto's government saw mounting tension with National Awami Party (NAP) in Baluchistan over the radical agenda of NAP. Since Bhutto dismissed the provincial government of Baluchistan, the NAP-JUI Jamiat-i-ulema Islam coalition in NWFP also resigned showing sympathy with them. Baloch people rose in armed struggle against the Islamabad government. Pak Army killed thousands of Baloch, Jailed them and tortured. Khan Abdul Wali Khan, son of Khan Ghaffar Khan the Frontier Gandhi, and Ataullah Mengal were imprisoned. However the situation and uprising was brought under control albeit temporarily.

Baloch people are continuing with their struggle of seperate land even today.

Z.A. Bhutto remained Parliament of Pakistan from Dec. 20, 1971 to Aug. 14, 1973. Thereafter he become Prime Minister and remained so till Gen. Zia took over from him. Bhutto remained in New York till Dec. 18, 1971 when Gen Yahya

Khan sent for him to return to Islamabad to take over from home as head of state. It was during his period in 1974 that Ahmediyas and Qadiyanes were declared a non-muslim minority in Pakistan.

REFERENCE

1. Diaries of Field Marshal Ayub Khan 1966-1972-Page 99 published by Oxford University Press, Karachi in 2007.
2. Three Presidents and an wide-lite, power and politics (Page 201) by Ambassador Arshad Sami.
3. Working with Zia (Page 210) by Gen. K.M. Arit.[6]

   Salig Harrison, Director of Asia Programme at the Centre for international policy and author of In Afghanistan's shadow in an article published an Feb 2008
4. Pakistan : Between Mosque and military Page 111-112 by Hussain Haqqani.
5. Working with Zia Page 210 by Gen. K.M. Arit.
6. Salig Harrison, Director of Asia Programme of the Centre for International Policy and Author of Afghanistan's Shadow. In artical published on Feb. 2008.

4

Gen. Zia-ul-Haq's Period

Gen. Zia-ul-Haq, Pakistan's third military ruler, who had called himself a 'soldier of Islam' took over reign of power from Z.A. Bhutto on July 4, 1977 overthrowing him and announced with assurance that he would hold general elections in the country within three months. What to talk of three months, elections were not held untill 1985. Ostensibly he had toppled Bhutto on the point of differences, allegations and counter-allegations between Pakistan people's Party (PPP) and Pakistan National Alliance (PNA). A sentence spoken by 'Gen. Zia at a Press Conference in Lahore on Sept. 1, 1977 that this country can be kept together by Armed Forces and not by politicians,' spoke volumes of the thinking of his mind. Right from 1958 when Gen. Ayub took over the governance of the country, Pak Army did not allow democracy even to take roots, what to speak of seeing it flourish. They saw in themselves as the real saviour of the nation. This trend increased in intensity and magnitude during Gen. Zia's rule. They tried to divide the political leadership and find fault with simply to impose overt or covert military rule suiting their whims and fency. Under the pretext of saving the nation, they imposed military rule and strengthened army establishments, provided cosy and lucrative placements to serving and retired general(s) and made sure that they lead a comfortable life full with luxury. Considering themselves as the custodian and guardian of the nation, they rendered civilian governments powerless whenever ostensibly in power. Every decision taken by such a civilian government was vetted by the Army and had to be okeyed for implementation. Gen.

Zia had Contributed his own agenda of Islamaization which was a mixture of Islam and muslim doses in his military rule thinking that Pakistan is the only country that has monopoly on these two subjects. He carried out Islamaization of Pakistan's civil society vigourously which simply produced Mulla, Mullas and more Mullas. Gen. Zia is on record stating to BBC in April 1978 that his mission is to purify and cleanse Pakistan.[1] In the process, he passed a number of laws which could be called anti womenfolk. Islamaization in certain ways was a blow to the traditional way of tribal leadership. Mullahs, infact, brought degeneration of tribal 'Jirgah' and gradually they were replaced by 'Mullahs' in Mosques. Gen. Zia institutionalised Islamaisation of Pakistan.

Through Islamaization, Zia controlled the trend of westernization of Pakistanis. The young girls had started wearing tracks just like Iranian female youngsters. Elderly women were not taking to cover their head. One of the highly educated doctor in fact, sophisticated and cultured Pakistani gentlemen working with a foreign mission in early ninetees once told that the women folk who had started dressing in western style till Gen. Zia took over switched to wearing 'chador' and covering themselves in full with cloths. And he was happy about it. Men folk started growing beard and reading 'Namaz' five times a day. Gen. Zia combined religion with politics and curtailed freedom of mind, action and thoughts. Even Army officers and sepoys were asked to read Namaz, instead of dancing and music in the officers mess, as the case may be. The officer class of Pak Army who were recruited and trained by Gen. Zia in his ideology in this fashion have now reached a stage where they are holding senior position and within next four-five years they are to take over full command of Pakistan Army. These officers of Gen. Zia's times are known as 'Zia Bharti'. IMA Dehradoon trained officers or those who have influence of British Army would be over soon and Indian Army should be prepared to face a different situation in dealing with them six-eight years hence. So far, comparatively it was easy to deal with senior most Army officers with exception of those from ISI hierarchy, Put Islamic fundamentalism oriented officers shall have to be dealt with by India in future.

A noted philosopher and political activist Noam Chomsky opined in Feb. 2008 that Pakistan is a paradigm example of a failed state that has undergone an extremely dangerous form of radical Islamaization since 1980. In his book "Failed States, Chomsky writes" I am afraid to say Pakistan is the paradigm example of a failed state and has been for a long time.' In order to make Pakistan a complete Islamic state, 'Shariat' was introduced and Jannat-i-Islami, a religioo-political party, moved closer to Gen. Zia. A few other religious and sectarian outfits also followed suit. Maulana Madoodi who died in Sept. 1979 was close to Gen. Zia. Zia-ul-Haq, was so much after glorifying Islam that he ordered to rewrite all school text books which gave them history of depicting supremacy of Islam and muslims and clearly stated that Islam could not co-exist with Hindus justifying demand for a separate Muslim state which resulted in the birth of Pakistan in 1947. These text book continue generating hatred towards Hindus and India in the fragile and innocent minds of Pakistan students. The re-written text books were full of false, concocted, twisted and wrong facts and these facts are bound to impact the minds of young school children. Once these wrong facts go into their mind, it is difficult to obliterate them and then they start harbouring a ground against India. For example it is written that 1965 Indo-Pak war was won by Pakistan simply because Indian Army was Frightened of Pakistan Army and Pakistanis. Books were full of historical revisionism, half truths or no-truth at all and fabricated theories showing supremacy of their army, nationals and nation. Muslim were portrayed as victims of many onslaughts form other religious. They conveniently forget that in India people from all religious-Hindu, Muslim, Sikh or Christian live like brotheren. All people respect all religions, their rituals and traditions and even participate in them. They help each other Hindus go to Khawaza Moinuddin Chisti's 'Dergah' in Ajmer to pay obeisance. Whatever odd incidents take place they are only because of rogue elements.

In 1979 under the pretext of Nizam-e-Mustafa, a number of ordinances concerning women folk were introduced like Hadood (limits) which dealt with 'zina' (adultary), 'zina-bil-jabra' (Rape) etc. In 1982 an ordinance dealing with 'Quisas' and 'diyat' was introduced by Council of Islamic Ideology (C11). In 1983 Zia opined that democracy is not an Islamic form of government and formed a Commission called Pakistan Commission on the status of women 1983 under Begum Zari Sarfaraz. CII was authorised to examine all laws repugnant to Islam. Roedad Khan opines in his book 'A dream gone sour' (Page 168) that-"if Zia had lived, he would have taken us back to the middle ages."

The second plan of Gen. Zia was to get rid of Z.A. Bhutto for which he had already made up his mind but was only looking for execuses. Bhutto had maligned the Army and even challenged their fighting capabilities etc. which was just not liked by the Army. The fact was that both Zia and Bhutto had developed hatred for each other. Ultimately Bhutto was hanged on April 4, 1979 for complicity in the murder of a political opponent.[2]

Zia had efficiently handled so many vexed problems of his period in a turbulent Pakistan, of course, some of them were his own creations. He released all Balochis who were detained by Z. A. Bhutto government and withdrew all operations against them in Baluchistan which were started in Feb. 1973 after dismissal of Provincial government by Bhutto.

Afghan cell which was originally formed in Foreign Office in 1973 was reactivated in 1978 with Roedad Khan, Secretary Interior Ministry as its member. Shah of Iran was dethroned in Jan. 1979 and it had its repurcussions in Pakistan. But Gen. Zia had misread the soviet intentions when they invaded Afghanistan an Dec. 24, 1979.[3] The majority view of the Afghan cell was that the objectives of soviet aggression in Afghanistan was to reach the warm waters of the Arabian sea and that aggression against Pakistan was inevitable. But Gen. Zia opined that the next step for the Russians would be to turn toward Pakistan once the Afghan resistance is suppressed which would take the Soviets about two years.[4]

Gen. Zia introduced separate electorate for muslims and non-muslims and postponed the general elections fixed for Nov. 17, 1979. On Nov. 21, 1979 US Embassy Building in Islamabad was set on fire by miscreants who were protesting US involvement in desecration of Holy Kaba. Gen. Zia had to deal with the influx of thousands and thousands of Afghan refugees who entered Pakistan from Afghanistan after soviet Invasion in Dec. 79 Gen. Zia seized this opportunity and got America shell out millions of dollars and arm and ammunitions to Pakistan. Zia's Islam was used by CIA and Americans against soviets in Afghanistan to oust them. Money in dollars come from CIA to ISI and all and sundry in ISI became rich and richer overnight.

In 1980 only, observing Islamic tenets, Gen. Zia introduced compulsory 'Zakat' @ 2.5% which was vehemently opposed by shias who said it can't be done under compulsion according to shia seet. This created sectarian divide which continues even today.

Soviet invasion of Afghanistan brought major upheaval for Pakistan which changed the future course of Pakistan's place in the world map. About three million Afghan refugees entered into Pakistan in 1980 itself soon after the soviet invasion. They mostly settled in Baluchistan and NWFP.

USA asked Gen. Zia to organise resistance to Russian invasion. He created and assisted 'mujahideen' (Islamic militants) to handle operations against soviets. Their recruitment, training and fight against them kept Gen. Zia., Pakistan Army and ISI very busy throughout soviet occupation of Afghanistan. This period brought economic boom for Pakistan since USA pumped rather rained millions and millions of dollars in the name of fight against Soviets. Gen. Akhtar Abdul Rehman ISI chief conducted and controlled the operations against soviets while Brig. Mohammad Yous of was ISI representative in Afghanistan from 1983 to 1987 giving shape to the fight on ground in the Afghan soil. One of the money changer who also owned a foreign crockery shop which had other articles also of international availability told me that the Blue Area market of Islamabad, where he also had his shop, used to be thronged by wives of Pak Army Generals. They would enter the shop and in a second order the whole lot to their homes. The then ISI chief Gen. Akhtar's (June 79 to March 87) son Humayun Akhtar Khan, a PML MNA, was reported to have spent 'unbelievable amount of funds' during two elections and this report was filed in 'The News' international of Jan. 31, 1999 of Islamabad (Pakistan). Even ISI became financially independent with American dollars. While dollars were kept by ISI personnel for themselves, most of the arms and ammunition received from CIA to fight soviets in Afghanistan was passed on to mujahideen fighting in Kashmir and also to Pak Army. The terrorist Islamic outfits received a shot in the arm receiving highly sophisticated arms which they used to put under earth in the form of arms cache in the jungles of Kashmir. Most of the arms and ammunition including stringers were stored in Ojheri Camp ammunition depot located in between Islamabad and Chaklala airport. Fire broke out in this Camp on April 10, 1988 compelling Gen. Zia to return to Islamabad cutting short his visit to Kuwait where he had gone to attend Organization of Islamic Conference (OIC)'s mini summit.

An outfit under the name of 'Al Zulfiqar' alleged to be headed by Z. A. Bhutto's son Murtaza Bhutto cropped up to give thorough and tough resistance to Gen. Zias military rule. Zia changed Pakistan's constitution in order to have powers which could not be challenged in a court of law, introduced 'Shariat' and downgraded educational standards by introducing 'madersa' education. A madarsa student was considered equivalent to an university graduate. Gen. Zia saw Islam in every object, subject, space, time and matter.

Even Army discipline was slowly and gradually brought down to madarsa environment. Saudi Arabia also powred money into Pakistan to fight Soviets and it hijacked Pakistani Islam to Saudi version of Islam.

Then Gen Zia was confronted with a conglonnerate of twelve opposition political parties formed under the banner of Movement for Restoration of Democracy (MRD) in Feb. 1981. However, he held elections-non-party elections-on Feb. 25, 1985 which were boycotted by MRD for not restoring the 1973 constitution. Zia appointed Mohammad Khan Juneja as Prime Minister who acted against the policy of Gen. Zia and within no time contained the wild spread Islamaization process to a large extend and demanded even the constitutional amendments made by Zia should be nullified and abrogated by the National Assembly. Junega's conduct was just opposite the expectation of Gen. Zia and both fell apart soon. Junejo had earlier compelled Gen. Zia to lift Martial Law on Dec. 30, 1985.

Meanwhile the fire that engulfed Ojhri ammunition depot on April 10, 1988 at 10 am rocked both Islamabad and Rawalpindi twin cities. Yet the following day i.e. April 11, President Zia stated that 200% security measures were taken by the Army for the safety of ammunition depot yet accident are accidents and cited ammunition fire incidents of 1944 in Bombay, 1969 ammunition blasts in Lahore itself, the Bhopal leakage of gas and nuclear gas leakage at chernnobyle in USSR. Arms and ammunition received from CIA were stored in this depot yet Gen. Zia denied that the military stuff dumped at Ojheri camp was meant for Afghan mujahideen. An enquiry committe was set up under the Corps Commander 10th crops which led to the sharp differences between Prime Minister Juneja and the Army Generals when a 300-page report was submitted to him on April 24. Muhammad Khan Juneja was so angry that he had made his mind to dismiss Gen. Akhtar Abdul Rehman former ISI Chief and Lt. Gen Hamid Gul the current ISI chief as they were accountable for disaster. Angered by Juneja's action containing Islamaization and other actions like 'dismisal to be' of thees officers etc., Gen. Zia dismissed Juneja on May 29, 1988 himself and dissolved the National Assembly.

Lahore High Court on Sep. 27, 1988 declared the Presidential order of May 29, 1988 dissolving National and Provincial Assemblies as unconstitutional but refused to restore them. Supreme Court upheld the Lahcre High Court's decision on Oct. 5, 1988 and stressed the need for holding fresh elections on Nov. 16 and 19. Gen. Mirza Aslam Beg had approached Supreme Court through a letter asking for reversal of its judgement to restore the government of Mohammad Khan Junejo by President Zia-ul-Haq. Frontier Gandhi Khan Abdul Ghaffar Khan, who passed away on Jan. 20, 1988 had wished to be buried in Jalalabad. It was also to be arraged by Zia. He was always surrounded with one or the other problem.

Gen. Zia was honest, pious and always smiling. Down to earth a simple man. It never came to notice so far that he shiphoned off CIA given American dollars meant for Afghan war. During his last visit to New Delhi in 1987 before his sad demise, while his motorcade was negotiating a round about on Janpath and Akbar Road crossing, this writer happened to be walking on foot to catch a bus. Since VVIP was moving, the policemen pushed me aside and I stood in a corner watching the General pass through. He saw me and raised his hand in salutation smilingly. In response I greeted him with folded hands and bowed with respect. His humbleness and wishing me, a pedestrian, still vibrates in my memory.

General Zia made all out efforts to make Pakistan a nuclear power-and all the efforts of all the rulers of Pakistan was and is India-specific. It made a significant head way during his rule from 1977 to 1988. In 1987 Pakistan had achieved breakthrough in 'Islamic Bomb' and soon it started clendestine activities in J & K by way of recruiting Kashmiri Youths, lure them with money or by way of administering threats or invoking religious sentiments, sent them to militants camps in Pakistan run by Pak Army. ISI and other religious extremists outfits for training in militancy and they were ask to carry out militant acts on return to Kashmir after being trained in Pakistan. They were provided with arms and ammunition, other logistics and communication channels as well. Since Pakistan could not sustain a long drawn overt fourth war with India, it devised covert ways of carrying out low cost offensives and proxy war in Kashmir observing guidelines given by Maj. Gen. Akbar in early fifties. Since operation 'Gibraltor' launched on Aug. 8, 1965 and operation 'Grandslam' failed miserably, Gen Zia prepared a plan in 1984 for Kashmir which was supposed to mature in 1991. The plan was to prepare Kashmiri mujahideen to stage an indegeneous uprising to seek self determination. Militant Islamic outfits, encouraged by Gen. Zia's Islamaization drive planned to send militants in Kashmir secretly which were aided and abetted by ISI and Pak Army to target installation, security forces, communication points etc. The Pakistan-sponsored militancy was to be given a tinge of domestic uprising of Kashmiris for self determination. Kargil misadventure was also a part of this very planned strategy. As recently as on Feb. 4, 2004 Gen. Pervez Musharraf, All-in-All of Pakistan of his years, while speaking to Pakistan newspaper editors in Islamabad stated that Pakistan has two vital interests. Being a nuclear state and second, Kashmir Cause. Gen. Zia managed, through ISI, to raise on outfits called Muhajir Qaumi Movement in March 1984 out of all Muhajir Students Organisation (APMSO) an organisation of urdu speaking migrants from India who chose to settle down in Pakistan after 1947 partition. Gen Zia-ul-Haq developed close proximity with china by way of allowing them to open Karrakoram Highway connecting China with central Asia.

By and large, Pakistan somehow had started a dislike for Gen. Zia's type of governance, his over emphasis on Islamization of Pakistan polity, Army, creation of laws against women folk curtailing their freedom etc. They no longer wanted Zia's continuance in ruling the nation. America had ceased to attach any more importance since the Afghan war was already over by April 14, 1988 which had brought ISI very close to CIA. Zia was not liked by Moscow either. ISI's policies were in contrast with that of Foreign Affairs Ministry of Pakistan. Gen Zia was criticised for prolonging Afghan war in order to prolong his own rule in Pakistan. He had even announced general election to be held on Nov. 16, 1988. But.

On Aug. 17, 1988 Gen. Zias plane C-130 exploded mid-air and 31 persons perished with him including former ISI Chief Gen. Akhtar Abdul Rehman and American Ambassador to Pakistan. A sabotage was suspected.

Ghulam Ishaq Khan stepped into his shoes as President of Pakistan.

Gen. Zia never liked the constitution of Pakistan of 1973. In fact, he was for Presidential form of government rather than Democracy and always held opinion that democratic form of government does not promote Islamic concepts and was unsuitable for Pakistan. In conformity with his line of thinking, he even held a referendum on Dec. 19 1984 in which he was the only candidate for the President and the question put to voters was " Do you elect Gen. Zia as the President of Pakistan for a further period of five years ?"

Thus each Ruler having his own agenda required help form his intelligence agencies to keep him abreast and informed of all the happenings in the state including consipiracies against him in order to retain his position. A specialized agency was required to execute the assigned tasks quietly for which IB and ISI became handy. Since most of the rulers were from Army they encouraged Intelligence system staffed by army personnel since their loyality was to army rulers only and thus Inter Services Intelligence suited them. But whenever civilian government was in power they encouraged Intelligence Bureau which was started by Police and other civilians. But be it ISI or IB or MI, Kashmir was and is a Jugular vein for them. All of them work relentlessly against Indians and India.

Recently (May 20, 2008) Asif Zardari, PPP Co-Chairperson stated to visiting Indian Foreign Minister Pranab Mukherji when asking him to withdraw Army from J & K "the Army by design, wherever it is, by its nature is crude whether it is your army or any other army. If you had a police force there, even it was 5,00,000 strong, police training is different and they have to go back to their wives. They don't have to go back to their cantonments and they live in a normal world."[5] As such, they preferred Intelligence Bureau.

During Gen. Zia regime (July 5, 1977 Aug. 17, 1988) Army grew from 4,00,000 to 4,50,000 and its inventory of equipment increased in quantity and quality.[6]

Intelligence agencies during Gen. Zia's rule flourished and flourished. ISI chief were very powerful because they had to keep an eye on domestic upheavals because of Bhutto's autocratic and whimsical attitude, insurgency in Baluchistan, formation of political outfits and then Zia had to keep a watch on the developments staged by PPP and Ultimately Bhutto was ordered to be hanged. Afghan war made ISI-personnel as well as organization very rich dollars-wise. They were trained by CIA in modern intelligence gathering Techniques which brought them close to CIA in day-to-day functioning resulting into lasting relationship. ISI gained considerable experience during soviet fight in Afghanistan, got hardened and adopted independent nature in functioning. By Feb. 1989 when last soviet troop withdrew from Afghanistan, the ISI diverted their trained personnel to Kashmir. Developments in Iran, Afghan rufgess influx, development in nuclear field, friendship with China etc. were such subjects where Zia had to integrate, ensconce and settle his ISI men. ISI grew in stature, expanded its wings, started terrifying even their own countrymen and ultimately become a state within a state. ISI was a graffity and omnipresent. CIA made ISI financially independent because of Afghan war. You turn a stone in any city of Pakistan and you find an ISI/IB/MI/FIU/ local Intelligence man who are engaged in collection of intelligence. Involvement in Afghan war made them expert and experienced. During Zia's rule, it was ISI which was running the country. In the process, a whole directorate was engaged to keep a watch on India, Indians, their mission in Islamabad and Karachi. For Kashmir Affairs there was entirely different division known by the name of Joint Intelligence North (JIN).

Islamic radicalism originated from Zia's period continues to hound Pakistan even today and would engulf the world in times to come if not contained timely and effectively.

After Gen. Zia took over the region of the Country, Sindhis and Shias became his suspects. He ordered ISI and IB to monitor the activities of Sindhi nationalists and shia organisations in Pakistan soon after the victory of Iranian revolution in 1979. The dictator in Gen. Zia was in reality afraid of PPP which had already started a Movement for Restoration of Democracy (MRD) in early eightees. As such he wanted an Intelligence Organization to keep an eye on PPP leaders. What else could be more reliable and dependable than an agency under his own command i.e. ISI.

All these subsequent events kept on expanding the role of ISI since 1950 making it more and more powerful in sustaining military rule and keeping a tab on opposition political parties by each passing day which made it "Invisible Government" as described by Pak newspaper "The Frontier Post", (Peshawar dtd, May 18, 1994) and as 'Our secret Godfather' Published by "The DAWN" Karachi (April 25, 1994). Today ISI is a state within a state.

REFERENCE

1. Gen. Zia's interview to BBC Correspondent Brian Barron.
2. Nawab Muhammad Ahmad Khan on 10/11 Nov 1974. Bhutto was arrested for this murder on Sept. 3, 1977.
3. First small batch of Russians entered Afghanistan an Dec. 24, 1979. but in large number they entered on Dec. 27, They pulled out on Feb. 15, 1989.
4. Pakistan—A dream gone sour by Roedad Khan Page 97.
5. The Times of India May 23, 2008.
6. The History of the Pakistan Army-Page 272 By Brian Cloughley.

5

Ghulam Ishaq Khan's Era

It was on Aug. 17, 1988 itself Ghulam Ishaq Khan was made acting President. He was elected President on Dec. 13 backed both by PPP and IJI. Prior of his taking over as President and Gen. Zia's death on Aug. 17, general elections were held in the country on Nov. 16 for National Assembly and Nov. 19 for all the four Provincial Assemblies where Benazir Bhutto and her party PPP won 39% of votes. Intrigues and venality played prominent part in this election. Election were declared by Gen. Zia because in reality he wanted to continue army rule under cover keeping facade of civilian government. On Gen. Zia's death Gen. Mirza Aslam Beg who was vice chief of Army Staff till then took over as Chief. Both Ghulam Ishaq Khan and Gen. Beg continued the policies of Gen. Zia's. Afghan war with the aim of achieving strategic depth (a word coined by Gen. Beg himself) was continued. Jihad in Kashmir not only continued but rather was carried out with renewed vigour and greater enthusiasm where by Kashmiri youths were selected and lured by way of offering money or administering threats to undergo militant training in Jihadi camps in Pakistan where they were imparted training in militant activities by ISI instructors. Fresh developments in nuclear fieled were achieved. Gen Beg field waned to make Pakistan's nuclear capability known to the world particularly to USA and India although Gen. Zia had already made it known, particularly to India, Ttrough Dr. A.Q. Khan, the father of the Bomb, Mushalid Hussain a journalist and editor of the Muslim and Kuldeep Nayyar Indian journalist who published a scoop in the Indian Observer on March 1, 1987. It was one of the operations of Gen Zia through which they made their nuclear capabilities public just to restrain India from carrying out op Brasstack any further. Kuldeep Nayyar was fed the information when Mushahid Hussain invited him to Pakistan and introduced him straight way to Dr A.Q. Khan who rather volunterred information of Pakistan having capability of making a nuclear bomb.

Gen. Zia with the help of Gen. Hamid Gul who succeeded Akhtar Abdul Rehman as ISI Chief planned a Islamist hotch-potch which was given a shape by Brig. Imtiaz Ahmed in the form of Islamic Jamhoori Ittehad (IJI) to contest against PPP and its leader Benazir Bhutto. IJI consisted of Islamic parties viz Jamiat-e-Ulema-e-Islam (Darkhvest), Jamiat-e-Ahle Hadith (Lakhvi), the Azad group (Fakhr wasti), the Hizb-e-Jihad, the Nizam-e-Mustafa group, the Jamiat-e-Mushaikh, and Pakistan Muslim League (PML). Later on, on Oct. 10, Jamaat-e-Islami also joined IJI to contest Nov. 16 general elections. ISI funded IJI and provided guidance. Benzir Bhutto, who had returned to Pakistan in April, 1986 only, won the election on the platform of PPP. Many stalwarts like IJI President Ghulam Mustafa Jatoi and secretary General Tikka Khan (of 1971 Bengladesh war who had later on joined PPP was defeated by Sheikh Rashid from Rawalpindi), retried Air Marshal Ashghar Ali Khan of Tehrik-e-Istiqhal (a party formed by him), Maulana Ahmed Shah Noorani (JUP chief), syed Ali Mardan Shah known as Pir of Pagaro, Ghulam Ahmed Bilour (Vice president of Awami National Party ANP) and Ghous Bux Bizenjo (PNP chief) lost the election. Benazir Bhutto was nominated as Prime Minister on Dec. 1, 1988 since her party PPP had emerged as the single largest party with 93 seats for National Assembly followed by IJI claiming more than 60 seats. President Ghulam Ishaq Khan lifted emergency and dissolved the Emergency Council. Benazir Bhutto restored banned trade unions, and students unions and various other organization. In Punjab, Nawaz Sharif (IJI), in Sindh, Qaim Ali Shah (PPP), in NWFP Aftab sherpao and in Baluchistan Zafrullah Khan Jamali (IJI) took over as Chief Ministers,

However, Benazir's victory was somehow not liked by Gen. Aslam Beg the Army chief as well as by Gen. Hamid Gul the ISI chief. Since Benazir was the first women Prime Minister of an Islamic country, her becoming PM was not liked by Islamic seminaries of Pakistan either coming out with the plea that a women could not lead the country. Pakistan Army and Benazir did not pull on well with each other and ISI kept on hidden operation against her in practical terms. She was later on accused of challenging the institution of military directly or indirectly, there were agitations in her home province-sindh, she had replaced ISI chief Gen. Hamid Gul with a retired General. Kallue who was a persona-non-grat for Army cheif, was in confrontation with IJI chief Nawaz Sharif particularly in Punjab and above all corruption was alleged against her and her party PPP. Meanwhile Rajiv Gandhi also visited Islamabad in Dec. 1988 to attend SAARC meeting but this was also not liked by ISI. Gandhis visit resulted in signing an Agreement on Dec. 31 between India and Pakistan not to attack each others nuclear facilities. The meeting between Benazir and Rajiv Gandhi was termed by certain elements as Benazir being soft on India to the utter dislike of Pakistan Army, the President and certain political personalities like PoK President Sardar Abdul Qayyum. In May 1989 her policies on Afghanistan which differed from Pak Army's plans and that of Pak Foreign office also came under severe criticism though soviets had withdrawn the forces by Feb. 14, 1989. She was considered to be too close to America which was viewed as damaging to Pakistan's interests. ISI wanted all out efforts for Islamist govt.'s installation in Afghanistan and Benazir proved to be an impediment. ISI had escalated militant activities in J & K causing insurgency and uprising of Kashmir giving it a tinge of indigeneous revolt. Kashmiri youths were sent to Pak for Jihadi training and training in Islamic fundamentalism. Beg and Gul combination proved to be most dangerous and damaging for India which was not effectively countered by India.

In June 1989 Benazir visited Washington to meet George

H. W. Bush where the latter demanded assurances regarding not possessing nuclear weapons. CIA director William Webster also met her explaining that America knew about Pakistan's nuclear programmes and Pakistan military. Back home, in an IJI meeting, Jamiat-e-Ulema-e-Islam leader Maulana Sami-ul-Haq said "Pakistan' nuclear weapons capability simply cannot be safe under the leadership of a westernised women. She cares more for American approval than for ensuring the Umma's first nuclear bomb.[1]

Meanwhile Gen. Aslam Beg chief of Army staff and Lt. Gen. Hamid Gul, chief of ISI kept a watchful eye on Benazirs over all actions at home and abroad on all fronts. Benazir no control over the Army nor could it stop the nuclear programme which resulted in terming her as a weak Prime Minister in the eyes of America. Moreover, in Sept. 89 Gen. Beg ordered a military exercise under the code name Zerb-e-Momin (The blow of the believer).

Op. Midnight Jackal

There was a nexus of powerful people headed by Nawaz Sharif, the then Chief Minister of Punjab, who were prepared to go to any extent-constitutional or unconstitutional-in their efforts to topple Benazir Bhutto in the National Assembly. A conspiracy was hatched against Benazir Bhutto by a group of military officers including some who were serving or had served in the ISI. In order to catch the conspirators, Intelligence Bureau launched an operation under the code name "midnight jackals" to record secretly all the conversation that took place at the conspirators RVs. In all 12 tapes were recorded with the conversations between Brig. Imtiaz, Maj. Ameer, IJI Senator Gusher, Malik Mumtaz, PPP MNA Arif Awan IJI MNA Malik Naeem and PPP MNA Rashid Bhatti during the period Sept. 28 to Oct. 6, 1989. Some of the tapes reflect the thinking of anybody who was somebody regarding ISI. For example transcript of tape No. 3 (recorded on Oct 3, 1989) quotes, Brig Imtiaz, "I want to tell you that Indias R&AW, USA'S CIA, Israel's MOSSAD and many other agencies over the world have been afraid of ISI. The Indian know that they have to first destroy ISI-You must have heard of the exercise "Brass Tasks" I must tell you that India, during that exercise would have launched a full fleded attack on Pakistan, during which it would capture one of Pakistan's provinces. The Indian had planned it in a manner that they would find the Pakistan Army in the contonments and there by it would be caught unawares. But it was the ISI which procured top secret exercise papers from India and started disseminating them to Army". On Sept. 5, 1992 Gen. Aslam Beg in a press statement said that after the failure of the no confidence motion against Benazir, he had received tape recorded evidence against two ISI officers i.e. Brig. Imtiaz and Maj. Ameer. Gen. Beg further said that though there was insufficient evidence to court martial imtiaz and Ameer, he had ordered the retirement of the two officers from the Army Service. (Both of them were serving army officers when the incident took place). Soon after Nawaz Sharif became P.M. and he appointed Brig. Imtiaz as chief of the Intelligence Bureau. In early 1991 he appointed, Maj. Ameer to head the Federal Investigation Agency's Immigration wing.[2]

It was on Aug. 2, 1990 Saddam Hussain had invaded Kuwait. Benazir had different perception for Iraq war than that of Gen. Beg. He recommend dismissal of Benazir Bhutto to the President Ghulam Ishaq Khan which was done on Aug. 6, 1990. At the time of her dismissal she and her husband were charged with several corruption cases, internal dissentions and friction, persistent and scandalous horse trading, unlawful and undemocratic practices, tendencies of opportunism and selfishness etc. Benazirs dismissal was expected from the very beginning but it was accelerated by the alleged actions of her husband Asif Ali Zardari who was known to be charging 10% commission on government contracts and was known as 'Mr ten per cent' as also having opened an stock exchange in the Prime Ministers House, a charge later on vehemently denied by Benazir Bhutto. She blamed military Intelligence (MI) for her dismissal from the seat of power. Benazir on her intelligence outfits had no inkilling what so ever of her dismissal fill it actually came through.

Benazir's dismissal brought Ghulam Mustafa Jatoi of National Peoples party as caretaker Prime Minister on the very day of dismissal of Benazir Bhutto i.e. on Aug. 6, 1990 for three months i.e. fill Oct. 24, 1990 the date of general elections.

Election were held on Oct. 24, 1990 for electing 217 National Assembly members (207 for muslims and 10 for non-muslims). Provincial Assemblies polls were held on Oct. 27. Islami Jamhoori Ittehad (IJI) won at Centre as well as in provinces. PPP did not fare well. IJI which was continuing from 1988 consisted of Islamist parties like Pakistan Muslim League (PML), Jamaat-e-Islami (JeI), Jamiat-ul-ulema-e-Pakistan (JUI), Jamiat Mashaikh and a few other smaller groups whereas Peoples Democratic Alliance (PDA) consisted of Tehrik-e-Istiqlal, Tehrik-e-Nifaz-e-Fiqah-e-Jaltaria (TNFJ) etc. IJI won more than two third of seats in National Assembly. Since Nawaz Sharif and his IJI was backed by these Islamist parties, he was under obligation or say duty-bound to fulfill all the requirements of these components to make the country 'Darul Islam' which was the main aim and plank of Islamists of Pakistan. This move pushed the country further to 'Mullaism' and Islamic fundamentalism Though normal and routine general elections were scheduled in 1993 only but holding mid-term elections was necessitated because of Benazirs dismissal mainly on the ground of incompetence and of the corrupt regime of PPP. In election IJI had won by majority. As such IJI Chief Nawaz Sharif became Prime Minister. The ouster of PPP enraged America and they openly lent their support to PPP and went to the extent of threatening to stop American aid to Pakistan. American observers had reported election as fair and impartial yet they noticed that the people of Pakistan had strong anti-US feelings. ISI went all out to make IJI win and spent Rs. 150 million to defeat PPP. The other party contesting election was Peoples

Democratic Alliance (PDA).

On Nov. 6, 1990 Mian Nawaz Sharif was elected leader of the House and Prime Minister. He declared continued Pakistan's support to oppressed Muslims of Kashmir, Afghanistan and other parts of the world and refused to strike any compromise on Pakistan's 'peaceful' nuclear programme. In Oct. 90 US President Bush refused to certify that Pkistan was not involved in nuclear weapons programme. Military Sales to Pakistan were stopped even F-16 for which Pakistan had paid in full in advance and in dollars were stopped from being delivered. However, when Nawaz Sharif took over leadership of the country, Ghulam Haider Wyne in Punjab, Jam Sadiq Ali in Sindh, Mir Afzal Khan in NWFP and Mir Taj Muhammad Jamali in Baluchistan became chief Ministers. Nawaz Sharif, no sooner he became Prime Minister dashed to Riyadh in Nov. 10 to meet the Royal family as well as Emir of Kuwait, condemned Iraj's invasion of Kuwait and promised help in the form of troops to save the royal palace etc. His stand on the issue of the gulf war was in contrast with that of his chief of Army staff Gen. Aslam Beg whose thinking was that the Royal family had outlived its usefulness and that Pakistan might consider a more appropriate regional policy.[3]

There existed several discords between Nawaz Sharif and Benazir Bhutto. When Gen. Asif Nawaz Janjua took over as chief of Army staff from Gen. Aslam Beg on Aug. 17, 1991, he tried for a patch up between them in the interest of the nation and to strengthen the parliamentary democracy. Gen. Asif Nawaz escalated operations in Kashmir more vigourously for which USA threatened Pakistan that US would declare it as terrorism sponsoring state. Resultantly, ISI/IB/MI and other intelligence outfits were made still stronger by Pakistan to work against India and Indians in carrying out militant activities in Kashmir and elsewhere in India.

In August 1991 a coalition of opposition parties known as People's Democratic Alliance (PDA) staged a twelve-hour hunger strike led by PPP to protest the governments decision against establishing speedy trial courts. In June 92 Army operation in Sindh began and 600 persons were arrested. In October 1992 Benazir Bhutto, Ghulam Mustafa Jatoi, Malik Qasim and other opposition leaders protested against Nawaz Sharif government by joining a "train march' form Karachi. In November 1992 she was teargassed during her march from Rawalpindi to Islamabad while demanding Fresh polls. Nusrat Bhutto was teargassed in Lahore.' Nawaz Sharif accused Benazir Bhutto of "open rebellion."

Nawaz Sharif, though himself a moderate muslim, had to face tricky situations created by Islamists for example, when Babri Masjid was pulled down in 1992 in Faizabad (India), there was a lot of reaction amongst Islamists all over Pakistan. They went berserk in demolishing all Hindu temples throughout the country. Nawaz Sharif did try to stop but by that time damage had already been done.

There were demonstration by violent crowds infront of Indian Embassy in Islamabad. Islamists supported Saddam Hussain of Iraq when he invaded Kuwait in Aug. 10 but Nawaz sided with Saudi Arabia in Iraq's war. Saudi Arabia reciprocated this gesture of Nawaz Sharif by way of striking a deal with Gen. Pervez Musharraf in the year 2000 to take him to Riyadh instead keeping him in jail by Gen. Musharrf after overthrowing him in a bloodless coup on Oct. 12, 1999. Nawaz Sharif also desired a moderate Mujahideen government in Afghanistan after soviets withdrew but ISI wanted Islamist government led by Engineer Gulbadin Hykmatyar to rule Kabul. On April 16, 1992 Najibullah surrendered and he was kept under UN coustody when his forces defected after Soviets stopped assistance. Kabul had fallen to Abdul Rashid Dostum and Ahmed Shah Masud and they wanted Kabul to be led by Burhanuddin Rabbani. Nawaz was also saddled by sectarian clashes at homefront, ISI's high handedness in all affairs of Pakistan, various faction of Afghan mujahideen vying with each other to take over Kabul and support to them by ISI, Pak Army's thrust of militants into Kashmir to create various factions of mujahideen so as to keep

Indian security forces confused and on their toes. It was difficult for India for sometime to find out asto which faction of mujahideen was responsible for which militant action. There was great political turmoil. USA had threatened Pak with declaring it a terrorism sponsoring state in 1992.

Suddenly on Jan. 8, 1993 Gen. Asif Nawaz Janjua expired because of over exercising which probably effected his heart. President Ghulam Ishaq khan wanted to appoint chief of General staff Gen. Farrukh Khan as COAS but on the objections of Nawaz Sharif, he appointed Gen. Abdul Waheed Kakar on Jan. 12, 1993 as chief of Army staff. Mrs Asif Nawaz raised finger towards Nawaz Sharif for the death of her husband but Nawaz showed restraint and maintained his cool like a true statesman. Relations between Nawaz Sharif and Gen. Asif Nawaz Janjua were strained. Differences also persisted, rather increased, between President Ghulam Ishaq Khan and the Prime Minister Nawaz Sharif because of personal vendetta. On April 17, Nawaz Sharif even went on Air to PTV to address the nation in which he made a tirade against the President. He is the root cause of all intrigues, Nawaz opined. Enraged, President dismissed Nawaz Sharif government following morning i.e. on April 13, 1993 and appointed Balkh Sher Mazari as caretaker Prime Minister. Nawaz Sharif filed a case in the supreme court on April 19 against this dissolution. On May 26 supreme court restored the government of Nawaz Sharif overturning the action of the President. President had charged him with corruption and mismanagement. This led to further and increased bitterness between the president and the Prime Minister compelling Chief of Army Staff Gen. Abdual Waheed Kakar to intervene. After failing to bring any compromise or patch up between them, he asked both of them Ghulam Ishaq Khan and Nawaz Sharif to resign simultaneously and they resigned on July 18, 1993. An ex-world Bank functionary Moeen Qureshi was made acting PM and Chairman of the senate Wasim sajjad acting President. Fresh elections were ordered to be held on Oct. 6 and 9 respectively for NA and all the four Provincial Assemblies.

The first action of caretaker PM Moeen Qureshi was to pevalue Pakistani rupee by 6% on July 22, 1993. On July 26 he dashed to United States for four days which was branded as a private visit. He dissolved local bodies on Aug. 15 and released a detailed and comprehensive list of defaulters and beneficiaries of loan write-offs on Aug. 27 and imposed a ban on defaulters to participate in the forthcoming election on Oct. 6 and 9. He also got an ordinance passed on Sept. 27 to award death penalty for drug trafficking. It also passed an ordinance on Oct. 7 to prevent post election defections by politicians, ordered closure of 15 ministries and 10 embassies of Pakistan since the economy was in bad shape. In Aug. 1997 former PM Moeen Qureshi cautioned the nation saying that this is the last chance for the parliamentary form of government of the kind we have in Pakistan. If this experiment does not succeed then 1 think we must consider a presidential form of Government.

Incidently, on Aug. 27, 1993 The weekend post section of The Frontier Post newspaper of Pakistan published an interesting item in which it depicted ten (10) persons as most scandalous personalities. They were Fratanullah Marwat (Politician), Anita Ayub (Actress), Altaf Hussain (Politician) Nawaz Sharif (Politician), Maulana Smeeul Haq (Politician) Ghulam Mustafa Khar (Politician), Reema (Actress) Brig. Imtiaz (Political advisor), Khalda Riasat (Actress) and Imran Khan (Cricketer).

REFERENCE

1. PAKISTAN BETWEEN MOSQUE AND MILITARY—PAGE 216-17 BY HUSSAIN HAQQAMI

2. The News—report by Kuleem Omar did Sept. 24, 1992.
3. Pakistan at the Cross current of History—by Lawrence Ziring Page 2 19-220.

6

Return of Benazir Bhutto to Power

Elections for the National Assembly on Oct. 6, 1993 saw Benazir Bhutto back to power for the second term with 86 votes in NA out of 201 Assembly seats. The Islamist parties received a very small percentage of overall votes. Total six (6) seats (2 each from NWFP and Baluchistan won by Islami Jamhoori Mahaz (IJM) and 1 each from Punjab and NWFP won by Muttahida Dini Mohaz (MDM). Muttahida Qaumi Movement (MQM) boycotted the election of National Assembly which benefited PPP and PML(N). A very senior journalist of an urdu newspapers, during a casual discussion, lidely well before the elections gave his assessment regarding the outcome of election that the Islamic parties would get six (6) seats only. All the arguments put forward against his assessment were rejected outright by him offering very convincing facts. And when the election results were made open, it was realised how accurate his assessment was. By way of Obiter dicta, one word for Pakistani Journalists--Almost all of them,be they from urdu newspaper or English ones, they are extremely well informed, very well behaved, polite, learned, broad minded and helping. Mr. Najam Sethi of Friday Times, Lahore, Shaheen Sehbai and many more have made their mark in the field of Journalism. Ms. Maleeha Lodi has even made her way to diplomatic life from journalism. They are indeed world's best. Their balanced view of the happenings world over and depth in analysing events is indeed superb. But on the question of Kashmir, all of them invariably hold just one view that Kashmir should be given to them. They have to abide by the official line of government of Pakistan which consists of Troika, that Kashmir belongs to Pakistan, and India is in Ijllegal occupation. Pakistan has named this part of Kashmir as Indian Occupied Kashmir. There is another hurdle for them. In any Pakistani journalist gives his balanced views or if they write an article which depicts Indian view accurately and they justify it on Kashmir affairs and militant activities by Pak sponsored Islamic fundamentalists, then journalist would have a taste of states agencies-IB/ISI/MI/ Local intelligence outfits etc. Mr. Najan Sethi had visited India in the year 1999 and it was reported in media that he had made a speech that had been critical of the government in his journal and had expressed his opinion about the ruling family in a BBC interview. High Commissioner of Pakistan in New Delhi Mr. Qazi sent home a critical report on his speech. On his return to Lahore form New Delhi he was arrested and tortured by[18] ISI. Even one 'Sarkari' MNA Syed Zafar Ali Shah filed a petition before the Election Commission to decide whether Mr. Sethi was a Muslim or not; and if was found to be a non-muslim, he demanded that Mr. Sethi's name should be struck from the voter's list because he had made a speech against Pakistan in New Delhi.[1] Ultimately Chief Election Commissioner dismissed the petition and ISI chiey also cleared him. Journalists have to slip out quietly out of the country to escape the clutches of agencies if they report any article in favour of India.

Anyway, when Benazir Bhutto won Confidence vote on Oct. 19, 1993 she got 121 votes against 72 bagged by Nawaz Sharif and become Prime Minister. Undeterred, by his defeat, Nawaz Sharif replied to Benazir's statement "people do not want change of the face, they want to change the system." By replying that "I am ready to cooperate unconditionally with Benazir Bhutto to change this system and to solve the problems of the country." The following day i.e. on Oct. 20, she addressed the nation stating that "we will protect peaceful nuclear programme and will not let anyone to harm our national interests." On the issue of Kashmir she rowed to mobilise international opinion against Indian atrocities in occupied Kashmir and struggle to end them. A few months ago in May 93 Lt. Gen. Javed Ashraf Qazi had taken over as DG ISI who promised to make ISI invisible again. Benazir had inherited a mismanaged economy from Nawaz Sharif, there were floods, cotton crops was substantially damaged because of disease. Increased violence in Kashmir and Punjab, sponsored by Pakistan, made America keep Pakistan on "terrorist watch list." There were diplomatic tensions between India and Pakistan. Viilence in Karachi escalated. Indian Consulate in Karachi was closed down by Pak government in 1993. Sectarin clashes between Shias and Sunnis were the order of the day. Mastermind of World Trade Centr's bombing on Feb 26., 1993 was reported hiding in Pakistan whose rea name was Abdul Karim although he was known as Ramzi yousug. He was ultimately arrested in Feb. 95 although ISI protected him quietly for two years. A new President was also to be elected. Though Benazir tried for a consensus candidate on Oct. 27 but 14 candidates including three from PPP and five from PML(N) fielded themselves. Presidential election was held on Nov. 13, 93 and Farooq Leghari won the race by polling 274 votes against 168 of PML Candidate acting President Wasim Sajjad. Sardar Farooq Leghari, a Baloach, was an ex-civil servant who entered politics in 1973 by Joining PPP. Leghari at the time of taking over the presidency stated "I will never be an interventionist President" referring to the fact that his predecessor Ghulam Ishaq Khan was intervening. He was also of the opinion of repealing 8th amendment of the 1973 constitution that bestowed power on the president to interfere, intervene and dismiss the National Assembly and the government. Lo and behold, Farooq Leghari himself used 8th amendment, dismissed his own party's government of Benazir Bhutto on Nov. 5. 1996.

In the month of September 1993 the Acting President Wasim Sajjad had promulgated three Ordinances (1) Wealth Tax Ordinance (2) Asking Pakistan Banking Council to publish the names of loan defaulters exceeding Rs. 10 Lac and those who got their loans written off after 1985 and (3) providing death penalty to and confisation of property of drug traffickers. A list of 160 drug barous was released in Sept. itself[2]. Paula Newbers sums up the year 1993 for Pakistan in the following way. Even in the annals of Pakistan's fractious and byzantine politics, 1993 was an unusual year. By year's end, the country had survived five governments, four Prime Ministers, three President, two Army Chiefs, and one remarkably engineered election that returned Prime Minister Bhutto to office. Bhutto in back, but she in not the same leader she was when she assumed office for the first time in 1988. Nor is Pakistan the same country she inherited form General Mohammed Zia ul Haq after 11 years of military rule.[3] Bhutto hyperbolically calls Kashmir the jugular vein' of Pakistan. The bilateral talks in January 1994 with Indian prime minister Narashimha Rao quickly ended when neither government could translate that diagnosis into policy. The Pakistani position hardened so that Kashmir become the focal point of its India policy. Pakistan then renewed its attempts to pass a resolution in the UN Human Rights Commission condemming abuses in the valley. (The resolution was finally withdrawn with pressure from Iran, China and more than 40 others who would otherwise have abstained.[4]

On Feb. 25, 1994 Governors Rule was imposed in NWFP and PML(N) government headed by Pir Sabir Shah was suspended by President Farooq Leghari Pir Sabir Shah approached the supreme court against dismissal of his government which ruled on April 22 that Sabir Shah's government would stand restored on April 25 when Presidential order imposing Governor's Rule lapses. Acting Governor Maj. Gen (Retd.) Khurshid Ali summoned the NWFP Assembly on April 22 1994 and asked Pir Sabir Shah to seek vote of Confidence. On April 24 though Awami National Party (ANP) and PML(N) including Pir Sabir Shah himself boycotted the session, Aftab Sherpao who secured 42 votes was elected Chief Minister of NWFP and his government sworn in on April 29. On June 5, 1994 Nawaz Sharif wanted President Leghari to explain involvement in Mehran Gate scandal, accused the government of corruption and demanded his resignation from the Presidentship. He organised mass contact programme against price hike, corruption, victimization and warned of a 'long march' while addressing a rally at Mingora on July 15. However, on July 19, he made offers of talks with the government on 8th amendment of constitution and floor crossing other Constitutional amendments including women's seat. Though government agreed but talks did not materialise since tensions continued to rise. PML(N) Lagislators asked Nawaz Sharif in a meeting in Lahore on July 24 to lead a long march to Islamabad. On Aug, 14, Nawaz threatened to lead a 'train march' from Karachi to Peshawar respectively while addressing an Independence Day Rally in Karachi and urged the government to quit or face protest action. On Aug. 17 he repeated his pledge to launch protest action.

The year 1994 was significant for Pakistan in the sense that it was credited to have become world champion in cricket squash, snooker and hockey though the following year i.e. 1995 the allegation of match fixing were levelled against Pakistan's cricketers.

Late 1994 and early 95, ISI assisted Taliban in Afghanistan in a big way. By December 1994, 3,000-4,000 religious students moved from Madarsa's to join Taliban. By Feb. 95 Taliban forces reached some 25,000. On May 10, 1995 Islamic fundamentalists/terrorists burnt down 14th centaury shrine of Sheikh Nooruddin Wali. It was done by an Afghan national Mast Gul who belongs to Ahle hidth sect and who joined Al Umer Mujahideen in July 2000. Mast Gul returned to Muzaffarabad, after burning the shrine and Khankah mosque in Chara-e-Sharif, on August 1, 1995 to a hero's welcome by a cheering crowd of several thousands.[5] April-May 1994 alone saw some 400 Afghan Mujahideen (because they fought in Afghanistan) were infiltrated into Kashmir. In June 1994 Commander Manzur shah, the leader of Jamiat-ul-Mujahideen, declared that the sole objective of the escalating Jihad in Kashmir is to incorporate it into Pakistan.[6] Pakistan continued to play mischeif by carrying out militant activities throughout

1995 through ISI sponsored and aetivafy supported Islamic terrorists and fundamentalists in Kashmir.

In 1995 Pakistan was rated second most corrupt country by Berlin based Transparency International (TI). In Sept. 95 a bunch of about 40 army officer had planned a coup to take over the Government, Pakistan Army by way of killing corps Commanders, President and the Prime Minister. Brigadier Muntasir Billah known as 'Billa', a Baluch Regiment officer of a dubious past, not only gave birth to the idea that the country could only be salvaged through his vision and version of Islamic revolution, he also thought that an immediate military intervention was required to liberate Kashmir. He offered to play key role and convinced another dozen senior and middle cadre officers of the army to join him. The plot was incidently and accidently discovered while Brig. Billa alongwith a colonel of army aviation corps was himself transporting arms to Rawalpindi for this purpose. At Attock checkpost he and caught while his vehicle and the one that followed it full of arms was searched in Sept. 1995. Before launching the major adventure aimed at removing the political and military leadership of the country in early October 95, the group strengthened its ties with Harkat-ul-Ansar and Hizbul Mujahideen the two groups dedicated to 'Jihad' against infidels all over the world. Ironically, it was the arrest of Harkat activist in Muzaffarabad, a couple of weeks ago, that provided military authorities with the initial clue about the plot.[7] Major General Zaheerul Islam Abbasi, who was DG Infantry and former military Attach to New Delhi, Colonel Kiyani, Col. Zahid, Col Amyade etc. were involved in the plot. Abbasi was the man who had been removed form his command in the Kargil ared of Kashmir by Gen. Asif Nawaz and given a non-operational desk role at GHQ after having undertaken an unauthorized and costly foray into Indian held territory in 1990. loosing many men including a Brigadier. Abbasi would have been fired had it not been for the reported intervention of another Tablighi Jamaat General Javed Nasir.[8] These army officers were arrested on Sept. 26, 1995 from Rawalpindi.

The government of Pakistan of the day or its agencies including Army Intelligence. might not have come to know in time about the impending coup against the Army Chief his corps commanders, Precident and the Prime Minister to overthrow and kill all of them but certain quarters knew well in advance that such and such coup in about to take place in November 1995 to be staged by lower leadership of colonels who will then take over the country for reconstruction. And it was known as early as first week of March 95. However, according to a formal statement of the Defence Minister, Mr.Aftab Shah Mirani (Nov. 14, 95) the 'conspirators' planned to arrest 'key personalities' from G.H.Q. Conference Hall during a corps commander's conference, kill the participants and impose a self styled Shariah rule in the country." (The failed 'coup' Islam and the Army By Brig. A.R. Siddiqiui. The Nation did Aug. 12, 1996). Currents of this would-be-coup' got passed through the electric lines and in Pok they were felt. Concerned desks were alerted by March itself. But the nose for news was wanting. One Vikram Sood had written one article where in he said "it is no longer possible to assume that a civil service examination passed years ago qualifies a person to be an Intelligence Officer.[9] Analyse and one would find how true his words were. The impending coup was originated and planned from Karachi.

In 1995 in Kashmir six western tourists, one of them American, were kidnapped by ISI sponsored militant outfit by name of 'Al Farhan' which brought pressure on Pakistan from America. Though Benazir adopted a tough line on Kashmir simply to please the Army high ups of Pakistan, she tried to distinguish between Kashmir insurgency and that of Punjab insurgency. She was branded as going soft on India or 'disloyal' or a security risk for Pakistan' by Nawaz Sharif Mayhem in Karachi continued, In 1995 about 2,000 persons were killed which included politicians, litterati and glittarati. There was fend between mujahideen outfits in Afghanistan which had it repurcussion on Pakistan, its government and its Army. Benazir got Taliban trained, about 70-75 in a first batch, and sent them to Afghanistan to save their merchandise on way to central Asian Countries. President Leghari started asserting his authority in managing and stablizing various issues which were disliked by Benazir since she wanted to establish her own authority. Cricketeer Imran Khan and Nawaz Sharif sided with Murtaza Bhutto in joining opposition to Mrs. Benazir Bhutto. Gen. kakar retired inspite of request from Benazir to continue in his post of chief of Army staff atleast for another year. She held high opinion of Gen. Abdul waheed Kakar. But Gen. Kakar, as an old British soldier, opted to retire as per rules. Gen. Jehangir Karamat took his place in Jan. 1996. Same year Osama bin Laden also shifted to Afghanistan from Sudan to join the fight against America where, he was joined by the Taliban. Benazir Bhutto's IMF backed adverse economic policies brought financial difficulties for common man which was opposed by Jamaat-e-Islami when a confrontation broke out between masses and the government on June 24, 1996 in which three IJI workers were killed which further ignited the situation. Qazi Hussain Ahmed Amir of IJI openly demanded that the party's (IJI) 'Dharna' would continue till the corrupt and tyrant government of Benazir was ousted. Train services were disrupted, all roads leading to Islamabad were blocked and country come virtually to a standstill. There was extreme delay in the implementation of Supreme court's judgement regarding regularisation of High Court judges. Benazir Bhutto strongly criticized, rather humiliated, judiciary and the presidency during her regime. Extra-Judicial killings in police custody in Karachi continued. On Sept. 20, 1996 Benazir Bhutto's brother Murtaza Bhutto was killed along with 7 of his members by the police right near his home in Karachi. It was rumoured that Benazir's husband Asif Zardari got him killed because of some tiff with him while disembarking from an aircraft. Murtaza Bhutto's widow Ghinawa Bhutto accused Zardari and the then Director of Intelligence Bureau for this killing. Telephones of political leaders, Judges of the superior courts and senior higher ranking military and civil officers were bugged. Economic situation of the country which was already worst worsened further. The coffers of the country were almost empty. Her husband Zardari was called Mr. 100% while during her 1st term of Primership he was called as Mr. 10% President Leghari punctuated her administering repeated cautions. But when things did not improve, he dismissed Benazir Bhutto's government on Nov. 5, 1996 for which there was little or no condemnation from Public. President appointed Malik Meraj Khalid as caretaker Prime Minister. Khalid, an 80 year old PPP veteran was known for his honesty and efficiency. Leghari also simultaneously declared general elections to be held on Feb. 3, 1997. Malik Meraj Khalid took over as Prime Minister of Pakistan on Oct. 5, 1996 itself. The Caretaker Prime Minister knew the corrupt people As such he laid emphasis on Election and Accountability. His thinking can be know by his statement." We have engulfed ourselves in the fire that has been caused by us alone and we are dying in the process. We kill one another and then raising the voice of protest, term it to be the conspiracy of Jews and Hindus. We do not need any enemy to crush us, as we are already besieged by our self created differences." Accountability Ordinance was promulgated on Nov. 18, 1996. Since there existed, in the past friction between the president and the Prime Minister in order to remove them, a council by name of Council for Defence and National Security (CDNS) was floated on Jan. 6, 1997 during Khalid's Primership, as suggested by Gen. Jehangir Karamat, Cheif of the Army staff to bring harmonious relation between the three pillars of the governance i.e. the Prime Minister, the President and the chief of Army staff which normally is known as Troika in Pakistan's parlance. CDNS was proposed to consist of 10 members headed by the PM to advise the government on everything right from National Security to economic issues. It included P.M. President, Defence and Interior Ministers, Chairman Joint chief of staff committee (JCSS), Naval and Air cheifs, cheif of Army staff. Formation of CDNS was objected to by many politicians arguing that it brings Armed Forces in Constitutional process at the posts of political representatives. So much so, even a petition was filed before Lahore High court on Jan. 16 to declare the formation of CDNS ultra vires. Benazir Bhutto approached the Supreme court of Pakistan on Jan. 16, 1997 against the dismissal of her government but on Jan. 28 it upheld the dissolution order passed by the President and rejected her petition.

When Taliban took over Kabul in 1996, ISI pressed Nawaz Sharif to immediately recognise Taliban Government in Afghanistan which he did.

Return of Nawaz Sharif

In the general elections of Feb. 3, 1997 Muslim League of Nawaz Sharif won with landslide margin. Jamaat-e-Islami did not participate in the elections. Imran Khan formed his own party Tehrik-e-Insaf (TI) and contested election. Nawaz Sharif's PML-N voted to power on Feb. 17 in National Assembly obtained 181 votes in his favour in the 217 member National Assembly. The NA unanimously passed the 13th Constitutional Amendment on April 1, whereby President of Pakistan lost his powers of dissolution of National Assembly and the government under Article 58(2) (b) i.e. the 8th amendment of the constitution was undone. It had its ramifications on the provincial Governors as well. It made the presidency virtually powerless. Prime Minsiter had taken powers to appoint defence services chiefs. Former PM Benazir Bhutto also lent her support to it since she was also a victim of Article 58(2) (b) when Farooq Leghari dismissed her government. This Article had been exercised five times by the president Zia-ul-Haq in 1985 against Muhammad Khan Juneja, by President Ghulam Ishaq Khan thrice against Benazir Bhutto in 1990, twice against Nawaz Sharif in 1993 and again in 1993 after his government got restored by the supreme court and by Sardar Ahmed Khan Leghari in November 1996 when he dismissed Benazir Bhutto's 2nd term government.

On Feb. 18, 1997 Nawaz was sworn in as P.M. Director, Intelligence Bureau Massod Sharif was sacked the same day i.e. on Feb. 18.

8th amendment that gave power to the President (Gen. Zia-ul-Haq) at that time was passed in Dec. 1985. In fact, he exchanged democracy with Presidential powers conferred on him by 8th amendment. He played a clever game to become absolute Monarch.

On July 1, 1997 National Assembly Got 14th amendment passed with 181 votes against none to stop defection of the members of parliament to other parties. With this amendment he brought his party members as well as other members of Parliament under his control since the amendment prohibited crossing of floor and deviation form party line on any crucial issue national or otherwise.

On August 13, 1997 Anti-terrorism get was passed which was signed by the President on Aug. 17 making it law.

Chief Justice Sajjad Ali Shah of the Supreme Court of Pakistan nominated five new Supreme court judges to the existing 12 to raise the strength to sanctioned 17 judges. Since two of the so nominated judges were from Lahore High Court, who had decided cases against Nawaz Sharif's Ittefaq Industries, he never wanted to clear their names and say 'yes' to the proposal forwarded by the chief justice. Nawaz Sharif did not want to appoint more judges to the Supreme Court lest any of the so appointed recommended judges consent for his (Nawaz Sharifs) dismissal on the ground of old corruption cases. Two of the proposed judges were the root cause of not okeying the list sent by CJ Sajaad Ali Shah. As such, tension between the Judiciary and the Executive developed in early 97 which later on culminated into a Constitutional crisis dividing the Judiciary. Nawaz Sharif tried to remove the chief Justice himself. In response on Oct. 29, 1997 sajiad Ali Shah declared Anti defection law passed by Nawaz Sharif government as unconstitutional and suspended the operation of 14th amendment of the Constitution. Nawaz Sharif criticised this action of CJ in the National Assembly on Oct. 29 and affirmed the supremacy of the Parliament. Chief Justice filed a Contempt of Court petition in the Supreme

Court against such discussion in the National Assembly by Nawaz Sharif and five others on Oct. 30 and also asked the President to notify elevation of five High Court judges without seeking Prime Ministers advice. Same day, Nawaz Sharif asked the President not to act on the order for 30 days but on Oct. 31 he agreed to CJ's demand. Nov. 4, Supreme Court issues notice to Nawaj Sharif on contempt petition. On Nov. 4, the jugdes so cleavated to the Supreme Court took oath of office. On Nov. 17 Nawaz Sharif appeared in SC and denied having committed or committing contempt of court. Same day, National Assembly amended contempt law. On Nov. 18, Supreme Court issued contempt notice to National Assembly Secretary for not submitting complete record of proceedings. On Nov. 19, supreme court charge sheeted Prime Minisiiter and eleven others in contempt case. PM also asked the President to sign the contempt of court Amendment Bill on Nov. 19 itself and immediately. The following day i.e. Nov. 20 SC asked the President's not to assent the Contempt of court Bill. Thus the President House became the venue of all these activities instead of the supreme court. On Nov. 28, 1997 when the contempt cases were being heard in the supreme court over the criticism of Chief Justice in Parliament, PML(N) led by Nawaz Sharif himself and accompanied by seven PML(N) legislatures, stormed the Supreme Court and demanded CJ's resignation. Cheif Justice asked the President to arrange Army protection for Judges. Meanwhile, ruling party MPA's of PML(N) in Bahawalpur took out a procession and charged judges of superior court corruption. Resultantly, a crisis of serious nature errupted. ISI Cheif Nasim Rana, COAS Gen. Jehagir Karamat President Farooq Leghari intervened to cool off the tempers. CJ Sajjad Ali Shah was urged to withdraw the contempt petition which he flatly refused. Then President Leghari suggested that the contempt case hearing be delayed by alteast a fortnight to which CJ agreed. During this interregnum Nawaz Sharif played a clever game and hit at the root of CJ's original appointment itself. He got a case filed in Baluchistan High Court on Nov. 26', 97 challenging the original appointment of Sajiad Ali Shah as CJ. On Nov. 26 itself SC Quetta Bench held his appointment in abeyance but the very following day i.e. on Nov. 27, a 5-member supreme court Bench annulled Quetta Bench's verdict on CJ's suspension. Meanwhile SC's Peshawar Bench endorsed the order of Quetta Bench which created rowdy scenes in the supreme court by way of obstructing hearing in the 13th Amendment case. Prime Minister Nawaz Sharif accused President Leghari of causing a political crisis in the country. Justice Saiduzzaman assumed Administrative control of the supreme court on Nov. 28, President Leghari was asked to sign a summary denotifying the appointment of CJ Sajjad Ali Shah after the observation of Quetta and Peshawar Benches of the Supreme Court which became a 'majority of Judges'. Leghari never wanted to sign it and refused. Instead, he offered to resign himself from the post of Presidentship.

Earlier on Oct. 17, 7-SC Judges had requisitioned Full House Court meeting to discuss government-Judiciary tussle over the appointment of judges but CJ Sajjd Ali Shah rejected the request on Oct. 18. Unyielding attitude or stand on this point ultimately led President Leghari to resign on Dec. 2, 1997. Sajjad Ali Shah already made his exit on Dec. 28 and with this the judicial activism ended and the Judiciary stood tamed by Nawaz Sharif who emerged strongest-ever Prime Minister winning on all fronts albeit for a very short period. On Dec. 3, 1997 justice Ajmal Mian was sworn in as Acting Chief Justice. Hearing began on Dec. 10 on the petitions challenging the appoint of CJ Sajjd Ali shah. Ultimately on Dec. 23 SC majority Bench declared the appointment of CJ Sajjd Ali Shah as illegal rand Justice Ajmal Mian was sworn in as Chief Justice.

Before Farooq Leghari's proposal to resign, Gen. Karamat met him to urge to find a solution to the problem created by frictions between PM, President and the Chief Justice. On President Leghari's offer to resign as a solution to the problem, Gen. Karamat is also reported to have offered to resign in case President did so. Gen Karamat never wanted President

Leghari to resign.[10] Mushahid Hussain, a journalist-turned politician who became a close friend of Nawaz Sharif stated on Dec. 3, when the crisis ended, that it is a sign of maturity and strength of democratic institution. Nawaz Sharif considered it as his personal victory.

The Chairman of the Senate Wasim Sajiad became Acting President and issued appointment letter making Ajmal Khan as Chief Justice of Pakistan.

Retired Justice Rafiq Tarar, who was a close friend and choice of the father of Nawaz Sharif, was elected as President on Dec. 31, 1997 securing all time high record of 374 votes out of a total of 457 valid votes cast. Even Ghulam Ishaq Khan secured 348 votes in 1988. Though PML(N) had 227 votes, it was able to muster support of many independent members of the National Assembly for the party's hand picked nominee. 'The Muslim,' an english daily commented on his election as: "With the nomination of Justice (Retd.) Rafiq Ahmed Tarar as the Country's next head of State, Pakistan would have from Jan. 1, 1988 its first President from amongst the indigenous Taliban." The country started ringing with the cry that a Punjabi has been appointed as President which was unwise. The media even quoted 41 top posts occupied by Punjabis in the political and bureaucratic field. Sectarian clashes, oppression of Ahmadias, victimisation of Christians continued. Breakdown of Civil Society, criminal violence, corruption and nepotism was the order of the day. Pakistan economy dipped to a new low. Nawaz Sharifs aim appeared to capture absolute and total power and behaved like a dictator and monarch. On Jan. 10, 1998 Benazir Bhutto filed three charges of corruption against Nawaz Sharif with the state-run Anti-corruption commission. Nawaz Sharif government had already filed 15 references in various corruption cases involving Benazir and Asif Zardari and Nusrat Bhutto for taking out of Pakistan huge funds and stocking it in various foreign banks as well as creating properties in foreign countries. Plunder of millions of dollars was the charge both Nawaz and Benazir slapped against each other.

Blasphemy is a common charge heaped on Christians and other minorities in Pakistan. Since it is such a sensitive topic nobody comes forward to defend the one who has been falsely accused. In one of the cases where Ayub Massih, a catholic was convicted and sentenced to death on April 27, 1998, Bishop John Joseph Chairman of a human Right Commission established by Catholic Bishops Conference shot himself to death on 6th May (Wednesday) in the courthouse itself at Sahiwal where Ayub Massih was tried and sentenced to death. Hindu girls are abducted kidnapped, forcibly converted and married off to Muslims If any parents of such forcibly converted girls raise any objection, blasphemy law-a potent weapon is slapped against them and there is absolutely no remedy. Hindus live in constant fear for this reason. In one of the instances in early 1998 one Arib Bheel, an SC doctor in Khipro led a protest march of his community against kidnapping of two Bheel girls. But to the shock of the entire country he was charged with burning the holy Quran. There is religious discrimination and harrassment of Hindus and Christians. Even Judiciary does not come to the rescue of minorities.

Social violence continues in Pakistan and it continued in 1998 as well. A blood-thirsty system called karo-kari which takes human life is also prevalent in Pakistani society. It can be called honour killing as well. If a women is suspected of having an illicit relation with a man, she is traded as 'Kari' by her folk and the suspected man is 'Karo'. Both are considered a black blot of degradation on the honour and nobility of the suspected woman's family or tribe. Consequently, instant murder of both becomes a social obligation for the family or the tribe in order to save its so called honour and regain lost glory. In the year 1998 about 475 persons lost their lives in Karo-Kari. Among them 318 were women and remaining were men. 70% of the victims were under the age of 25. In the year 1999 the number rose to 500. Karo-Kari is deeply rooted in the feudalistic socieity of rural sindh. Gen. Pervez Musharraf did try to ameliorate the situation but did not succeed much.

His decision to pronounce the honour killing as a first rate murder was very constructive and a bold move. He sincerely wanted to pull the society in rural Sindh out of Dark Ages.[11] In Sindh province another prevalent custom is to marry a girl to Quran whose main aim is to prevent the family property from giving outside the family. Secondly she would concentrate on Quran only and would not think of raising a family. In Baluchistan and parts of NWFP, women is treated as a commodity 'Savera' is called to name this custom. One Tribe wanting to palliate a murder or settle some other dispute with another by offering one of its girls in marriage to the aggrieved one among the latter. In yet another custom 'Watta Satta' two families exchange their pair of siblings to same family property.

Inspite of upheavals and precarious situation inside the country, there was no slackeness in Pakistan's efforts to keep Kashmir supplied with militants. Lt. Gen. (Retd.) Hamid Gul advised these militant on Jan. 16, 1998 that they should expand their area of operation and tire out the enemy by targeting its Army bases even outside Kashmir. Gen. Gul a former ISI chief issued this call while he was attending an Iftar party hosted by Markaz-ul-Dhawat Al-Irshad which was also attended by Prime Minister Barrister Sultan Mehmood, his successor Sardar Adul Qayyum Khan, Sardar Sikandar Hayat Khan and other leaders of Azad Kashmir.[12] Gen. (Retd.) Mirza Aslam Beg in an article wrote that (1) Kashmir is an unfinished part of the agenda of the partition of the sub-continent and as such Pakistan cannot absolve itself of its historical obligations and commitments. Any predilection to do so would amount to timidity and national dishonour, never to be forgiven by the posterity and (2) The commitment made by Nehru can not be bypassed through Kautalian lies, distortious and political rigmaroles. In the year 1998 he wrote that the Kashmir war of liberation is also in it 8th year now.[13]

Information Minister Mushahid Hussain alongwith Punjab province Governor Shahid Hamid and other provincial ministers visited the Headquarters of Lashar-e-Taiba in Muridke (about 30 km from Lahore) in April 1998 and appreciated the work of the organization. He not only hailed the activities of Markaz Dawa Al Irshad (centre for preaching) which trains and maintains LeT, but also said the true concept of Jehad was being taught by the Markaz. Markaz cheif Hafiz Mohammad Saeed welcomed Hussains visit and said such trips by high-level government representatives would remove all misconceptions about the organisation. Hafiz Saeed continued Markez's involvement in militancy in Kashmir saying after the liberation of Kashmir, his organization would launch a 20-Crore Indian Muslims who he claimed had been living a second and third grade life.[14] Pakistan's aid to Kashmir militants alarmed even the united states of America. It said "Pakistan's official support to Harkat-ul-Ansar is cause for concern on the part of our government. It will have an impact on US policy towards Pakistan. As a result of insurgencies in Kashmir and the north-east, more than 25 bombings last year (i.e.1997) occurred. In Delhi these attacks appeared to be aimed at spreading terror among the public rather than causing casualties. In October 96 the HUA was designated a foreign terrorist organisation pursuant to the anti-terrorism and effective death penalty. Act of 1996. The Islamic militant group has carried out a number of operations against Indian troops and civilian largest in Kashmir. The HUA has several thousand armed supporters located in Azad Kashmir (PoK) and in the southern Kashmir and the Doda regions of India composed mostly of Pakistanis and Kashmiris and including Afghans and Arab veterans of the Afghan war"[15] HuA was formed in October 1994 following merger of Harkat-ul-Jihad Al-Islami and Harkat-ul-Murahideen. It is a Pakistan based terrorist organization.

REFERENCE

1. http: / / The fridaytimes. com/news 6.htm dt 10.18.99 Naram Sethi case: the worse type of Mc Carthysim by. Irshad Ahmad Haqqani Editor Daily Jang.

2. The Nation: Year Planner 1994.
3. Foreign Policy (Summer 1994): Dateline Pakistan: Bhutto's Back by Paula Newberg.
4. Ibid.
5. Two Research Papers by - Yossef Bodansky. published by Freeman Centre for Strategic Studies. Houston, Texas USA.
6. Ibid.
7. The News—Oct. 16, 1995 The rebellion that looks like a Childrens theatre—article by Kamran Khan.
8. Crossed Swords—Pakistan its Army and the wars within-by Shuya Nawaz Page 477.
9. The Hindustan Times June 21, 2006 Intelligence Quotient by Vikram Sood.
10. Crossed Swords: Pakistan, its Army and the wars within. By Shuya Nawaz Page 489.
11. DAWN- dt. June 15, 2000 It is time to burry the Karo-Kari system article by Shahid Ali Seehar.
12. The Frontier Post Jan. 17, 1998—Gul asks Kashmiris to expand area of operation.
13. Our Kashmir Policy—The Frontier Post-dt. Feb. 27, 1998 by. Gen. (Retd.) Mirza Aslam Beg.
14 Times of India April 22, 1998. Pakistan Minister visits militants training camp. By Shahid Ahmed Khan.
15 The Times of India May 2, 1998—Report by T.V. Parasuram mentioning state Department of US Govt. report.

7

Pakistan Goes Nuclear

Pakistan launched intermediate Range Gauri Ballistic Missile (IRBM) on April 6, 1996 with a range of 1500 km. United States advised Pakistan through Gen. Jehangir Karamat, who had visited US, to put it back by six months. In order to achieve nuclear parity with India and the right quantum of deterrence and then unilaterally restrain it at that threshold was the aim of Pakistan as per Gen. Aslam Beg's statement. He claims that Pakistans missile programme similarly was undertaken in the early 1987 on the explicit information gained that India was on the road to pursue its missile as well as chemical weapons development programmes.[1] Ghauri series is based on North Korean Liquid Fuel Rocket Technology whereas Shaheen Missiles incorporate Chinese solid fuel technology.

China's help to Pakistan on Nuclear Front:–

1974 : China assigns 12 scientists to help Pakistan develop a nuclear device.

1975 : China helps Pakistan build nuclear weapons research centres.

1977 : China and Pakistan plan to build and Test Pakistans first nuclear bomb, but the fall of Pakistans government suspends the operation.

1983 : China gives Pakistan complete design for a nuclear weapon and enough enriched uranium for two bombs, according to US Intelligence.

1986 : China reported by gives Pakistan enough tritium gas for 10 nuclear weapons, as well as enriched uranium.

1989 : China allows Pakistani scientists to observe a nuclear test.

1994–96 : China helps build 300 megawatt nuclear power plant at Kahuta.

1995 : A Chinese Company seats 5000 ring magnets used to make weapons grade uranium to nuclear research laboratory at Kahuta.

1996 : To avoid US reactions, China pledges not to provide assistance to unsafe guarded nuclear facilities in Pakistan. It also signs the Comprehensive Test Ban Treaty (CTBT).

1998 : Pakistan Tests its first nuclear Bomb.

On May 28, 1998 Pakistan went nuclear. Its nuclear programme was kept under wraps since 1983. Pakistan conducted five nuclear implosion at Chattar blast site in Rasko are of Chagai range of Baluchistan province on this day to claim 7th country in the world among the countries having weapons grade nuclear programme. Pakistan which was witherto known as a drug trading country felt enchanced in its prestige and confidence. On May 30, just 2 days after, it carried out another test–two in number. Raskoh where the tests were conducted is 100 Km off chagai Dr. Samar Mubarak Mund, Director General of National Development Complex (NDC) led the team of scientists which included Dr Fakharu Hasan Hashmi and Dr. Javed Arshad Mirza to conduct these tests of May 28 and 30. Test were successful. The team returned to Islamabad on May 31. While they were being welcomed at Chaklala airport, Dr. Samar Mubarak Mund announced that Pakistan is ready to test fire its medium range Shaheen-I missile carrying nuclear war heads upto 700 km and in working on Shaheen-II which can travel 2000 km.

The nuclear tests of May 28 made USA lift economic sanctions against Pakistan and granted a package of 5.5 billion dollars. In December 98 USA refunded the long outstanding amount of F-16s, of course on its own term. USA had advised

Pakistan not to conduct nuclear tests, yet Pakistan, went ahead ignoring US advise. When it comes to Pakistans own interests, it was observed that Pak Army kept aside US influence on it. There was some indecisiveness among prominent personalities in Pakistan whether it should also explode bomb visa-a-vis India. The Pakistan Times editorial advocated prudence on May 12 98, Lt. Gen. (Retd.) Rafaquate and Air Marshal (Retd.) Ashagar Khan opined Pak should not take any step in haste and watch for some time (May 15 and May 13 respectively), PPP senator Raja Rabbani opined on May 16 that Pakistan should not take any step in haste, Munir Ahmed Khan, Ex. Chairman Pakistan Atomic Energy Commission while speaking on PTV stated on May 17 that immediate test would not have the desired impact of Pakistan was not able to give a matching response. Lt. Gen. (Retd.) Talat Masood, a Defence Analyst opined (May 17) that Pakistan should not go for a test in haste and iresponsible manner. Reasons put forward by these personalities were that economic and other consequences should carefully be weighed before deciding to go nuclear. There should be a matching response lest the Test may prove to be counter productive and expose Pakistans weakness. This lot also wanted to extract maximum benefits from west particularly from USA for showing restraint. The benefits could be in the form more and open support on the position of Pakistan on Kashmir or US promising to provide a nuclear umbrella, defence supplies, debt relief and economic assistance. But there were other personalities who wanted Pakistan to give a befitting reply to Pakistan. Benazir Bhutto the leader of the opposition who was in London at that time taxed to Nawaz Sharif "what are you waiting for ?" and advised him to explode. In London on May 12 she said Pakistan has no choice but to conduct its nuclear test of its own and that too within a month Pakistan should respond. Former ISI chief Gen. Hamid Gul said on May 12 at Islamabad that Pakistan was urged to come up with an equally matching and powerful response. Abdul Sattar, former Foreign Minister wanted Pakistan to give befitting reply by taking proper measures on May, 12 at Islamabad. Gen. K.M. Arif desired (Islamabad May 12) that it is imperative for Pakistan to give a befitting and matching response. Jamaat-e-Islami chief Qazi Hussain Ahmed (Islamabad May 12) immediated nuclear test and opined that failure to so would boost India's hegemonic designs. Naib JI Amir Ghafoor Ahmed also wanted (Islambad May 12) to carry out nuclear tests. Dr. Qdeer Khan, the Nuclear scientist said (Islamabad May 13) that Pakistan is well placed to meet, any security threat. Dr Shireen Mazari, Editor 'Pulse weekly in an interview to PTV on May 17 wanted Pakistan to go for a immediate nuclear test. Foreign Minister Gohar Ayub Khan stated at Islamabad on May 13 that Pakistan can go for a nuclear test within 48 hours. Barrister Sultan Mehmood AJK Prime Minister and All Islam Pasand Parties strongly favoured a matching Pak-response to the nuclear test. Of course Pak opposition leader desired Nawaz government to mobilize public opinion in favour of conducting nuclear test.

The Federal cabinet met on May 14, 1998 to decide on the issue since a great deal of indecisiveness prevailed. Cabinet after taking all aspects into consideration authorised the Prime Minister Nawaz Sharif to take final decision himself on the issue. Nawaz Sharif in turn appointed a 4-member cabinet committee headed by Foreign Minister Gohar Ayub Khan and other members of which were Lt. Gen. (Retd.) Majid Malik, information Minister syed Mushahid Hussain and Raja Zafrul Haq Religious Affairs Minister. The Senate also resolved (May 14 itself) that they would support any step the Government took in this regard and also support the government and reject any unilateral discriminatory pressure from any quarter on matters pertaining to Pakistan's national security. It also condemned the adament stand of India to Continue and pursue its aggressive designs and just to acquire nuclear weapons to establish its hegemony in the region.

Pakistan's nuclear test perhaps can not be clamied to have taken place as a reaction to India action of May 11–13,1998 when it exploded in Pokhran ZA Bhutto in 1965 said "If India builds the bomb we will eat grass but we will get one of our own." Pakistans effort's in this direction started soon after Bangladesh war was over in Dec. 1971. ZA Bhutto had taken over reins of the country form Gen. Yahya Khan. Bhutto called a meeting of country's eminent scientists on Jan. 20, 1972 at the residence of Nawab Sadiq Qureshi, former Governor of Punjab, in Multan to discuss as to what contribution scientific community of the country can give in national defence and security. The meeting was attended by about 70 scientists which included Dr. Abdul Salam, chief scientific Advisor; Dr. I.H. Usmani Chairman PAEC; Dr. Z.A. Hashmi, Education Secretary, Munir Ahmed Khan, the Incharge of nuclear power and reactor division of the International Atomic Energy Agency in Vienna. Dr. A.Q. Khan was not invited in this meeting since he was still in holland and had not joined the PAEC. Z.A. Bhutto apprised them of the pain of defeat and humiliation of 1971 war and asked them specifically if they can meet India's Challenge and promised all resources they need. When they asked for 5 years time to accomplish the task, Bhutto gave them 3 years. A scientist S.A. Butt reassured Bhutto that it would be possible in three years as desired by him. Later, Butt, a nuclear scientist was to play a leading role in the procurement of various nuclear components and parts for the Pakistan Atomic Energy Commission. He was the man behind an elaborate procurement apparatus which the western press deliriously described as a net work of 'beg, borrow or steal." Bhutto announced that from that day Munir Ahmed Khan would be the chairman PAEC to step up Pakistan's pursuit of nuclear capability in real earnest. The Multan meeting was a watershed mark in the development of nuclear science and technology.[2]

Dr. Abdul Qadeer Khan is considered as father of Pakistan's nuclear programme. He was sentenced to a 4-years prison term in absentia by the Dutch government as for back as November 14, 1983 for stealing nuclear technology. Much later in October 1989, the Director General of the Pakistan Institute of Strategic Studies, Ross Masood Hussain declared at an international seminar in Italy that Pakistan had 'begged, borrowed and stolen" nuclear weapons technology adding "we did whatever had to be done'. In March 1995 late Gen. Zia-ul-Haq declared that they had acquired nuclear weapon capability in 1987. Then in 1990 both Gen-Mirza Aslam Beg and Pakistan President Ghulam Ishaq Khan separately declared that they would not hesitate to use a nuclear bomb against India there by confirming that they were already in actual possession of the Bomb[3] The first enrichment of uranium was done on April 4, 1978. The plant was made operational in 1979 and by 1981 it was producing substantial quantity of uranium. A.Q. Khan claimed that Pakistan can detonate a Hydrogen Bomb quickly[4]. On June 5, 1997 Dr AQ Khan confessed that "every Indian city is well within our target." We have satisfactory arrangements to safeguard the Kahuta Nuclear Plant from enemy attack. If any enemy dares aggression, we will teach him a lesson. We can also violate Indian Air space as and when we desire." On July 23, 1997 Pakistan had successfully tested two missile systems - ANZA and BAKHTARSIKAN.

Pakistan Atomic Energy Commission Chairman Ashfaq Ahmad had admitted that Pakistan had 40 Nuclear Establishment (till 1998). Pak Foreign office officially had informed India to have five 5 nuclear plants with Pakistan.[5]

1. Karachi Nuclear Power Plant
2. DG Khan Chemical Plants Complex for uranium processing and refining
3. Kundian Fuel Fabrication Complex
4. Rawalpindi - Pakistan Institute of Nuclear Science and technology
5. Kahuta Dr AQ Khan Research Laboratories.

Muslim world welcomed the nuclear tests of May 28 and 30. Irans Foreign Minister Kamal Kharazi apprised Pakistan on June 2, 1998 that "muslims in the middle east who were worried about Israel's nuclear capability now feel confident because our fellow Islamic nation bases the know-how to build nuclear weapons."

Baluchistan Cheif Minister Sardar Akhtar Mangel threatened to resign in protest against the failure of the Federal Government to Take it into confidence before the nuclear tests in Chagai region were conducted.

Lt. Gen. Javed Nasir, former ISI Chief lamented the jubilation shown by Indian and Pakistanis after their respective nuclear tests, as he considered nuclear rivalry to be of dangerous for regional society. He opined that "to say the least, Indian and Pakistanis do not have foggiest idea as to what can happen to them and to their generations if a nuclear confict is initiated even accidently." Air Marshal Rashid Shaikh of Pakistan Air Force is another opponent of nuke testing who argues that sanction would surt the country at a time when economic revival should have been higher priority. He regarded nuclear deterrence to be a recipt for collective suicide and urged that Pakistan should instead rely almost wholly an conventional forces for its security Lagainst India.[6]

The main architect of Pakistan's nuclear power Dr. Abdul Qadeer Khan is a Bhopal born (1936) scientist who migrated to Pakistan with family in the year 1952. In January 2004, Dr. Abdul Qadeer Khan admitted his involvement in an international network of nuclear weapons technology proliferation from Pakistan to Iran, North Korea and Libya. On Feb. 5, 2004 President Gen. Pervez Musharraf made it known to the world that he had pardoned Dr Khan. On Aug. 23, 2005 he confirmed that Dr. Khan had indeed supplied gas centrifuges and its parts besides uranium hexafluoride to North Korea but on May 29, 2008 Dr. Qadeer Khan in his first western media interview since 2004 denied his involvement in the spread of nuclear arms to above said countries. He stated that Musharraf and Pak Government had forced him to confess such a thing and that he was made a scapegoat for the national interests. He said "it was not of my free will. It was handed into my hands." He declared that he would never co-operate with any investigator from International Atomic

Energy Agency (IAEA) and that since Pakistan is not a signatory to Nuclear Non-proliferation Treaty (NDT), he had not violated any International Law. He also declared that details of his clendestine nuclear supply network were his internal affairs and his Country's affairs. Rebuking President Pervez Musharraf on May 29, 2008, Dr. Khan said "the country has gone to dogs in the last 10 years, people are hungry and prices are rising." Blaming the team leader (Pervez Musharraf) he stated that "the team leader is to be responsible for the failure of the Team but all those who were with him did not assert themselves and do a proper Job."

REFERENCE

1. DAWN April 26, 1998 Ghauri won't rock the region by General Mirza Aslam Beg.
2. The Frontier Post April 4, 1994 A Historic Meeting Recalled article by Farhatullah Babar.
3. The Times of India. June 1, 1998—Islamabad's Nuclear Capability dates back to 83–Dinesh Kumar.
4. Times of India June 1, 1918, report by L.K. Sharma.
5. Nawa-i-Waqt Feb. 21, 1998.
6. The Frontier Post at Feb. 16, 1999.

8
General Karamat Quits

The problems facing the country continued inspite of the fact the Pakistan became a nuclear power. 204 people got killed in sectarian violence in 1997. Gen. Jehangir Karamat COAS time and again punctuated PM Nawaz Sharif but his cautions fell in deaf ears. So much so, the COAS even threw a cleverly contrived caution that the Armed Forces have a constitutional duty to sea things go smooth and in good spirit reminding him that in the name of religion and ethnic identity, violence should not be the answer. He exhorted the nation to keep truce and calm and called upon Nawaz Administration to fulfill his government's responsibility and obligations to achieve the aim which Pakistan was created for and embrace people of different religious and ethnic background and that he would not tolerate constitutional crisis. Nawaz Sharif did not take all this in good spirit. Meanwhile, General Karamat, in a speech on Oct. 6, 1998 at the Naval Staff College, Lahore suggested formation of a National Security Council (NSC) to provide stability to the political system.[1] Nawaz Sharif did not like this advise from his chief of staff since he was riding a high horse after defeating SC cheif Justice Sajjad Hussain and wining on other political fronts like forcing the President to resign etc. nominating a President of his own choice. Nawaz Sharif considered it as interference in political attairs of the country and demanded Gen. Jehangir Karamat's resignation which he tendered on Oct. 7, 1998. Gen. Karamat was a literary and soft man. On his exit, Gen. Mirza Aslam Beg commented that "Army does not forget insult." However, his exit did exhibit supremacy of civil authority over the third arm of TROKA i.e. Military Establishment albeit temporarily as the later events proved.

Nawaz Sharif chose Lt. Gen. Pervez Musharraf to take over as chief of Army staff to replace Gen. Jehangir Karamat on Oct. 7, 1998 superseding Lt. Gen. Ali Quli Khan and Lt. Gen. Khalid Nawaz. Gen. Lt. Ali Quali Khan was not made COAS simply because he was related to Gohar Ayub Khan. Both of them sought retirement from Army. Gen Pervez Musharraf was chosen, as providence would have it for Nawaz Sharif, inspite of some black marks in his ACRs. His ACR clearly said that he is not fit for the appointment of the chief of Army Staff. ISI and other Intelligence outfits had reported that he was not 'suitable' for the post. They reported that Gen. Musharraf was a person who was 'quick in taking action and could easily be aroused. Takes action without deep thought.'[2] Nawaz was advised by his close friend Rashid Ahmed that he (Nawaz) would not be able to survive with a military commando (Gen. Musharraf) when he was not able to pull on well with a man like Gen. Jehangir Karamat. Since power was at its peak with Nawaz, he did not bother for any advise whatsoever.

Nawaz Sharif abhored criticism of his government even by the media. He set his intelligence men after a number of Journalists who wrote against his policies. Actions and adventures, even though they were justified in their write ups. Sindh was burning with all sorts of conflicts. Journalists criticised him for Undertaking 28 visits to 22 countries in his 32 month rule. He visited Turkey (14th June 1997), Malaysia (31th July 1997), Turkmenistan (15th October 1997), Britain (23 October 1997) Iran (8th December 1997), Turkey (18th December 1997), Bengladesh (15th January 1998), Britain (28th January 1998), China (10th February 1998), Saudi Arabia (24th March 1998), Italy (17th April 1998), Hong Kong (5th May 1998), Saudi Arabia (6th June 1998), Britain (13th June 1998), Qatar (27th June 1998), Sri Lanka (28th July 1998), Britian (8th September 1998), United States (19th September 1998), United States (30th November 1998). During 1999, Sharif visited the United Arab Emirates (UAE), Saudi Arabia, the United States and a few other countries.[3]

In October 1998 Governor's rule was imposed in Sindh

province and summary military courts were established. These courts awarded death sentence to two persons. With the result the Supreme Court had to intervene in Feb. 1999 to declare these courts unconstitutional.

On Oct. 1, 1998 an organisation by the name of Oppressed Nations Movement (PONM) was formed which gave a call for forming a loose confederation of Pakistan as was originally envisaged in the Lahore Resolution of 1940. PONM was formed as a result of unhappiness because of domination of Punjabis in all aspects of Pakistan. Pakistan Army was dominated, by and large, by Punjabis. They had rather captured the political life of the nation. Vibrant and dashing as Punjabis are, they possess a dominating nature. This characteristic is not liked by people from other provinces like Balochis, Sindhis or Pakhtoons. Together they raised a voice to redraft the constitution of Pakistan where all nationalities could be equal. To implement this line of thinking, they formed PONM. It Central Convenor was Senator Ajmal Khattak and it consisted of Awami National Party (ANP), Pakhtoon khwa Qaumi Party (PQP). Baloch National Movement (BNM) and Baloch National Party (BNP) led by their leaders. Mohammed Afzal Khan led PQP, Dr. Abdul Hayee Baloch led BNM. PKMP, PQP and Seraiki Qaumi Movement were also active members of PONM.

Kargil Misadventure and Perfidy

Insurgency in Kashmir was rooted in the ideology of Pakistan's Islamists carefully nurtured for decades by the Pakistan military.[4] In September 1998 when Indian troops of 121 infantry Brigade came down to lower heights from Kargil, the Force Commander of Northern Areas stationed in Gilgit who was commanding Pakistan's Northern Light Infantry (NLI) along with corps Commander X Corps decided to take on the posts so vacated by the Indian Army during winters. Meanwhile there was change at the level of chief of Army start in Islamabad. Gen. Jehangir Karamat resigned and his place was taken over by Gen. Pervez Musharraf on Oct. 7,

1998. At that point of time Gen. Pervez Musharraf was Commanding II Corps stationed in Multan. October 1998 onwards for five months, NLI, Islamic militants from Harkat-ul-Mujahideen (they were already designated as Foreign Terrorist Organization by US in 1997), Al Badar, Let and even some of personal bodyguards of Osama bin Laden moved from Camps in Jalalabad and occupied these vacated places after erecting well-dug trenches in the high mountains. All these militants were hosted, trained and equiped by NLI. Gen. Musharraf himself visited the Northern Areas twice during the winter of 1998-99. NLI had positioned its nine battalions. Somehow their movements went unnoticed by Indian side. Pak Army did notice the gap in India's strategic intelligence. On Feb. 20, 1999 when PM A.B. Vajpayee visited Lahore to meet PM Nawaz Sharif, the Kargil operation was already on. On Feb. 21, 1999 Lahore Declaration was signed by Shamshad for Pakistan and Raghunath for India. Nawaz Sharif claims that he was not aware of what was in place in Kargil. Gen. Musharraf has counter claims and he states that everybody was on board. It is indeed strange that the ISI which is supposed to report to PM on operational matters did not report to him as to what NLI was doing in Kargil heights. However, On May 6, 1999 the infiltration/incursion by Pakistan Army components in Kargil heights was detected by India. At least 130 of India's unheld posts had been occupied by NLI and other Pak supported militants. It was indeed strange that neither UNMOGP, nor CIA with all their aerial reconnaissance Vehicle were able to detect the incursion. Indian Army launched Operation Vijay, carried on aerial strikes and neutralised stinger missiles. The stringer missiles supplied by CIA to Pakistan to fight Soviet in Afghanistan were kept behind by Gen. Zia-ul-Haq and later on passed on to NLI to fight in Kargil heights and use against Indian Air Craft. It is these Stinger missiles which USSR became afraid of after loosing a few aircrafts which were accurately hit by Afghan Mujahideen and forced Russian forces to withdraw from Afghanistan. Had stinger missile not been there with Pak forces supplied by CIA, probably history would have been different Soviets would not have withdrawn from Afghanistan. A stinger brought down M-17 helicopter, a MIG-27 and a MIG.21 also went down. Indeed, Pakistani invasion took India by surprise but it is also equally true that Pakistan's efforts behind Kargil drama to internationalise Kashmir issue miserably failed and it rather backfired both at the national and international fronts. The entire civilized world took it as aggression. Even China told Pakistan to back off. In the Pakistan Army, young officers felt deeply betrayed. Pakistan was definitely panicky lest India opens up other fronts on the Indo-Pak border as it did in 1965 by opening up Lahore and Sialkot fronts and almost reached Lahore. In December 1999 when TIME interviewed Gen. Musharraf one of the questions asked was: "In New Delhi you are held responsible for last summer's war with India. How do you hope to normalise relations with India.? Musharraf's reply was 'I was Chief of Army staff, so I take full responsibility for whatever my army does. However, Kargil has to be seen in the total perspective of Kashmir, and such far reaching decision are not taken by one man alone. Everyone was on board, including the Prime Minister'. But the Pakistan Army has a history of acting on its own.[5] But Nawaz Sharif has a different version of the Kargil mischief. He told to the press corps on June 12, 2000 that he was not privy to the Kargil operation until May 1999 when the operation was well under way; begin as it did in January of that year. The operation was totally secret; even the chief of Air force and Navy were kept in the dark; the army leadership was pushing an agenda that ran contrary to the policy of civilian government, if he (Nawaz Sharif) had not contacted US President Bill clinton, the conflict could have resulted in a nuclear exchange with India; and finally, that if he knew about her operation, he would not have invited Indian Prime Minister A.B. Vajpayee to Lahore and begun the process of normalisation.[6] However from this incident onwards, relationship between P.M. Nawaz Sharif and the cheif of Army staff Gen. Perverz Musharraf became strained and culminated in the removal of Nawaz Sharif on Oct. 12, 1999 when the Army staged a coup d'etat. The civilian supremacy over military establishment was torn off by Gen. Musharraf that day.

One more word of caution on Kargil. Pakistan's Harkat ul-Mujahideen chief Fazlur Rehman Khalil stated soon after the winter season the mujahideen will launch a major offensive against the Indian troops and open a number of Kargils inside India and that Mujahideen would oppose any move aimed at division of Kashmir as it was not in the interest of Kashmiri people and would not serve Indian and US interests.[7]

Dr. Maleeha Lodhi, Pakistan's Ambassador to Washington form 1994 to 97 described Kargil as a "strategically flawed and unsustainable plan of guerilla action." (Newsline July 1999).

Ms Benazir Bhutto claimed that when she was Prime Minister, Gen. Pervez Musharraf had presented an early version of his Kargil plan to her which was ready as a 'war-game' and Pakistan was to claim that it was 'mujahideen operation'. But she put down her foot stating that "if anything like this happens, it will be a big setback for Pakistan. We will be forced to withdraw." But after she was out of office, the General went ahead with his plan. She desired to have the episode investigated so as to find out who was responsible for this humiliation. The former Prime Ministers remarks confirm the widely held view that General Musharraf planned the Kargil invasion using the 'Mujahideen' as a cover and was then forced to refuse to accept the bodies of Pakistani regulars because to do so would have meant accepting that the Pakistan army was involved.[8] The war game plan so presented by Gen. Musharraf was vetoed by the then PM Benazir.

Ahmed Rashid a famous writer of Pakistan, says: "Quote 'And when Sharif was first briefed by the Army in January 1999 about executing the Kargil operation, he gave the go ahead but then told nobody in the government, made no economic or foreign policy preparations for the resulting international fall out and went ahead on his own to invite Indian Prime Minister Atal Bihari Vajpayee to Lahore in February 1999. The Kargil operation was deemed necessary by the Army in order to revive the ten-year long Kashmir struggle that was being beaten back by huge Indian troops deployment and military action, but Sharif was party to the decision." unquote.[9]

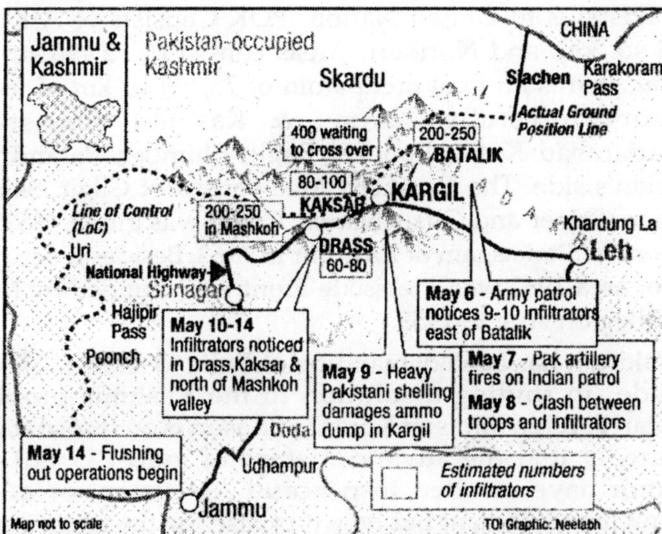

Courtesy – Times of India

According to a Radio news, Kargil misadventure resulted in 737 casualties including 45 officers 13 ISI and 68 SSG personnel for Pakistan. 270 Pakistani soldiers bodies were recovered, 262 burried, 8 pons handed over to Pak after its initial refusal to accept them. Pakistan had thrown 8 battalions into this action. India's casualties were: 471 killed and 1060 wounded.

Indias total tally of solidier killed and wounded form 1948 till 1999 was follows.

	1948	1962	1965	1971	1999
Killed	1104	3250	3264	3843	471
Wounded	3152	548	8623	?	1060

Compare it with the American loss is Vietnam war. As per American Congressman Charles Wilson in 1985, America lost 58,000 men in Vietnam war.

On Oct. 22 1947 Pak raiders invaded Kashmir. State of Azad Kashmir that came into existence on Oct. 24, 1947 under Sardar Muhammd Ibrahim. Maharaja Hari Singh of J&K Riyasat signed letter of accession to India on Oct. 26, 1947 and on Jan. 1, 1948 India takes the care of invasion of Kashmir by Pakistanis to United Nation. POK Consists of AJK area 5,703 sq. km. and Northern Areas consist of 72,496 sq. km. i.e. Pakistan is an total orcupatoin of 78,199 sq km of Indian territory forcefully. Jammu & Kashmir consists of Muzaffarabad Kothi, Poonch, Bagh, Bhimber, Palandri on Pakistan's side. The Northern Area consist of Gligit. Skardu. Diamer, Ghizer and Ghanchearea. China was gifted 4853% of territory in Shakasgam of Kashmir in 1963. Besides it occupied 20% of area 1962 war. Plebiscite Front was founded by Mirza Afzal Beg on Aug 9, 1955.

Pakistan has been demanding of India to show a "flexible attitude" in finding a solution to the Kashmir problem. Pakistan Foreign Minister Khurshid Kasuri is on record stating repeatedly that the advanced stage of indo Pak talks on Kashmir have resulted in peaceful Agreement or atleast nearing the settlement but he won't disclose the facts. Even if it is true, only five(5) persons know the details of solving the Kashmir puzzle until how. Though nothing was heard from Covt. of India, Kasuri says that the proposal would first be placed before the Pakistani parliament and then only would be made public. Mr. Francois Gautier, a French national and Editor-in-Chief of Paris based La Revue de L' Inde cautions Indian authorities against demilitarisation of Jammu & Kashmir emphasising that once the Army goes from J&K, it would result in chaos and Pakistani gamble of 20 year Proxy war will have paid. He further opines that Kashmiris have forsaken 'Sufism' and allowing Aurangzeb's spirit to take over. Mr Joseph sepp Blatter a 71 years Swiss national recently gave a clarion call to India to 'Wake up-Wake up". Though the call was given in the context of football game but it is equally valid and applicable to Kashmir front. CIA has asked us to tighten the security of His Holiness the Dalai Lama in view of threat to his life from Lashkar-e-Toiba (LeT). Gen. Pervez Musharraf's four proposals for solving Kashmir issue were also highly unfavourable to India. Demilitarisation or Joint Management Pakistan war to win on this point and allowing Pakistan to set its foot in the valley. Taking the cue from settled issues like Aland Islands–a dispute between Sweden and Finland or between Italia and Austria on South Tyrot or Anglo Spanish Control over Gibraltor or Noumea Agreement on New Caledonia, a fresh colony etc. are not comparable with Kashmir issue simply because the Christains inhabited all these colonies whereas in Kashmir the big question involved is a religious one i.e. Hindus and Muslims besides the question of territory. In fact the crux of matter is that Pakistan is interested in possession of territory only. It is simply using Kashmiri muslims as a ploy but they are not interested in these muslims. This point Kashmiri muslims are not understanding. As Such, Kashmir and Andorra or for that matter Kashmir and Trieste are uncomparable. Gen Musharraf dropped Pakistan's age old demand of plebescite. It is not for nothing Musharraf did so. He pretty well knew that this demand has become obsolete and would not fetch any support from America or European union or Russia or even China. Mr M.P. Bhandara an eminent personality of Pakistan, MNA and Industrialst had already said decade ago that the UN resolutions on plebscite had become obsote and non-enforceable ISI-instigated and supported demand for 'Khalistan' is still simmering. Mr. John Thomson, President of Toronto's Mackenzzie Institute has stated that support for Khalistan exists to some extent in Canada and could rise. ULFA with active support from ISI demands independent Assam. Under Operation PINCODE, ISI has tried to create disturbances in North Eastern states of India through DGFI of Bengladesh. Pakistan had demanded in thdramal of Indian security Forces from Kupwara, Baramullla and Srinagar. Why? Simply because should India agree or in Gen. Musharrafs terminology, show flexibility.' the vacated areas would be occupied by under-cover pro jihadi and Pak Army elements under civilian garb to Co habit with locals. Indian Army Chief Gen. JJ Singh put his foot down and did not allow withdrawal of troops from these areas. Otherwise more or less another Kargil would have been created. It was also Pakistan's intention to facilitate the infiltration of miltants in J & K through these areas should Indian Army withdraws from these areas. Since it did not happen, Pak Army Rangers have started cutting the fencing wire on LoC and infiltrate militants in Jammu & Kashmir. Gen. Musharrafs statement on Jan. 12, 2002 that "Kashmir runs in our blood. No Pakistani can afford to sever links with Kashmir" reveals the hidden resolve of ISI and its resolute efforts in de-stabilising India. Pakistan Army is not going to relent even if the Kashmir riddle in solved. Pakistan Army is itching to revenge dismemberment of their country (mulk) in 1971. Hardly a few people in India know that at the time of induction or comission in Pakistan Army,a soldier or officer is administered oath that he would take revenge from India for 1971 dismemberment of Pakistan by India. While advocating support for Kashmir cause, former ISI DG Lt-Gen. (Retd.) Asad Durrani gave out the following policy directions at a seminar organised by "The News" at Islamabad on Feb. 23, 2000:

(*i*) Since India will not attack Pakistan, Do not scumb to their threats. (How true ! India did move its Army right upto borders and even gave a call for "aar par ki ladai" but did not go 'par'.

(*ii*) International Community is not likely to declare Pak a terrorist sponsoring state. As such, international threats should be resisted.

(*iii*) Destroy India from within, for which Pakistan has the capability. (Flooding India with Quetta printed fake Indian currency of Rs. 100, Rs. 500 and Rs. 1000 denomination and disturbing India's economic equilibrium is one example of this policy direction. Bomblasts from muslim organization like SIMI is also a step in the direction of destroying India from within.

(*iv*) World community would question Pakistan on terrorism anywhere regardless of whether Pak extends support in Kashmir or not.

(*v*) Keep local resistance in Kashmir alive and appeal to international community about pathetic conditions of Kashmiris in J & K.

Gen. Musharraf always harped on India showing flexibility. Gen. Durrani ex-ISI DG assessed the situation also what is happening and anticipated the events and influenced the policy and action. Thereafter followed the developments of the situation and events so as to have complete control over them. Directly or indirectly Pakistan and its ISI influenced the situation to be adverse to India and directed their developments. It provided access to China in Construction of Gwadar (Baluchistan) sea port which in turn has direct access in the Persian Gulf to hunt for Oil. China is also constructing an Airport of International standard there, has agread to establish six (6) new nuclear power plants to be located at Qadirabad - Bulloki link Canal, Dera Ghazi Khan canal near Taunsa bridge, Tunsa - Punjnad canal near Multan, Nara canal near Sukkur, Pat Feeder canal near Guddu and Kabul river near Nowshera. Construction of Karrakoram Highway linking China with Rawalpindi, military cooperation with countries surrounding India like Nepal Bengladesh, Myanmar and Sri Lanka, Irrawady corridor and Coco Islands in Yangoun, building of sea port at Chittagong and Hamban Tota (Sri Lanka), plans to divert the direction of the river in Tibet which in India is known as Brahmputra etc. are a few instances which should make India anticipate the future outcome. Who anticipates the future and influences the developments? It could be politicians or Bureaucrats in Indian context. It falls mainly on Intelligence Organization to fill the Bill since politicians come and go. And there are no more Raj Gopalacharis, Govind Ballabh Pants, Pilloo Modis and a number of the likes. How many Purushottam Dass Tondons, Minoo Masani, Sardar Ballabh Bhai Patels or Chandra Bhanu Gupta are there to anticipate the future and then influence the situations, make policy to counter these future developments ? Even amongst Bureaucrats, eminent writers have come out with opinions not so encouraging. "It is no longer possible to assume that a civil service exam passed years ago qualifies a person to be an Intelligence officer. Each rookie believes to have fair chance to make it to the top slot."[10] Yet another writer[11] stated that "the agencies are amataurs showing no sign of becoming professional bodies. lack of accountability, their working carefully hidden from public gaze". In such situations how can they anticipate the future and influence developments ? There are fair chances of lapses at every stage. Even CIA could not utilize the advance information furnished by French Intelligence on 9/11. Le Monde claims to have given a fresh report of Jan. 2001 to a Paris-based CIA operative regarding plan to hijack an aircraft by Islamic radicals. Much on this topic is soon to be revealed by the former CIA Chief George Tenet in his memoirs. Canadian police had prior warning of Kanishka Bombing exploded on June 23, 1985, MI-5 let 7/7 bombers slip through twelve times etc. etc.

Gen. Durrani former DG ISI's dictum "destory India from within" has always to be remembered. It is under this dictum, ULFA is being assisted by ISI to demand independent Assam. Foreign Minister Mehmud Kasuri stated, time and again, that Kashmir issue is near solution, anticipating the situation that more than 50 terrorist camps are operating in Pakistan. Islamic militants will take Training in these camps and then infiltrate into India. Z.A. Bhutto had said that "they will eat grass but produce nuclear bomb" and they have done that. Pakistan was almost at the verge of bankruptcy. Yet it imported missiles from North Korea to be used against India-specific targets. It is also preparing to deploy Gen. Next nuclear missile Shaheen-2 bringing most of the Indian cities within its striking range. To understand the design of ISI against India, one has to be 10 times cleverer than those of ISI people. Gen. Musharraf holds the view that "India is a hegemonic power. Low-intensity conflict with India will continue even of Kashmir issue is solved." ISI has already chalked out strategy for the next 15 years to augment its national defence. During the last 3-4 years Pakistan spent more amount on improving nuclear capability than in the past 30 years. It claims to have far better tanks than India adding that it has enough resources and that the two pillars of the country - Defence and Economy - are strong, Gen. Musharraf does not want to involve people and says "It was for senior leaders of India and Pakistan to take decision. You cannot more forward on intractable issues if you involve peoples."

CIA has predicted Yugoslovatic-like fate for Pakistan and its becoming a failed state by 2015.

Justifying the Kargil action, one writer says "the need to reassure the Kashmiri people was never felt with the result that they thought that their sacrifices were forgotten and political regimes were out to gain their own advantages through the usual meaningless dialogues. Something like Kargil was therefore just waiting to happen it come as a surprise because all the warning signs were ignored and the sacrifices of the Kashmiri people taken for granted." Justifying ISI's action the wniter further says "Contrary to what is being propogated by India, the ISI has consistently acted to keep situations within acceptable thresholdes inspite of pressures to act otherwise."[12]

Pakistani english daily 'The Frontier Post' of October 22, 1999 published an online newsitem from New York stating that the state owned Pakistan Telecommunication Company Limited (PTCL) was used for leaking national defence secrets to the Indians as well as for personal monetary benefits by a minister and top authorities. The complete news report is reproduced here with for the use of the readers. The conversation between the then COAS Gen. Musharraf who was then in China and his Chief of staff Lt. General Mohammed Aziz which appeared in the Hindustan Times of 12.6.1999 is also reproduced in full. The newsitem claims that the conversation was recorded by SBD section of PTCL then headed by Nuruddin Bugai under directives of DG Intelligence Bureau Col. Iqbal Niazi. There were other claims also of having intercepted the talks between Gen. Musharraf and his cheif of staff Lt. Gen. Aziz but I am not dwelling into it for the moment. The report says "these tapes were handed over to the former Information Minister who leaked the tapes to Indians through a journalist." The report further refers to an interview of Dr. Qadeer Khan with an Indian journalist in 1987 regarding Pakistan processing Nuclear device. Adrian Levy & Catherine scott-clark in their book "DECEPTION Pakistan, the United States and the global nuclear weapons conspiracy writes (Page 148 to 151) that "Gen Zia wanted to deliver a threat that would force India to back down" in view of operation Brass Tacks in December 1986 authorised by Rajiv Gandhi and launched by General K. Sunderji. Lest 1971 is repeated Gen. Zia asked the nuclear scientist "AQ Khan to arrange an interview that would play loudly in India, in which he would reveal just a little more of the secret work at KRL." Khan approached Mushahid Hussain who was then editor of the Muslim' newspaper and one Indian journalist happened to be an old friend and syndicated columnist of 'the Muslim'. Meanwhile Mushahid Hussain was to get married and he had sent an invitation to the Indian journalist, All of them grabbed the opportunity together and deliberately leaked the story of Pakistan possessing a nuclear device and its willingness to assemble and deliver a bomb should it be sufficiently provoked." However the planning of Gen. Zia was successful and the Observer of London broke the story on March 1, 1987 quoting Khan as saying "what the CIA has been saying about our possessing the bomb is correct. They told us Pakistan could never produce the bomb and they doubted my capabilities, but they now know we have it."

On using nuclear weapons against India even Gen. Pervez Musharraf admitted (Dec. 30, 2002) that he had conveyed messages to (Indian) Prime Minister Atal Bihari Vajpayee through every international leader who came to Pakistan that if Indian troops moved a single step across the international border or the line of control they should not expect a conventional war from Pakistan. And that he was prepared to nuclear-bomb if New Delhi had launched strikes into its territory.[13]

REFERANCE

1. Crossed Swords Page 498 by Shiuja Nawaz.
2. Ibid Page 500.
3. The Friday Times June 9, 2000 On board the Chief Executive's plane—by Amir Mir.
4. Pakistan between Mosque and Military by Hussain Haqqani Page 235.
5. The News on Sunday - Kargil was not an aberration. article by (dt June 18, 2000) Farrukh Sallem.
6. The Friday Times June 16, 2000. Sharif's Statement and the issue of civil Military Relation - By Ejaz Haidar.
7. The Nation dt 15-12-1999.
8. Weekly Independent Dec.-6-12, 2001. ISI bugged me as Premier–Complied by Hussain Sajjad.
9. The Nation dt. November 12, 1999. The coup in Perspective-article by Ahmed Rashid.
10. The Hindustan Times dt. June 21, 2006. Article by Vikram Sood.
11. V. Balachandran March 18, 2007.
12. The News Aug. 5, 1999 Learning from Kargil of Jehangir Karamat.
13. The Hindustan Times Dec. 31, 2002 cross Border Fire: Pervez: I was ready nuke India—report by Mubashir Zaidi & Agencies form Islamabad on Dec. 30, 2002

9

General Pervez Musharraf Takes Over and Gives Up

On July 4, 1999 Prime Minister Nawaz Sharif dashed to US to meet President Bill Clinton who put pressure on him to withdraw from Kashmir. He ordered NLI troops and ISI sponsored muslim mujahideen of LeT and other militant outfits to withdraw from Kashmir (Kargil heights) to end the stand off with India. This order he issued on July 12, 99 which caused friction between Nawaz Sharif and his chief of Army staff Gen. Pervez Musharraf. Earlier throughout June-July, 99 border Skirmishes erupted between India and Pakistan over muslim militants and NLI troops who had seized hill top positions on the Indian side of Kashmir. When the intrusious were detected by Indian Security forces, they adopted a threatening posture and started action to evict them from Kargil and Drass Sectors. Meanwhile, on July 16, 1999 Army chief Gen. Musharraf came out with a note of discord saying Nawaz Sharif and his government were in on the plans of infiltration of India-held Kashmir.

On Sept. 20, 1999 America had warned Pakistan of a possible coup stating that it would oppose any attempt to overthrow the government through unconstitutional means. On Oct. 9, Gen. Musharraf visited Sri Lanka to attend an official function from where he was to return on Oct. 12. Nawaz Sharif alongwith his ISI Chief Gen. Ziauddin paid a one day visit to UAE on Oct. 12 and returned to Islamabad same day, announced sacking of Gen. Pervez Musharrf and appointed ISI chief Gen. Ziauddin as the new Chief of Army staff with immediate effect. Nawaz did not allow the plane

Pk-806 which was bringing Gen. Musharraf back to Pakistan to land any where in Pakistan. The aircraft remained in the sky and it almost exhausted fuel. Desperate, Gen. Musharraf contacted Gen. Usmani in Karachi who took over the Karachi Airport and asked Gen. Musharraf's aircraft PK-806 to land at Karachi. Had Nawaz Sharif allowed Gen. Musharraf to land, perhaps Nawaz still would have been in power and history would have been different. In the meantime when ISI chief Gen. Ziauddin reached GHQ to take over as chief of Army staff, he was mestrained saying that he could do so only after Gen. Musharraf returns to Rawalpindi form Sri Lanka. Perhaps, it was this abuse of power by the head of state which compelled coAs Gen. Musharraf to take over the reins of the country on Oct. 12, 1999 and dismiss Nawaz Sharif Government. Not allowing him to land in Pakistan was immediate provocation that swung Gen. Musharraf to take this action. That night he halted at Karachi itself. He called a meeting of Corps Commanders on Oct. 13 which was presided over by himself and took a decision not to impose martial law and instead he proclaimed Emergency on Oct. 14, 1999 after taking over the control of the government from Nawaz Sharif in a dramatic coup. The civilian rule of almost eleven years ended abruptly.

Whenever there was political turmoil or political uncertainty or misrule, Army took over the governance overthrowing civilian rule. The first Martial law was imposed on Oct. 7, 1958. Successive Martial laws in 1969 by Gen. Yahya Khan in 1977 by Gen. Zia-ul-Haq and then in Oct. 1999 by Gen. Pervez Musharraf (though Musharraf named it Emergency but in essence it was Martial law): once again in Nov. 2007 by Gen Musharraf, were imposed which weakened the democratic process and enabled Army to emerge stronger, independent, effective and sole player even in the domestic political life of the nation.

Roedad Khan former secretary Ministry of Interior of the government of Pakistan has summed up the military takeovers nicely as follows: "But ultimate power in Pakistan–that in highest power over citizens, unrestrained by law—continues to reside where the coercive power resides. Its power to abrogate the constitution, dissolve the parliament and sack elected governments with impunity is not affected by the repeal of 58(2) (b). Nawaz Sharif's biggest Challenge in the days ahead, therefore, will be managing relations with *'Le pouvoir'*, the defacto sovereign, because it is their will which is ultimately obeyed by the citizens. It is an ironical fact that in the history of Pakistan no central government, whatever its mandate, has ever lost power on the floor of the house in consequence of a vote of no-confidence brought against it. It is a unique feature of our stunted, pallied democracy that parliamentary strength does not guarantee the stability or survival of government and loss of power is invariably brought about by extraneous forces. It would, therefore, come as no surprise it in spite of the Mandate of Heaven–or perhaps because of it-Nawaz Sharif's tryst with destiny ends in a puft of smoke." (This he wrote about two years ago when Nawaz Sharif was at the peak of his power. Thereafter in the same article he wrote as follows. "It is now abundantly clear that whatever the constitutional position, in the final analysis de facto sovereignty in Pakistan (Majestas est summa in civas ac subditoes legibusque soluta potestars i.e. "highest power over citizens and subjects unrestrained by law" in the words of French jurist Jean Bodin) resides neither in the electorate, nor the Parliament nor the executive, nor the Judiciary, nor even the Constitution–which has superiority over all the institutions it creates. It resides, it resides anywhere at all, where the coercive power resides. In practice, it is the pouvoir occulte which is the ultimate authority in the decision-making process in Pakistan. They decide when to abrogate the constitution; when it should be suspended; when elected government shall be sacked, and when democracy should be given a chance. The political sovereignty of the people is a myth. To apply, the adjective sovereign to the people in today's Pakistan is a tragic force. Of course, if the term is used in the strictly legal sense, sovereign power under our constitution also resides in our Parliament (now suspended). But, as Dicey says, the world sovereignty is sometimes employed in a political rather than in a legal sense, and in that sense that body alone is sovereign in a state the will of which is ultimately obeyed by the citizens."[1] what a brilliant analysis is given by the learned retired bureaucrat who had many feathers to his cap. His book Pakistan–A Dream gone sour is masterpiece of work on political developments in Pakistan.

On Oct. 14, 1999 Gen. Musharraf suspended the constitution, become chief Executive, appointed an eight member National security council on Oct. 25 to function as Pakistan's supreme governing body. On May 12, 2000 supreme court validated the Oct. 12. 99 coup and granted Gen. Musharraf both executive and legislative authority for three years from the date of coup under the doctrine of necessity plea. He addressed the nation on Oct. 17, 1999 clarifying that the military take over is not martial law, only another path to democracy. The armed forces have no intention to remain in charge any longer than is absolutely necessary to pave the way for true democracy to flourish in Pakistan." He also placed a seven-point agenda before the nation:–

1. Rebuild national confidence and morale.
2. Strengthen federation, remove inter provincial disharmony and restore national cohesion.
3. Revive economy and restore investor confidence.
4. Ensure law and order and dispense speedy justice.
5. Depoliticise state Institutions.
6. Devolution of power to the grass roots level.
7. Ensure swift and across the board accountability.

The Army overthrow Nawaz Sharif under secret operation. "OPERATION SOLIDARITY" in Oct. 1999 whereas Zia-ul-Haq overthrew Z. A. Bhutto in 1977 under operation "FAIRPLAY".

To begin with Gen. Musharraf indeed had all good intentions to make Pakistan a modern Islamic state, free of corruption and an enlightened state. He wanted all members of Parliament to be educated and prescribed minimum qualification of graduation to become an MP. He even took time to pick up his team and selected highly reputed, honest and competent bureaucrat like Mr. Tariq Aziz as his principal secretary. Aziz was above any controversial and dishonest deals. Gen. Musharraf appointed Lt. Gen. (Retd.) Mohammad Shafiq, as Governor of NWFP who took oath on Nov. 3, 1999 on the suggestion of the then corps Commander of Peshawar Lt. Gen. Saeed-uz-Zafar. Lt. Gen. Shafiq, who belonged to Kohat from where maximum number of persons had Joined Defence forces, had served as Inspector General Frontier Corps (IGFC) and was corps commander in Bahawalpur when Gen. Zia-ul-Haq's C-130 Aircraft crashed in the area on Aug. 17, 1998. Gen. Musharraf also tried to ensure, through his corps commanders that no official with a tainted background should get an important posting in any of the lucrative department including police.

The fact is that Gen. Musharraf, indeed, had no inclination to stage a coup though he was damn annoyed with Nawaz Sharif for so many reasons. Jean-Charles Bristard and Guillaume Dasquie write in their combindly written book "The Forbidden truth' that the October 1999 military coup led by Musharraf that originally toppled Sharifs regime was sparked by animosity, between the two camps, as well as Sharifs personal corruption and political megalomania" and "Concerns that Sharif was dancing too eagerly to Washington's tune on Kashmir and Afghanistan." (Page 32 of the book).[2]

Political parties which were allowed to operate within limits on the eve of military take over on Oct. 12, 1999 were:

1. Awami National Party (ANP) led by Wali Khan.
2. Balochistan National Movement. Hayee Group (BNM-H) led by Dr Hayee Baloch.
3. Baluch National Party - Sardar Akhtar Mengal (BNP).
4. Jamhoori Watan Party (JWP) led by Akbar Khan Bugti.
5. Jamiat-al-Hadith (JAH) led by Sajid Mir.
6. Jamiat-ulema-i-Islam (JUI-F) led by Fazlur Rehman.

7. Jamiat. ulema-i-Pakistan-Niazi (JUP.NI) led by Abdul Sattar Khan Niazi.
8. Millat Party - led by Farooq Leghari.
9. Milli Yekjheti Council (MYC) - an umbrella organization which included Jamaat-i-Islami or JI (Qazi Hussain Ahmed), Jamiat ulema-i-Islam, Sami-ul-Haq faction JUI(s), Tehrik-i-Jafria Pakistan (TJP) led by Allama Sajid Naqui, and Jamiat ulema-i-Pakistan (Noorani faction) (JUP-NO) led by shah Ahmad Noorani.
10. Muttahid a Qaumi Movement Altaf faction MQM(A) led by Altaf Hussain.
11. National People's Party (NPP) led by Ghulam Mustapha Jatoi.
12. Pakhtoon Khwa Milli Awami Party (PKMAP) led by Mahmood Khan Achakzai.
13. Pakhtoon Qaumi Party (PQP) led by Mohammed Afzal Khan.
14. Pakistan Awami Tehrik (PAT) led by Tahir-ul-Qadri.
15. Pakistan Muslim League–Functional group (PML-F) led by Pir Pagaro.
16. Pakistan Muslim League-Junejo faction (PML-J) led by Hamid Nasir Chattha.
17. Pakistan Muslim League-Nawaz Sharif faction PML(N) led by Nawaz Sharif.
18. Pakistan Muslim League-Qaud-e Azam fraction led by Mian Azhar.
19. Pakistan National Party (PNP) - led by Hasil Bizenzo
20. Pakistan People's Party (PPP) Benazir Bhutto.
21. Pakistan People's Party (PPP-SB) led by Ghinwa Bhutto w/o of Shaheed Bhutto.

22. Pakistan Tehrik-e-Insaf (PTI) led by Imran Khan.

In the year 2001, incidently, Pakistan Muslim League had the following factions.

PML (N)—Acting President Makhdoom Javed Hashmi

PML (J)—President Hamid Nasir Chatta

PML (Q)—President Syed Kabir Ali Wasti

PML (Jinnah)—President Azad Bin Haider

PML (Warloo)—President - Mian Manzoor Wattoo

PML (LM) (i.e like Minded group)—led by Mian Muhammad Azhar (formed an March 25, 2001)

PML (Saifullah Group)—President Saifullah Saif

PML (Qayyum group)—President Aman Khan

PML (Functional)—led by Pir of Pagara

All PML (N) factious were asked to unite on June 3, 2001 for a strong and stable Pakistan.

THE NATION OCTOBER 20, 1999

NEW YORK–The flight time between Colombo and Karachi is only 210 minutes. But as passengers on PIA flight 805 discovered last Tuesday. much can transpire in that span of time.

The VIP on board, General Pervez Musharraf was returning from a weekend attending the Sri Lankan army's 50th-anniversary celebrations and playing golf. Once the plane took off from Colombo, Musharraf's civilian boss, Prime Minister Nawaz Sharif, attempted to seize control over the military. Sharif fired Musharraf from his job, had his replacement announced on television and arranged that Musharraf's plane be prevented from landing at Karachi's airport, says a report in TIME.

What the Prime Minister didn't know, though he probably should have, was that the military saw it all coming. While Musharraf was in the air, incommunicado and oblivious to what was transpiring for most of the flight, colleagues on the ground surrounded Parliament and other government buildings, as well as Sharif's residence and those of a number of military and political allies. Sharif's brother Shahbaz Sharif was whisked from his Lahore home after getting a few slaps from a military man. Soldiers climbed a fence to seize TV station and secured Karachi's airport to await their cheif's landing.

The 6:50 p.m. arrival time came and went, but the General's plane remained in the air. From Karachi's control tower. The pilot was told to land elsewhere. He responded that he was short of fuel; the control tower told him to go to India or Nawabshah where police were waiting to arrest the General.

After the plane had circled for 40 minutes, both the airborne Musharraf and his men on the ground realized something was wrong. The General entered the cockpit and told the pilot to land; his loyalists at the airport reached the control tower and found the head of PIA, a Nawaz appointee, giving the orders. The plane ultimately landed with only five minutes' worth of fuel left.

Seven hours later, he was on nation wide television making a stern announcement: the elected Sharif government was overthrown. Forty-eight hours later, he declared that the Constitution was "in abeyance" and that the "whole of Pakistan will come under the control of the Armed Forces."

For the international community, the events in Pakistan last week were something new and distinctly frightening. When Sharif's government tested six atomic weapons in May last year, following the lead of neighbouring India, it became the seventh country to detonate a nuclear bomb. Last week it be came the first nuclear-armed nation in history to have a government overthrown by a military coup d' etat.

The US Defence Department hastened to note that Pakistan's atomic arsenal, believed to consist of some 25 bombs, had always been in military hands, never controlled by the country's Prime Minister or President, who is nominally Commander-in-Chief. Said Pentagon spokesman Kenneth

Bacon: "I don't think that anyting should change."

But clearly much has changed; Pakistan's nuclear status has placed the world on the edge of its seat. Sharif was boldly, perhaps recklessly, attempting to split his country's military while its chief was aloft and seemingly helpless.

That the attempt failed owes as much to the military's inherent unity as to recent moves by Musharraf to consolidate his control. Starting last month, he replaced two of the country's nine Corps Commanders, the backbone of military control, with men he could trust. India Pakistan's major military rival initially reacted to the coup by putting its armed forces on high alert. But within a few days, Delhi's leader were making sanguine statements, apparently convinced that the coup was a domestic situation, not an immediate regional threat.

Pakistan's return to military rule also belies the notion that the 20th century is ending on a wave of irreversible, global democratisation. Following the People Power Revolution in the Philippines, the 1988 return of democracy to Pakistan – which has been run by the army for 25 of its 52 years of independence – was one of the shining land marks on that road. A nation of 140 million people had regained a large parcel of democratic freedoms and fully embraced at least one: the ability to throw out the old guard via the ballot. In each general election of the past decade, they voted against the previous government.

There were, however, at least two major flaws in the system. First, the Constitution allowed the President, usually with military backing, to toss out the government at his discretion. This fate has befallen each administration: that of Benazir Bhutto in 1990 Sharif in 1993. Bhutto again in 1996. Always on charges of corruption and misuse of power. The bigger problem was that the same faces kept coming back: the political system was dominated by the PML and PPP.

Even more worrying are the triumphant crowings of

Islamic groups. Their post-coup celebrations were especially fevered, perhaps because the last military ruler of Pakistan, General Zia ul-Haq, used Islamization to lend legitimacy to his rule. Musharraf is reputed to be cut form very different cloth, but that hasn't stopped the Islamists from hoping for a conversion of political convenience.

By week's end, Pakistan's new government setup was still opaque. Musharraf announced a state of emergency that was still a half-pace short of martial law, and he said nothing about the possibility of future elections. There were expectations that the General would soon spell out specific plans for the new administration.

Most importantly at the end, Nawaz Sharif's relations with the military were shaky. Late last year, Musharraf's predecessor was forced to resign after he proposed setting up National Security Council, a suggestion the Prime Minister took as a threat. Musharraf was considered a tolerable replacement, and possibly a seatwarmer for Lt. General Khwaja Ziauddin, a Sharif family friend and head of the Inter-Service Intelligence (ISI).

Last Tuesday at 3:45 p.m., just after Musharraf had boarded the plane in Colombo, Sharif summoned the ISI's Lt. General Ziauddin for a meeting at his Islamabad residence. A camera crew taped the Prime Minister decorating his new military chief. The video was sent to PTV to be broadcast as a bulletin at 5 p.m. and again on the main news programme an hour later. Presumably, Ziauddin was then supposed to move quickly to clean out the top army brass. Police officers were on standby at Karachi's airport to arrest Musharraf, while other police waited at the small airport at Nawabshah. The men did't move fast enough. As soon as Ziauddin started calling his Corps Commanders, they quickly put into effect their counter-coup. Soldiers took over PTV before the 6 p.m. broadcast. At 6:30 p.m. three army trucks pulled up at Sharif's residence; soldiers went to the door and ordered the security men, house hold staff and gardeners to leave. "We handed over the keys and left the premises,' says one guard. Before Musharraf's plane touched down, soldiers had taken control of the airport and the radio and television stations, and put a number of Ministers under house arrest. At 9:30 p.m., a convoy of jeeps left Sharif's residence carrying Ziauddin. The Prime Minister was also taken into custody that night; both were taken to safe houses at Chaklala airbase.

However prepared Musharraf and his team were to take over, they had plainly given scant attention to what to do afterward. In the two days following Sharif's overthrow, the Generals attempted to get President Muhammed Rafiq. Tarar to declare an official nationwide state of emergency. The President declined, so Musharraf declared it himself and announced that the Constitution was being suspended.

Some predict the military will have to install civilians, partly to assuage the international community–including donors of millions of dollars in vital aid–but also to shield themselves from blame if they fail to turn Pakistan around.

'Coup was not Pre-planned'

NEW YORK–Nawaz Sharif was democratically elected, but he isn't a democrat. The former Prime Minister, ousted last week in a coup, acted more like a despot after his landslide electron victory 1997. He amended the Constitution to strip the President of the power to remove him. He sacked the Cheif Justice. He treated the country like a family estate, seeding national institutions with relatives and friends. And he did all this even as he led the economy to further ruin. So when Nawaz last week tried to oust his Army chief, Gen. Pervez Musharraf, the Generals ousted him instead, says a report in Newsweek.

So Pakistan's latest coup isn't any thing to worry about, right? Wrong. If Nawaz were a democrat, Pakistan at least would have a leader to rally be hind and an ideal to aim for. Now cynicism pervails. The country has the proven ability to build a nuclear bomb. But it can't master the more subtle science of effectively managing its own affairs. It's got a violent history with India, and it's also on a grim list of post-cold-war countries listing dangerously toward lawlessness.

"There is every danger of Pakistan becoming a failed state," exiled opposition leader Benazir Bhutto, who faces corruption charges at come, told Newsweek last week in New York. "Many Pakistanis have been talking about this that we need to wake up and save our own nation because the rest of the world can't save us"

The Generals now in charge probably share that concern. It seems the coup last week was not the result of meticulous planning by the military, but rather an immediate reaction to threats to its own interests. Musharraf was on a plane when Nawaz unceremoniously fired him; only then did the Army step in. Units loyal to Musharraf took over the TV station and the airports. Other soldiers arrested Nawaz, his brother and Lt. Gen. Khawaja Ziauddin, the head of ISI.

But the Generals were stumped about what to do next. They apparently tried to persuade Nawaz–who was incommunicado–to resign and dissolve Parliament. If Nawaz had agreed, the Army could have appointed a government of technocrats, as it did in 1993, when World Bank executive Moeen Qureshi led the country for 90 days. Two days passed before Musharraf finally suspended the Constitution, imposed a state of emergency and made himself Chief Executive. Late last week the Generals were huddled in consultations about how to form an "interim government."

US intelligence analysts furiously shuffled through field reports of the past several weeks to look for missed signals. They were well aware of tensions between Nawaz and the military. In recent months opposition politicians had warned of an impending crisis, as had Nawaz' own brother during a visit to Washington in September.

The worst of the tension seemed to pass, particularly after Sept. 29, when Nawaz formally confirmed Musharraf as Army cheif until fall 2001. But then last week Nawaz inexplicably moved against Musharraf. Senior officials in Washington seemed exasperated. Tellingly, nobody took up Nawaz' cause once he was under house arrest. Instead the message to the Generals in Islamabad, in the words of Assistant Secretary of State Karl Inderfurth, was that Washington expects "democracy and civilian government will be restored as soon as possible." Note the omissions: not Nawaz or his government restored, and not even at once or immediately. The White House cancelled a $1.7 million 4th health programme, but left open-at least for the moment-plans for President Bill Clinton to visit Pakistan and India early next year.

If Clinton does make the trip to Islamaband, he'll have plenty to talk about: Pakistan's nuclear programme, its volatile standoff with India and its substantial role in Afghanistan. During the cold war, the US Central Intelligence Agency used Pakistan for transshipment of weapons to Afghans and Islamists fighting the Soviet occupation. Rebel arms were partly paid for by heroin grown in Afghanistan and the tribal areas of Northern Pakistan. Now, Washington wants Pakistan's help to stamp out the drug trade. The problem only seems to get worse: last month the United Nations announced that Afghanistan had become the world's largest producer of raw opium, accounting for three quarters of global output.

So what can outsider do to encourage stability? Washington has been forced to recognize that, thanks to years of sanctions to protest Pakistan's nuclear-weapons program, the United States has virtually no influence within the Pakistani military. Back in the 1980s, roughly half of the senior leadership of the Pakistan Army had been through US traning schools. Now the figure is 10 per cent or less. "We have lost touch with a generation of Pakistani military leader," says inderfurth.

A Man of Action

NEW YORK–General Pervez Musharraf, Pakistan's new military ruler, is an economical man: he chooses his words carefully and counts every penny. He's mentally quick, according to a military insider, and likes to read speeches by Abraham Lincoln. But he is not an intellectual or a deep thinker. His coup was planned and executed with precision, says a report published Time.

He's also a man of action, with a reputation for geeting thing done. Friends say he likes taking on daunting tasks, reducing problems to their bare bones and looking for quick solutions. He is impetuous, perhaps, but so are many of the best soldiers. "He takes risks and believes that anything is achievable." Says a Major who served under General Musharraf when he was a Corps Commander." And he is cool under fire." Those who know him say he is a good manager, a listener, a leader.

From a military point of view, Musharraf has done all the right things on the way to the top: he received a solid grounding in an artillery regiment, he spent time as a commando he attended Staff College in Britain, he commanded one of Pakistan's army corps. His credentials are impressive from a political point of view as well. Born in Delhi in 1943, he is a neutral figure, able to straddle the permanent rivalry between the Punjabi and Pathan officers who dominate Pakistan's 520,000-man army. He is also viewed as a man of principle. Admirers say he is loyal and stands by his commitments. Musharraf is said to be a passionate nationalist, believing the army should help the government serve the country properly. "General Musharraf is not power-hungry," says Haroon Akbar, a family friend. "He does things which he believes are right."

Like many of Pakistan's senior army officers, Musharraf is an avid sports man. He plays a daily game of squash–fast, tough, requiring quick thinking. It's an activity that's over in half an hour. No strategic planning necessary.

THE NATION OCTOBER 18, 1999

Text of General Pervez Musharraf's speech

ISLAMABAD (APP)–Following is the text of speech by Chief Executive of Pakistan, CJCSC and COAS General Pervez Musharraf, delivered on October 17:

Bismillah-Ar-Rehman-Ar-Rahim My dear countrymen, Asalam-O-Alaikum.

Pakistan today stands at the crossroads of its destiny–a destiny which is in our hands to make or break. Fifty two years ago, we started with beacon of hope and today that beacon is no more and we stand in darkness. There is despondency, and hopelessness surrounding us with no light visible any where around. The slide down has been gradual but has rapidly accelerated in the last many years.

Today we have reached a stage where our economy has crumbled, our credibility is lost, state institutions lie demolished; provincial disharmony has caused cracks in the federation, and people who were once brothers are now at each other's throat.

In sum, we have lost our honour, our dignity, our respect in the comity of nations. Is this the democracy our Quadi-i-Azam had envisaged? Is this the way to enter the new millennium?.

Let us not be despondent. I am an optimist I have faith in the destiny of this nation: belief in its people and conviction in its future. We were not a poor nation as generally perceived. In fact we are rich. We have fertile land that can produce three crops a year. We have abundant water to irrigate these lands and generate surplus power. We have gas, coal and vast untapped mineral resources – and above all a dynamic and industrious people. All these await mobilisation. We have only to awaken. Join hands and grasp our destiny. For Allah helps those who help themselves.

My fellow Pakistanis, as you are aware I took over in extremely unusual circumstances–not of my making. It is unbelievable and indeed unfortunate that, the few at the helm of affairs in the last government were intriguing to destroy the last institution of stability left in Pakistan by creating dissention in the ranks of the armed forces of Pakistan. And who would believe that the Chief of Army Staff, having represented Pakistan in Sri Lanka, upon his return was denied landing in his own country and instead circumstances were created which would have forced our plane either to land in India or crash.

Providence ultimately intervened. Praise be to Allah that the plane landed safely when barely seven minutes of fuel was left. I salute all my officers and men for acting courageously in the supreme interest of the nation. Most of all I salute our people who stood solidly with their armed forces at that critical hour.

Quite clearly, what Pakistan has experienced in the recent years has been merely a label of democracy not the essence of it. Our people were never emancipated from the yoke of despotism. I shall not allow the people to be taken back to the era of sham democracy but to a true one. And I promise you I will Inshallah.

My dear countrymen. The choice before us on 12th October was between saving the body (that is the nation) at the cost of losing a limb (which is the Constitution) or saving the limb and losing the whole body. The Constitution is but a part of the nation therefore I chose to save the nation and yet took care not to sacrifice the Constitution. The Constitution only been temporarily held in abeyance. This is NOT MARTIAL LAW, only another path towards democracy. The armed forces have no intention to stay in charge any longer than is absolutely necessary to pave the way for true democracy to flourish in Pakistan.

Ever since 12th October I have deliberated, carried out consultations and crystallised my views about the future course to be adopted. I wish to share these with you today.

My dear countrymen, our aims and objectives shall be:–

One – Rebuild national confidence and morale.

Two–Strengthen federation, remove inter provincial disharmony and restore national cohesion.

Three–Revive economy and restore investor confidence.

Four – Ensure law and order and dispense speedy justice.

Five–Depoliticise state institutions.

Six – Devolution of power to the grass roots level.

Seven – Ensure swift and across the board accountability.

Good governance is the pre-requisite to achieve these objectives. In the past, our governments have ruled the people. It is time now for the governments to serve the people. The government I plan to institute shall comprise:–

Firstly – The President. On my request, President Rafique Tarar has very kindly agreed to stay.

Second–A National Security Council headed by the Cheif Executive with six members. These members will be Chief of Naval Staff, Chief of Air Staff, a specialist each in Legal, Finance, Foreign Policy and national affairs. A think tank to experts shall be formed as an adjunct to the National Security Council, to provide institutionalised advice and input.

Three – A Cabinet of Ministers who will work under the guidance of the National Security Council.

Four – The Provinces to be headed by a Governor, functioning through a small provincial cabinet.

All these appointments shall be made purely on the basis of professional competence, merit and repute.

Revival of Economy is critical. Our economy is in deep trouble and revolutionary steps are needed to put it back on track. The Pakistani people were subjected to betrayal of trust. Their hard earned money was frozen or taxed in violation of State commitment. We need to restore this trust.

The revitalise our economy in addition to measures like recovery of the looted national wealth-a task that will be ruthlessly be pushed, I am identifying policy guidelines. Some of which are:

— Rebuilding of investors' confidence through stability and consistency in economic policies, and economic security. The objective is to encourage the local investors, overseas Pakistanis and foreign investors.

— Increase domestic savings.

— Carry out Pragmatic tax reforms.

— Turn around the state enterprises towards profitability.

— Boost agriculture and revive industry.

— Strict austerity measures.

Next aspect is accountability. Lack of accountability has resulted in corruption of horrendous proportion, threatening the very basis of our society. The term 'Ehtesab' has been abused to an extent that it has lost its meaning. There is thus a need to re-establish faith in the process of accountability.

The process of accountability is being directed especially towards those guilty of plundering and looting the national wealth and tax evaders. It is also directed towards loan defaulters and those who have had their loans rescheduled or condoned. The process of accountability will be transparent for the public to see. My advice to the guilty is to return voluntarily national wealth, bank loans and pay their taxes before the hand of law forces them to do so with penalty. As a last chance I urge all defaulters to come forth and settle their debts within a period of four weeks, after which their names will be published and the law will take its due course. They owe this to Pakistan and I expect their spirit of patriotism to guide them.

Cementing the Federation is very vital. This will be achieved through devolution of power, from the centre to the provinces and from the provincial to the local government as actually enshrined in the constitution.

Media forms an integral part of statehood in this era of information. I have great regard and respect for the media; I trust it to play a positive and constructive role. I am a firm believer in the freedom of the press and am even considering to liberalise the policy on the establishment of private television and radio channels.

And now a few words on exploitation of religion. Islam teaches tolerance not hatred, universal brotherhood and no enmity, peace and not violence, progress and not bigotry. I have great respect for the Ulema and expect them to come forth and present Islami in its true light. I Urge them to curb elements which are exploiting religion for vested interests and bringing bad name to our faith. I would like to freassure our minorities that they enjoy full rights and protection as equal citizens in the letter and spirit of true Islam.

I wish to freassure the International community that there is no change in our foreign policy. We will continue to honour international obligations and commitments as in the past. It will remain our constant endeavour to promote peace and stability in our region. We would like to maintain our abiding policy of friendship and co-operation with all countries.

The strengthening of brotherly ties with the Islamic countries will be a central pillar of our foreign policy. We shall continue our efforts to achieve a just and peaceful solution in Afghanistan. We wish to see a truly representative government in Kabul. We will maintain and further reinforce our traditional and time tested friendship and co-operation with China. We attach the highest importance to our friendly relations with all major powers, especially the United States.

Here I would like to mention two key areas of our external relations; International security and disarmament and our relations with India.

Pakistan has always been alive to international non-proliferation concerns. Last year, we were compelled to respond to India's nuclear tests in order to restore strategic balance in the interest of our national security and regional peace and stability. In the new nuclear environment in South Asia, we believe that both Pakistan and India have to exercise utmost restraint and responsibility. We owe it to our people and also to the world. I wish to assure the world community that while preserving its vital security interests Pakistan will continue to pursue a policy of nuclear and missile restraint and sensitivity to global non-proliferation and disarmament objectives.

As for relations with India, let me at the out-set congratulate Mr Atal Bihari Vajpayee on assumption of office as the Prime Minister of India. I welcome his offer for friendly relations, and positively reciprocate.

At the turn of the century, South Asia stands at a crucial juncture of its history, 20th Century saw our transition to independence but the region has unfortunately remained mired in conflicts and economic deprivation.

Together Pakistan and India can change this scenario. For this objective both must sincerely work towards resolving their problems especially the core issue of Jammu and Kashmir. The people of Kashmir have made great sacrifices for the achievement of their rights promised to them by the United Nations. We shall continue our unflinching moral, political and diplomatic support to our Kashmiri brethren in their struggle to achieve their right of self-determination. India must honour the UN resolution and its own commitment to the people of Kashmir. It must also end its repression of the Kashmiri people and respect their fundamental human rights.

Pakistan would welcome unconditional, equitable and result-oriented dialogue with India. While, our armed forces are fully equipped and ready to defend our national sovereignty and territorial integrity, it is our desire that the situation on our borders with India an don the Line of Control should remain clam and peaceful. I take this opportunity to announce a unilateral military de-escalation on our international borders with India and initiate the return of all our forces moved to the borders in the recent past. I hope this step would serve as a meaningful confidence building measure.

My dear countrymen, to conclude my address let me say that;

We have hit rock bottom. We have no choice but to rise, and rise e will Inshallah. Our actions shall Inshallah speak louder than words. Therefore, my countrymen let us RISE To THE OCCASION AND SEIZE THE OPPORTUNITY.

Before I close I would like to give you a personal commitment. I herby undertake to declare my tax returns and assets to be documented to open for public scrutiny.

And now I would like to share a prayer that I wrote for myself:

O ALLAH

I PROMISE MY NATION SINCERITY, HONESTY INTEGRITY AND UNFLICHING LOYALTY. GIVE ME:

— THE VISION TO SEE AND PERCEIVE THE TRUTH FROM THE FALSE.

— THE WISDOM TO COMPREHEND THE PROBLEM AND FIND ITS SOLUTION.

— THE COURAGE TO DO JUSTICE AND THE STRENGTH TO DO THE RIGHT.

MAY ALLAH BE WITH US ALL:

AAMEEN

PAKISTAN ZINDABAD.

THE NEWS INTERNATIONAL, PAKISTAN AT 15-10-1999

General Musharraf takes charge of the Country

ISLAMABAD: Chairman joint Chiefs of Staff Committee General Pervez Musharaf has taken charge of the country by suspending the Constitution, the Senate, the National and Provincial Assemblies.

Proclamation of Emergency

ISLAMABAD: In pursuance of deliberations and decisions

of Chiefs of Staff of the Armed Forces and Corps Commanders of Pakistan Army, I, General Pervez Musharraf, Chairman Joint Chiefs of Staff Committee and Chief of Army Staff, proclaim emergency throughout Pakistan and assume the office of the Chief Executive of the Islamic State of Pakistan.

I hereby order and proclaim as follows:

(a) The Constitution of the Islamic Republic of Pakistan shall remain in abeyance;

(b) The President of Pakistan shall continue in office;

(c) The National Assembly, the Provincial Assemblies, and Senate shall stand supended;

(d) The Chairman and Deputy Chairman of the Senate, the Speaker and Deputy Speaker of the National Assembly and the Provincial Assemblies shall stand suspended;

(e) The Prime Minister, the Federal Ministers, Ministers of State, Advisors to the Prime Minister, Parliamentary Secretaries, the Provincial Governors, the Provincial Chief Ministers, the Provincial Ministers and the Advisors to the Chief Ministers shall cease to hold office;

(f) The whole of Pakistan will come under the control of the Armed Forces of Pakistan.

This Proclamation shall come into force at once and is deemed to have taken effect on 12th October 1999.

Provisional Constitution Order No.1 of 1999

ISLAMABAD: In pursuance of Proclamation of the 14th day of October, 1999, and in exercise of all powers enabling him in that behalf, the Chairman Joint Cheifs of Staff Committee and Chief of Army Staff and Chief Executive of the Islamic Republic of Pakistan under the Proclamation of Emergency of 14th day of October 1999 (hereinafter referred to as the Chief Executive) is pleased to make and promulgate the following Order.

1. (1) This Order may be called Provisional Constitution Order No.1 of 1999.

(2) It extends to the whole of Pakistan.

(3) It shall come into force at once

2. (1) Notwithstanding the obeyance of the provisions of the Constitution of the Islamic Republic of Pakistan, hereinafter referred to as the Constitution, Pakistan shall, subject to this Order and any other Order made by the Chief Executive, be governed, as nearly as may be, in accordance with the Constitution.

(2) Subject as aforesaid, all courts in existence immediately before the commencement of this Order shall continue to function and to exercise their respective powers and jurisdiction: Provided that the Supreme Court or High Courts and any other court shall not have the powers to make any order against the Chief Executive or any person exercising powers or jurisdiction under his authority.

(3) The Fundamental Right conferred by Chapter I of Part II of the Constitution, not in conflict with the Proclamation of Emergency or any Order made thereunder from time to time shall continue to be in force.

3. (1) The President shall act on, and in accordance, with the advice of the Chief Executive.

(2) No judgement, decree, writ, order or process whatsoever shall be made or issued by any court or tribunal against the Chief Executive or any authority designated by the Chief Executive.

Notwithstanding the abeyance of the provisions of the Constitution, but subject to the Order of the Chief Executive all laws other than the Constitution shall continue in force until altered, amended or repealed by the Chief Executive or any authority designated by him.

The Proclamation of Emergency issued on 28th day of May 1998, shall continue but subject to the provisions of Proclamation of Emergency dated 14th day of October 1999 and this Provincial Constitution Order and any other Order made there under. All persons who, immediately before the commencement of this Order, were in the service of Pakistan as defined in Article 260 of the Constitution and those persons who immediately before such commencement were in office as Judge of the Supreme Court, the Federal Shariat Court or a High Court or Auditor-General or Ombudsman and Chief Ehtesab Commissioner, shall continue in the said service on the same terms and conditions and shall enjoy the same privileges, if any.

General Pervez Musharaf

Chief Executive-Islamic Republic of Pakistan, Chairman JCSC & COAS Rawalpindi, 14th Oct. 1999

'SARTAJ AZIZ SAHEB SHOULD NOT EVEN ACCEPT A CEASEFIRE, BECAUSE THEN VEHICLES WILL MOVE ON THE HIGHWAY'

Lt. General Mohammed Aziz, Chief of Staff, in conversation with General Pervez Musharraf, Pakistan's Chief of Army Staff

WHAT FOLLOWS is the verbum record of the full telephone conversion between Lt Gen. Mohammed Aziz, Cheif of General Staff, at the Pakistan end, and his boss, Gen. Pervez Musharraf, Pakistan's Chief of Army Staff, who was then on a tour of China. The conversation took placed on May 20 last.

The conversation took place in Urdu and English. The portions translated into English are in italics. (Pakistan end) Lt. Gen. Aziz: This is Pakistan. Give me room No. 83315 (same room number). Hello.

(China end) Gen. Musharraf: Hello Aziz.

Lt. Gen. Aziz: The situation on ground is OK, no change, this area but it is not brought down by attack. One of their MI-17 arms (?) was brought down. Further, the position is, we had approached to our position. It was brought down.

Rest is OK. Nothing else except. there is a development. Have you listened to yesterday's news regarding Mian Saheb speaking to his counterpart. He told him that the spirit of Lahore Declaration and escalation has been done by your people. Specially wanted to speak to me thereafter. He told Indian PM that they should have waited instead of upping the ante by using Air Force and all other means. He (Nawaz) told him (Indian PM) that he suggested Sartaz Aziz could go to New Delhi to explore the possibility of defusing the tension.

Gen. Musharraf: OK.

Lt. Gen. Aziz Which is likely to take place most probably tomorrow.

Gen. Musharraf: OK.

Lt. Gen. Aziz: Our other friend (Lt. Gen. Ziauddin, DG ISI...?... or could be United States) might have also put pressure on. For that, today they will have discussion at Foreign Office about 9.30 and Zafar Shaeb (Lt. Gen. Saeed uz Zaman Zafar, GOC 11 Corps & Acting Chief) is supposed to attend.

Gen. Musharraf: OK.

Lt. Gen. Aziz: Aziz Saheb (Sartaj Aziz, Foreign Minister) has discussed with me and my recommendation is that dialogue option is always open. But in their first meeting, they must give no under standing or no commitment on ground situation.

Gen. Musharraf: Very correct. You or Mehmood (GOC X Corps, Rawalpindi) must have to go with Zafar. Because, they don't know about the ground situation.

Lt. Gen. Aziz: This week, we are getting together at 8'O clock because meeting will be at 9.30, so Zafar Sahib will deliberate it. We want to suggest to Zafar that they have to maintain that they will not be talking about ground situation. All that you say. So far as the ground situation is concerned. Subsequently, DGMOs can discuss with each other and work out the modus operandi.

Gen. Musharraf: Idea on LoC. Lt. Gen. Aziz: Yes. Hint is that, given that the LoC has many areas where the interpretation of either side is not what the other side believes. So, comprehensive deliberation is required. So, that can be worked out by DGMOs.

If they are assured that we are here form a long period. We have been sitting here for long. Like in the beginning, the matter is the same-no post was attacked and no post was captured. The situation is that we are along our defensive Line of Control. If it is not in his (Sartaj Aziz's) knowledge, then discuss it altogether. Emphasise that for years we are here only.

Gen. Musharraf: Yes, this point should be raised. We are sitting on the same LoC since a long period.

Lt. Gen. Aziz: This is their weakness. They are not agreed on the demarcation under UN's verification, whereas we are agreed. We want to exploit it.

Gen. Musharraf: This is in Simal Agreement that we cannot go for UN intervention.

Lt. Gen. Aziz: Our neighbour does not accept their presence or UNMOGIP arrangement for survey for the area. So, we can start from the top, from 9842 (NJ 9842). On this line, we can give them logic but in short, the recommendation for Sartaj Aziz Shaeb is that he should make no commitment in the first meeting on military situation. And he should not even accept ceasefire, because if there is ceasefire, then vehicles will be moving (on Drass-Kargil highway). In this regard, they have to use their own argument that whatever is interfering with you. That we don't know but there is no justification about tension of LoC. No justification. We want to give them this type of brief so that he does not get into any specifics.

Gen. Musharraf: Alright.

Lt. Gen. Aziz: In this connection, we want your approval and what is your programme.

Gen. Musharraf: I will come tomorrow. We are just

leaving within an hour. We are going to Shenzhen. From there, by evening, we will be in Hong Kong. There will be a flight tomorrow from Hong Kong. So, we will be there at Lahore in the evening, via Bangkok flight.

Lt. Gen. Aziz: Sunday evening, you will be at Lahore. We will also indicate that, if there is more critical situation then it (Sartaj visit) should be deferred for another day or two. We can discuss on Monday and then do.

Gen. Musharraf: Has this MI-17 not fallen in our area?

Lt. Gen. Aziz: No Sir. This has fallen in their area. We have not claimed it. We have got it clamied through the mujahideen.

Gen. Musharraf: Well done.

Lt. Gen. Aziz: But topwise side crashing straight before our eyes.

Gen. Musharraf: Very good. Now are they facing any greater difficulty in flying them? Are they scared or not? This also you should note. Are they coming any less nearer?

Lt. Gen. Aziz: Yes. There is a lot of pressure on them. They were talking about greater air defence than they had anticipated. They can't afford to lose any more aircraft. There has been less intensity of air flying after that.

Gen. Musharraf: Very good. First class. Is there any build up on the ground?

Lt. Gen. Aziz: Just like that but the movement is pretty sluggish and slow. One or two are coming near No. 6. Till now only one call sign in which one has not reached the valley so far. Now the air people and the ground people will stay back and then the situation will be OK.

Gen. Musharraf: See you in the evening.

The Frontier Post October 22, 1999.

Mushahid, others used PTCL for Leaking Defence Secrets

NEW YORK (Online)—State owned Pakistan Telecommunication Company Limited (PTCL), was used for leaking national defence secrets to the Indians as well as for personal monetary benefits by a minister and top authorities.

According to reliable sources, apart form handing over the tapes of conversation of General Musharraf and his Chief of General Staff Lt. Gen. Aziz to the Indians during the height of the Kargil crisis, dubious and shady deals amounting to approximately US$ 900 millions were signed by the secretary communication Akram Sheikh, Chairman PTCL Nasim Mirza and the former DG IB Col. Iqbal Niazi to award contracts to foreign and local companies including US-Sprint, MCI, AT&T, Iridium Satellite, Siemens, Ace-Tel, CyberNet and PakNet in consideration of commissions deposited in bank accounts abroad of these officials. Army authorities are trying to ascertain and confirm the facts of these cases through investigations.

Sources said the conversation of General Pervez Musharraf with his Chief of General Staff, Lt. General Aziz from China during the height of the Kargil crisis was recorded by the SBD section of PTCL headed by Nuruddin Bugai under directives of DG IB, Col. Iqbal Niazi. At that time Nuruddin Bugai was entrusted with the task of taping the telephone lines of important personalities by the former DG IB. Following the standing operating instructions (SOP). Nuruddin Bugai handed over the tapes to DG IB.

The sources said the tapes were handed over to former information minister, Mushahid Hussain, who leaked the tapes to Indians through a journalist.

It may by recalled that Mushahid was also instrumental in arranging interview of Dr. Qadeer with an Indian journalist in 1987, which later on created an enormous furore and Mushahid had to quit his job as editor of The Muslim.

A Pakistani national Baqai, who is an executive in New

York in Ace-Tel – the company with which a deal of 600 million dollars for the launching of PTCLOs mobile service was under consideration N is mentioned by the sources as an important component of the chain for the provision of the conversation tapes to the Indians. Two real cousins of Baqai, who live in India, are high ranking officials in two Indian ministries.

The links of the chain become complete when it is kept in mind that DG IB was deeply engrossed in the affaris of PTCL, particularly the award of contracts and signing of deals with foreign companies and to grant the security clearance form IB.

According to sources, the deal of $600 million with Ace Tel N a French company dealing in mobile telephone services N was approved after $45 million were received as kickbacks. The sources said, this amount was deposited in secretary communication Os account in Royal Bank of Canada, Toronto branch.

In the name of future technological advancement in telecoms, a US firm, Iridium Satellite, was also enlisted as one of the contractors for installation of the mobile system in PTCL at a cost of 290 million dollars.

The firm which is on the verge of bankruptcy, was a specialist in providing mobile telecom services on ultra-high frequencies, which cannot be bugged by the intelligence agencies. Six mobile telephone sets were gifted by Iridium Satellite to the former prime minister, secretary communications and DG IB for use as test samples.

It is believed that contacts with top Indian hierarchy were made by using these sets as part of back channel diplomacy during the Kargil crisis.

Another fraudulent and crooked deal was materialised with Siemens by chairman PTCL or upgrading the internal backbone system of PTCL. The sources allege that the deal was signed for an exaggerated amount of 12 million dollars, while its actual cost should not exceed $4 million.

The sources maintained that the commission was allegedly

deposited in the Columbia Federal Saving Bank, Washington DC and Barkeley Bank London accounts of the chairman PTCL.

The scam relating to the International Gateway Exchange involving US-Sprint, MCI and AT&T, was disclosed by former DG IB himself to this scribe sometime ago in a one-to-one meeting. At that time, DG IB in the presence of Joint Director General Shah Mehboob Alam while expressing his inability to do anyting about the scam of International Gateway Exchange had said, O In the evening I received calls from some very important persons to help them out. O

It is alleged that 32 million dollars were deposited in the foreign accounts of secretary communication, in this deal every month

The sources added that crores of rupees were also given to chairman PTCL by two internet service providers.

It is said that the sister of secretary communications looks after his accounts in Toronto. Akram Sheikh and the senior officials were in the Sates last month to sort out their shares to commission in the deals, reliable sources added.

In his first press conference on November 1, 1999 after taking over the government on Oct. 12, Gen. Pervez Musharraf expressed his desire to settle 'all differences' with India but the tone was aggressive and threatening. He declared "when I mean all differences, I mean the core issue of Kashmir first of all or simultaneously at least. But if there is any design to address other than Kashmir and sidelining the Kashmir issue, I am not part of it. Hostility will be met with hostility and peace will be met with peace. I will ensure the honour and dignity of this country. Nobody threatens us without getting a threatening response, anyone" withdrawal of his troops from Kargil had dishvelled his plans and he gave vent to his feelings in this press conference. He said "with India we would like to resolve all outstanding issues including the core issue of Kashmir for the benefit of South Asia. He in his maiden speech, also said that he would ensure Pakistan follows the policy of maintaining a minimum deference both in conventional and non-conventional fields for Pakistan's, security. Describing Indian nuclear weaponary for Pakistan. Gen. Musharraf wanted to contain India from flexing its muscle and become a regional power. In his opinion it was this desire of India i.e to be recognised as a regional power which retrains India form adopting flexible stand on various issues including Kashmir. He felt that if India's prominence as a regional leader is contained then India would be more flexible on Kashmir. It appeared that his main thrust would be to keep India engaged in anti-terrorist operations so that it does not emerge as a regional power.

Gen. Musharraf Concentrated 'India Experts' in his team. Corps Commander 10 Corps Lt Gen. Jamshed Gulzar, who was a Defence Attache in India in 1993, Foreign Minister Abdul Sattar who was Twice High Commissioner of Pakistan in New Delhi (incidently he was Director of India Desk in Pak Foreign Ministry during signing of Simla Accord) and a staunch supporter of Kashmir's self determination, DGMO Maj. Gen. Shahid Aziz who had served as a top analyst in ISI and chief of General Staff Lt. Gen. Mohammad Amir who ran External wing of ISI for three years and was a Kashmir Expert of Pak Army were some of the persons who consisted his 'India Experts Team.'

The Supreme Court on May 13, 2000 validated his coup dated of Oct. 12, 1999. In January 2000 the US government officials took steps to declare Pakistan a terrorist state i.e. a state which sponsor's international terrorism.

On June 20, 2001 before him visit to India to attend the Agra Summit held in July 2001, he appointed himself as the President of Pakistan replacing Mohammad Rafiq Tarar, thus virtually becoming all-in-all chief. This he did because he wanted to talk to India form the position of strength and as head of state as well. But in Agra his agenda was absolutely limited confined to Kashmir only in which he tried to play a tactical game. Gen. Musharraf disliked Simla Agreement and

Lahore declaration. During the Talks, on July 16, 2001 he invited a group of Indian editors to a morning breakfast. While talking to them he branded violence in Kashmir as "indigenous freedom struggle" and stated that is India could 'liberate' Bangladesh, Pakistan could have done Kargil in Kashmir." When this tet-e-tet was played on TV a hardened stand was taken by Indian side. India had poured its heart in welcoming him and it sincerely wanted to find an agreeable solution to Kashmir issue. Gen. Musharraf a Commando from SSG, had over-confidence in him in the sense that he thought he could easily take on the Indian Prime Minister Atal Bihari Vajpayee. Elated with Kargil intrusions which took Indian Army quite unaware, he undermined Indian position which was engaged in Bon homie with Nawaz Sharif while he was busy carrying out intrusions across LoC in Kargil and Drass sectors.

Gen. Musharraf realised that it was not easy to snatch Kashmir from India and the talks failed. He returned to Pakistan angry and empty handed even cancelling his prefixed programme of visiting Ajmer Sharif to pay obeisance. He blamed 'Indian hardliness' which obviously was a reference to shri L.K. Advani for failure of the talks.

A conglomerate of six religious outfits cropped up in June 2001 under the caption of Muttahida Majlis-e-Amal (MMA) headed by Maulana Shah Ahmed Noorani, leader of Jamiat-ulema-i-Pakistan (JUP) – the political representative of Barelvi School of Sunni Muslims. The alliance comprised of :–

1. Jamiat ulema-i-Islam (JUI–S) led by Maulana Fazlur Rehman.
2. Jamiat ulema-i-Islam (JUI–S) led by Maulana Samiul Haq. Vice President MMA.
3. Jamaat-i-Islami (JI) led by Qazi Hussain Ahmed. Senior Vice President MMA.
4. Jamiat ulema-i-Pakistan (JUP–N) led by Maulana Shah Ahmad Noorani. President MMA.
5. Markaz Jamiat Ahle Hadith (JAH–S) led by Professor

Sajid Mir. Vice President MMA.

6. Tehrick-i-Jafria Pakistan (TJF) renamed as Qauid-e-Mill at-e-Jafria headed by shia leader Maulana Syed Sajid Naqvi Vice President MMA.

Initiative was taken by the Jamat-e-Islami to form this politico–religion party whose core objectives were:–

1. To uphold Islamic laws and enact legislation in accordance with recommendation by the council of Islamic ideology (CII).
2. Restoring the 1973 Constitution of Pakistan.
3. To ensure free and fair general elections in the country exhibiting total transparency.
4. To rid Pakistani soil of American presence.

MMA had 15-point mainifesto for establishing 'Nizam-e-Mustafa'. One of the point was to extend moral, political and diplomatic support to all suppressed muslims world over but with particular emphasis on Kashmiris, Palestinians, Afghans and chechniyans. It also wanted to safeguard Pakistan's nuclear programme which according to their estimation was under threat because of the American presence in the country. MMA presented itself as the only alternative to Pro-western ruler Gen. Pervez Musharraf. It was able to form provincial government in NWFP. MMA supported Gen. Musharraf as President just was annoyed with him for his closeness with the US and also for the other reason that inspite of his promise that he would give up his uniform by the end of 2004, he continued to wear it. Gen. Musharraf's imposing and then lifting 42-days emergency on Dec. 15, 2007 brought disaster for MMA. The emergency brought a division with in the MMA. Some of the MMA components advocated participation in the forthcoming general elections while some others gave call for boycothin them. Maulana Fazlur Rehman (JUI) was for participating in the election while JeI's stand was that the polls would be rigged, and that participation would legitimize Musharrafs regime. JuI and JeI stuck to their stand and the result was MMA alliance tell apart by mid–December 2007.

In October 2001 Gen. Musharraf extended his term as COAS indefinitely and re shuffled top Army officers in order to remove the seightist risk from a few ambitious officers. As aftermath of 9/11 he withdrew Pak support for the Taliban regime in Afghanistan and declared Pak's joining US in the fight an "war on terror".

A controversial referendum was held on April 30, 2002 which made Gen. Musharraf win over by overwhelming majority of votes which also extended his rule for five more years. The elections two-term limit in the year 2002 on the Prime Minister which barred both Ms. Benazir Bhutto and Nawaz Sharif from contesting the post of PM again.

On October 10, 2002 general elections Pro-PML-Q won the majority seats in the National Assembly and Gen. Musharraf was sworn in for a fresh 5-years term on November 16, 2002 ending three year Army rule. Mir Zafrullah Khan becomes Prime Minister.

Attempts on his life were made Gen. Musharraf survived an explosive attack wreck a bridge in Rawalpindi on Dec. 14, 2003 just after his cavalcade passed under the bridge. A few days later he survived twin-attacks by way of car bombing. The assassination attempts were reportedly led by Islamits military officers on one occasion and by Al Qaeda on the other. So far nine (a) attempt were made on his life.

Air Force Chief Mustafa Ali Mir was killed on Feb. 20, 2003 in a mysterious Plane Crash. It might unfold after a few years.

On March 16, 2004 Gen. Musharraf ordered Army to launch the first of a series of operations against Al Qaeda hideouts in the tribal area of NWFP.

Parliament passed "President to hold another office Act on Nov. 30, 2004 which allowed him to hold dual office one of the chief of Army staff and the other that of the President of Pakistan. Confident by this Act, Gen. Musharraf reneged on Dec. 30, 2004 on his promise to quit the position of chief of

Army staff (COAs).

President's Uniform

1. Pakistan Peoples Party (PPP)–Patriots: were the first to suggest that the President Musharraf retain his uniform
2. Pakistan Muslim League (PML) Chief Shujat Hussain had, come out openly in favour of the Presidents uniform.
3. Punjab Chief Minister Pervez Elahi had also supported that President Musharraf would remian chief of Army staff as well as the President. His stand was if need be he would fight legal battle or for that matter even political battles.
4. Punjab Assembly adopted a resolution urging President Musharraf to retain his uniform.
5. Sindh Assembly passed resolution on Sept. 20, 2004 to retain his uniform.
6. NWFP Assembly opposed (Sept. 15, 2004) and asked Musharraf to doft his uniform.
7. Baluchistan Assembly had withdrawn the resolution of Presidents uniform of Sept. 16, 2004.

During the month of May 2004 atleast four significant bomb blast took place:–

(*i*) May 4, – Targeting Chinese Engineers. 12 Chinese engineers were injured.

(*ii*) May 24, Targeting Policemen in Quetta.

(*iii*) May 21, Gwadar Airport was attacked at midnight.

(*iv*) May 30/31, Two dozen Rockets fired on Mund hometown of Ms. Zubaida Jalal 850 km Southwest of Quetta.

Gen. Musharraf chalked out a strategy to augment the national defence for the next 15 years.

The Daily Times newspaper of Pakistan of June 23, 2004

reported criticism of President Musharraf done by Congressman Gary Ackerman who in a strongly worded statement called Gen. Musharraf "the pied piper of enlightened moderation". He further said " He did not pratise what he preached." Gen. Musharraf battled extremists and terrorists only in a limited way, that he had in reality strengthened the military's role in Pakistan governance rather than bring democracy."

Urdu newspaper "Khabrain" on Sept. 17, 2004 reported extract of a book "Pakistan's drift into Extremism "by Ali Abbas a visiting Harvard fellow. The report was as follows:

Army top brass discussed post 9/11 policy at Secret meet: Quote. A Secret meeting of Corps Commanders and important Generals was held on Sept. 14, 2001 to decide Pak policy after 9/11 terrorist attacks on US in 2001. The meeting was held at a nuclear shelter, in a departure form the practice of holding such meetings at the conference room in GHQ to protect it form spy satellites and other espionage activities. The DG ISI Lt. Gen. Mahmood called the meeting at a very short notice. President General Pervez Musharraf was himself called into the meeting half-an-hour after the meeting was over. Soon after arrival at the meeting, Gen. Musharraf received a phone call form US Secretary of state Colin Powell asking him to accept some conditions. When President Musharraf requested time to think over, Powell reportedly informed him that ISI chief Mahmood had already accepted some conditions on Sept. 13, 2004. On learning that President Musharraf was shocked and informed Powell that he would take his Generals into confidence and get back to him. The author said this was the reason for conflict between Gen. Mehmood and Gen. Pervez Musharraf. Reportedly, Gen. Musharraf was not in favour of being an ally of the US in war against terrorism but, as it turned out, Gen. Mehmood's assurance to the US had made the President change his mind." unquote.

It reveals how ISI directly deals with international issues without consulting Chief to Army Staff or the executive heads of the state.

The Federal government passed an amendment to the Anti-Terrorism Act and Contempt of Court Acts even as the opposition members abstained from voting. When the Bill was put to vote, all opposition members staged a walk out. Following the amendment of ATA, the Federal government had been empowered to effect inter-provincial transfer of cases. All cases relating to blasts, disturbances at places of workshop and court campuses would be registered only under ATA. The Bill had also made amendments to the term of imprisonment from 7 to 10 years and 14 years to 26 years under different circumstances. The new law came into force form Oct. 20, 2004.

On January 6, 2004 Gen. Musharraf declared that Pakistani soil would not be allowed to be used against Indian interest Leter on President Zardari also repeated this assurance that Pakistan would not allow any Anti–Indian activities form its soil.

Prime Minister Zafrullah Khan Jamali (Nov. 23, 2002 to June 26, 2004) was changed and chaudhary Shujat Hussain was appointed Prime Minister on August 30, 2004 as stop gap arrangement. On Aug. 27, 2004 Gen. Musharraf appointed Shaukat Aziz as PM. He alongwith Gen. Musharraf were given a 3-hour briefing by Maj. Gen. Zaki of ISI on Oct 4, 2004.

In the year 2004, a significant development in Indo–Pak relations took place. Both the countries allowed their Air space to be used by each other. But in internal matters Army started interfering through ISI even in non-army matters after parliament okeyed the formation of National Security Council. Muzaffarabad to Srinagar Bus service was started on April 7, 2005.

Note Please add from Page 116 A to here

In Jan. 2006, eighteen persons were killed while targetting Al-Qaeda in North of Pakistan. In North–West shias also took out a procession in which a suicide bomber killed 30 persons. In April 2006 during a Sunni gathering, two blasts took place in which 57 people were killed.

As said time and again Gen. Pervez Musharraf had all intentions of a good governance. He gave the nation of Pakistan an idea of 'enlightened moderation.' He had a vision for Pakistan. He wanted and ordered release of almost 2000 women languishing in Jail without being convicted and tasked council of Islamic ideology to review Hudood Ordinance and propose necessary amendments with a view to release women prisoners held in captivity for long. Gen. Musharraf sincerely wanted Pakistan to give up its image as a country of extreme Islam by Sept. 2006 religious intolerance grew in Pakistan. Forcible conversation of minorities to Islam, numerous attacks on non-muslims were the order of the day. Muttahida Majlis-e-Aimal (MMA) MPs opposed changes in reform in laws concerning rape. Gen. Musharraf desired that the present requirement for a women who can't prove rape to be charged of adultery and the requirement of four witnesses in rape cases should be done away with. He wanted such cases to be tried in civil courts and not in religious courts. A Bill for this purpose which was introduced in the Parliament in August 2006 was opposed by 68 lawmakers mostly form MMA, out of a total strength of 344 members of Pakistan's National Assembly. A walkout by the 68 MNAs could have destabilize the government. What could Gen. Musharraf do in that case?

Pakistan signed a peace deal with the tribal leaders and militants in North waziristan region an September 5, 2006 which was criticised by U.S. But soon after i.e in October Pakistan Army attacked a 'madarsa' near Pak–Afghan border killing 80 persons. Pakistan rebutted the allegation that Al Qaeda militants were hiding in Pak–Afghan international border. In an operation against Baluchistan insurgency. Pak Army killed Nawab Akbar Khan Bugti on Aug. 26, 2006 in Bhambore Hills. Baluchis right form 1947 were of independent mind Baluchistan had announced its independence on August

12, 1947 in the wake of Indian Independence Act. Bhutto's crackdown on them in 1973, branding them as terrorists, their demand of giving their Gwadar coast and natural resources back and then rape of a Baloch lady doctor Shazia Khaled in January 2005 had made them bitter. Nawab Bugti had reinforced the call for decivsive battle to liberate Baluchistan from Pakistan. In this case Gen. Musharraf indeed did a blunder. His action of handling the crisis was criticised by former COAS Gen. Aslam Beg (Retd.), Gen. Asad Durani former ISI chief, Gen. Hamid Gul, former ISI chief and Lt. Gen. (Retd.) Talat Masood. Getting a 79–year old Nawab Akbar Bugti, who was neither a Separatist Nor a supporter of violence served no purpose at all. Lahore – Delhi Bus Service Samjhauta Express was made a target and a blast was caused on February 18, 2007 killing 68 persons. Lawyers caused a number of demonstrations against the suspension of the chief justice. On May 12 in such a demonstration about 40 persons were killed in Police tiring.

On March 9, 2007 Gen. Musharraf removed the chief Justice of Supreme court Mr. Justice Iftikhar Mohammad Chaudhary which proved almost fatal for him. It invited most serious challenge to his authoritarian rule for nearly eight years. The removal of Chief Justice was followed by demonstrations and agitations by lawyers all over the country. Confrontation with lawyers generated slogans like 'Go, Musharraf Go.' On July 20, 2007 CJ Iftikhar Mohammad Chaudhury was reinstated by the supreme court itself. Removing Chief Justice was ill conceived move.

Another action which invited wrath form the fundamentalists and Islamic militants was that he ordered action on July 10, 2007 against these militants and fundamentalists who were hiding in Lal Masjid located close to Abpara in Islamabad. The military action against them remained in force from July 10 to 13 in which 105 suspected militants were killed.

On October 2, 2007, Gen. Musharraf designated Gen. Asfaq Pervez Kiani as next chief of Army Staff. Gen. Kiani took over the command of Pakistan Army on November 28, 2007.

Gen. Musharraf won October 6, 2007 Presidential Election with most of the votes but the Supreme Court put spokes on declaring the election results till it disposed off six petitions filed in the supreme Court challenging his candidacy. The vote was bocycotted by the opposition. On November 23, a 10 – member full court comprising Gen. Musharraf's hand picked Judges headed by Abdual Hameed Dogar of the supreme Court validated and upheld Musharraf's re-election held on Oct. 6 and asked the Election Commission to notify the result which the EC confirmed on Nov. 24, 2007 giving him another five years in the office. A Seven member bench headed by C.J. Dogar also threw out petitions challenging the Emergency and Provisional Constitution Order (PCO) and seeking reinstatement of the deposed Supreme Court Judges. At this point of time Apex Court comprised the Judges who took oath under the PCO.

Yet another blunder Committed by Gen. Musharraf was that he imposed Emergency on November 3, 2007 which was sort of second coup by him or yet another martial law. He kept the constitution in abeyance, saekad the chief justice who refused to endorse the Emergency, removed 60 other judges including 16 judges of the Supreme Court alongwith the Chief Justice who declared his act illegal and slapped strict curbs on the media. It was followed with widespread protests by media, lawyers and others from all walks of the society. Blasts rocked Pakistan. Judicial activism and extremism caused by Islamic militants were the causes which, according to Gen. Musharraf, forced him to proclaim Emergency.

Throughout the crisis in March 2007 regarding the ouster of the Chief Justice Iftikhar Chaudhury, Gen. Kayani maintained silence. Though professionally loyal to his chief Gen. Musharraf, he refrained from filing an affidavit against the ousted Chief Justice when Musharraf sought unsuccessfully to oust him in March. However, the two other Intelligence chiefs Brig. Ejaz Shah of Intelligence Bureau and Maj. Gen. Nadeem Taj who happened to be a relative also of Gen. Pervez Musharraf were very eager to hound the CJ out of his office. Gen. Kayani did not agree with Gen. Musharraf on many issues nor he shared all the attributes.

Since Gen. Musharraf clamped down a State of Emergency on November 3, 2007, the Council of Commonwealth suspended for a bloodless coup by Gen. Musharraf. However, Pakistan was readmitted into Commonwealth in 2004. Once earlier in the year 1972 Pakistan, of its own quit the Commonwealth protesting the recognition of Bengladesh but it rejoined it in the year 1989. Commonwealth is a 53–nation group.

On November 15, 2007 midnight, no sooner the National Assembly completed its 5–years term, it was dissolved by Gen. Musharraf. Incidently, it was the first NA to have completed its 5–years tenure during the past 35 years though the period was full of Jerks and jolts. On November 16, 2007 Senate Chairman Mohammad mian Soomro, a former Banker and a confidant of Gen. Musharraf was administered oath of Acting Prime Minister of Pakistan.

It was on November 28, 2007 Gen. Musharraf bade good bye to the Army and handed over power and office of the COAS to Gen. Ashfaq Pervez Kayani with a heavy heart and tears in his eyes. Thus Gen. Kayani became 14th chief of Pakistan Army. Earlier on May 23, 2007 Gen. Musharraf had declared that "his uniform is like a second skin to him which he cannot remove". Justifying army's presence in various institution he also said in the same breath that "when politicians do not know how to run the country's affairs, the army has no choice but to step in and put things right."[1] British High Commissioner to Pakistan Robert Brinkley had also in the month of May 2007 asked Gen. Musharraf to 'Separate' the office of the President and the COAS as demanded by the Commonwealth Political parties also put pressure on him to quit the post of COAS and PPP refused to have any deal with him while he continued to deal with both the officer i.e of President as well as that of chief of Army staff.

'Wukla Biradari' (lawyer brotherhood) was also very angry with Gen. Musharraf on the question of removal of the chief Justice Iftikhar Chaudhury, Advocate Ahmed Ali Kurd, while delivering a speech in early 2007 for demanding reinstatement of the ousted CJ gave vent to his feelings and said "we will strip his (Gen. Musharraf's) skin layer by layer to ensure that he takes off his uniform". In a symbolic reference to his uniform lawyers[2] tore a goat skin on November 28, 2007 in Multan.

Gen. Musharraf took oath of the office of the President on November 29, 2007 for a term of five years. US had also persuaded him to separate the two offices he was holding till then. Ms Condoeezza, Rice, US Secretary of state appreciated Gen. Musharraf's relinquishing the command of 7th largest Army of the world and handing it over to his hand-picked successor Gen. Kayani whom America also considers close to their nation. Ms. Rice also asked Gen. Musharraf to lift the Emergency while she described his step in giving up the post of COAS as a 'good first step'. While Ms. Benazir Bhutto stated that 'we are not in a hurry to accept Pervez Musharraf as a civilian President, former PM Nawaz Sharif. said Gen. Musharraf's retirement from army would make a lot of difference and desired him to lift the Emergency also, reinstate the ousted Judges in order to ensure the elections were fair. But a group of retired senior miltary officers were more blunt in expressing their views. In a joint statement signed and issued by these ex-servicemen, which included Air Marshal (Retd.) Noor Khan, Admiral feusihbokhari airchief marchal (Retd.) Abbas mirza, may. Gen (Retd.) Saeed Ahmed Wahla, Air Commander Auragzeb Azim (Retd.), Lieut. Gen. Talat Masood, Lt. Gen. Asad Durrani former ISI chief and Lt. Gen. (Retd.) Ali Quli Khan, said that Gen. Musharraf's actions had brought the Armed Forces of Pakistan into disrepute' and demanded he should step down not just as Army chief but also as President of Pakistan.[3] British Prime Minister Gordon Brown welcomed Pakistani President Pervez Musharraf action in handing over charge of Army describing it as an 'important part of the process' towards restoring democracy and urged him to follow up the move by ensuring that the free and fair elections were held in January 2008 as planned. Not everyone was impressed with the Generals modest retreat. One 'Time' magazine commentary, adding to epithets that have alluded to the military ruler as a thug and terrorist, observed that "praising Musharraf for stepping down as army chief is akin to praising the honesty of a thief, who, having stolen and broken a priceless vase, returns it in places with apologies.[4] William Dalrymple, a British author who has written extensively about India and Pakistan, put it bluntly, in an article for Britain's left-of-centre 'Guardian newspaper in 2005." As Pakistan shows rigid, corrupt, unrepresentative and flawed democracies without the strong independent institutions of a civil society – a free press, an independent judiciary, an empowered election commision can foster. Governments that are every bit as tyrannical as any dictatorship, "he wrote. "Justice and democracy are not synonymous" he added.[4]

State of Emergency was lifted by Gen. Musharraf as suggested by the US secretary of State Ms. Condolezza Rice on Dec. 15, 2007. Constitution was restored. General elections that were scheduled to take place on Jan. 2, 2008 were postponed to Feb. 18, 2008 in view of the disturbances caused by the public anger after the assassination of PPP chairperson Ms. Benazir Bhutto on Dec. 27, 2007 at an election rally in Rawalpindi.

On Feb. 18, 2008 polls were held in which PPP led by Asif Ali Zardari, Bhutto's widower, and PML(N) of Nawaz Sharif trounced Gen. Musharraf's allies of PML(Q) which used to be called 'Kings Party'. PPP won 120 of the 342 seats while PML(N) had bagged 90. Muttahida Majlis-e-Amal (MMA) – a religious coalition of six parties – that was the third largest group in the previous NA with 60 seats was routed and won only 3 parliamentary seats. So much so even Maulana Fazlur Rehman of JUI(F) lost his own seat in his hometown of Dera Ismail Khan though he won another. In fact, Pakistanis rejected religious parties completely. MMA was ousted form NWFP

Provincial Assembly and badly defeated in Baluchistan where it had a coalition government with PML(Q). ANP (Awami National Party) emerged as the single largest party with 31 seats. PPP won 17 and Independents 10 seats in NWFP. Jamaat-e-Islami had decided to boycott the polls. The Pakhtoon National Party–ANP– which had blessings from the family of Late Khan Abdul Ghaffar Khan, even uprooted a man like Maulana Fazulur Rehman. Mr. Anees Jillani an article "PLATFORM: Revenge by Democracy (the Hindustan times dt. Feb. 20, 2008) wrote "the people voted for the centrist parties in all the four provinces and have shunned fundamentalism and extremism. MMA lost partly because JI boycotted the polls in protest against the sacking of around 60 superior court judges by Musharraf and partly because of its poor performance while in government for the past five years in NWFP and Baluchistan provinces. The election results showed ethnic nationalism in the Pakistan Federation. But in Senate PML(Q) had a majority at that point of time.

On March 18, 2008 PPP nominated 52–year old Dr. Fehmida Mirza, a PPP stalwart and three–time member of the National Assembly for the post of the speaker. An women was nominated to be the speaker of the NA for the first time in the history of Pakistan. Her husband Zulfiqar Mirza was also MNA. Dr. Mirza, the first women speaker won 249 votes from the 325 members of the NA present and voting. Her opponent Mohammed Israr Tareen, a PML(Q) Candidate for the post supported by its allies scored jsut 70 votes.

For the post of Deputy Speaker, Faisal Karim Kundi, who defeated Maulana Fazlur Rehman of JUI(F) in Dera Ismail Khan constituency, was nominated. He won by 246 votes while his opponent Khushbakt Shujat of MQM which was allieved to Gen. Musharrafs party PML(Q) received just 68 votes.

On March 24, 2008 the Parliament elected 55 year old YOUSUF RAZA GILANI, A PPP member from Punjab and a Bhutto-aide, to the post of 22nd Prime Minister of the Country. PML (N) also joined the government and formed a coalition of PPP and PML (N). Gilani won with 264 votes in NA trouncing chaudhary Shujat Hussain, the opposition candidate from PML(Q) who secured only 42 votes. It was virtually 'no-contest'. When the NA speaker Ms. Fehmida Mirza announced Gilani's Victory, the visitors galleries that were stuffed and packed with the supporters of new incumbents to the NA ranted with the slogans" Go Musharraf Go" "Zinda Hai Bhutto Zinda Hai." No sooner Gilani was declared elected on March 24 , he set himself three main tasks (*i*) The release of the judges ousted by Musharraf (*ii*) to get the National Assembly pass a resolution for a UN investigation into the assassination of Benazir Bhutto (*iii*) and he would get a resolution passed apologising to the people of Pakistan for the 'Judicial murder' of Zulfiqar Ali Bhutto. Police immediately began removing barricades at the entrance to the judges colony where the deposed CJ Iftikar Chaudhary and other Judges were detained.

Yousuf Raja Gilani who born on June 9, 1952 in Karachi. His father Aalmdar Hussain was minister in fiftees in Pakistan government. His ancestors were reported to have signed the Resolution in 1940 which resulted in creation of Pakistan. A post -graduate in Journalism from Punjab University, Lahore, Gilani plunged into politics after the death of his father and joined Pakistan Muslim League in 1978. In 1985 election he was elected to the National Assembly as an Independent. He became Minister in Mohammad Khan Junejo's government but in 1988 he joined PPP and defeated sitting Punjab Chief Minsiter Nawaz Sharif. He rose to become vice chairman of PPP and joined Benazir's Cabinet in 1988-90 and remained speaker of NA (1993–96) during her second term. In 1997 he contested polls on PPP ticket but lost. He was made PPP's senior vice chairman in 1998. After Gen. Musharraf took over, Gilani was sent to jail for 10 years in the years 2001 by the Accountability Court for alleged corruption in making some illegal appointments while he was speaker of the National Assembly and was also fined Rs. 100 million. In October 2006 his prison term was set aside by Punjab High Court and he was released on bail. Though Gilani is from Multan city, his family is the custodian of a sufi shrine in Sindh Known as Musa Pak: Gilani's father's sister was married to syed Ali Mardan Shah, Pir of Pagara an influential political personality ofSindh. Pir of Pagara also heads a political party by name of PML. Thus Gilani has good political hold in Sindh as well.

After becoming Prime Minister, Gilani was under pressure from Americans to crack down on Islamic militants from Taliban and Al Qaeda more resolutely and effectively. Differences between Gen. Musharraf and PPP PML(N) combine persisted on various issues including the issue of re instatement of ousted Judges alongwith Chief Justice Iftikhar Mohammed Chaudhary. Among many other wrongs, presidents Musharraf's worst blunder was to have removed the chief justice on March 9, 2007. The political atmosphere further worsened when the supreme court restored the ousted CJ on July 20, 2007. On August 6, 2008 PML(N) chief Nawaz Sharif and PPP leader Asif Ali Zardari decided to initiate the process to impeach the President. Same day Gen. Musharraf signed a notification to restore eight Judges only. In view of the developments about his impeachment, Gen. Musharraf cancelled his trip to Beijing to attend the Olympic games and vowed to use all constitutional powers to thwart efforts to remove him from office. So far in the history of Pakistan right from Aug. 14, 1947 no talks were even in the air to impeach the President of Pakistan. Gen. Musharraf's blunder in firing the chief Justice triggered a mass movement by lawyer traternity all over the country against the military rule. All this and Gilani's swinging action against militants in Waziristan and Pak-Afghan border annoyed them and they targeted him (Gilani) on September 3, 2008. The militants fried two shots which hit his motorcade just three days before the Presidential election. The bullets hit the window glass of the bullet-proof car but the PM Mr Gilani was not in the car. Gilani's press secretary Mr. Zahid. Bashir said that unknown assailants fired multiple sniper shots in what he described was a murder attempt: The vehicle under attack was on its way to the airport to pick up the PM who had been in Lahore. Pakistani Taliban

For Impeachment of President

National Assembly member :	342
Senate Strength	100
For Impeachment two third of 442 member required	295
Zardari and Sharif were counting on 269 members form NA and 36–39 from Senate.	

They need 295 votes out of 442 members of the combined Strength of National Assembly and the Senate.

claimed responsibility for the attack and also threatened to carry out more strikes against leaders. The spot where the incident occurred was close to the one where four supporters of former PM Nawaz Sharif were shot at one Dec. 27, 2007 a few hours before Sharif was due to address his election campaign rally in Rawalpindi.[6–A]

On March 31, 2008 a 24–member Coalition Cabinet was sworn in by President Pervez Musharraf. The PML–N ministers–to–be wore black bonds to protest against the head of state (Gen. Retd. Pervez Musharraf). This was the first time when cabinet members were sworn in wearing black bands in Pakistan.[6–B] The formula adopted by the ruling Pakistan Democratic Alliance (PDA) was that 11 minister from PPP, 9 from PML–N, 2 from AND and 1 each from the JUI–F and the FATA would from the ministry. Important portfolios of ministers were allotted to :–

From PPP:–

1. Shah Mehmood Qureshi – Foreign Ministry
2. Ms Sherry Rehman – Information

3. Raja Pervez Ashraf	– Water & Power
4. Qamar Zaman Kaira	– Kashmir Affairs
5. Senator Farooq Malik	– Law, Justice, Human Rights
6. Chaudhary Ahmed Mukhtar	– Defence
7. Nazar Muhammad Gondal	– Narcotics

From PML–N–

1. Chaudhry Nisar Ali Khan	– Senior Minister
2. Senator Ishaq Dar	– Finance, Economic Affairs
3. Khawaja Asit	– Petroleum and National Resources
4. Sardar Mehtab Abbasi	– Railways.
5. Rana Tanveer Hussain	– Defence Production

From ANP

1. Ghulam Ahmed Bilour	– local governments Rural Development
2. Khawaja Mohammad Khan Hoti	– Social Welfare

From JUI–F

Rehmat ullah Kakar

FATA:

Hameedullah Jan Afridi.

However, PML–N chief Nawaz Sharif withdrew from the coalition ministry on Aug. 25, 2008 but continued support from outside.

Zardari had unveiled proposed constitutional changes on May 25, 2008 that would strip Gen. Musharraf of his powers but Gilani, the Prime Minister ruled out any confrontation with President Musharraf. Nawaz Sharif had persistently been demanding the ouster of Pervez Musharraf.

In the face of democratic upsurge during the period 2007-8 the kings party (PML–Q) disintegrated as rapidly as it was created in the year 2001. Nawaz Sharif was hell bent to see Musharraf not only impeached but prosecuted as well for violating the constitution and dismissing his lawfully elected democratic government in Oct. 1999. Gen. Musharraf right from 2001 till his resignation maintained a dual policy words Taliban Jihadi etc. of both Ali Qaeda and religious extremist parties. Overtly he showed as if he was in control of them but his ISI was actually arming Jihadis who were killing US forces mainly in Afghanistan. US did realise it albeit belatedly. But by then Musharraf had already earned 11.8 billions from US alone for Pakistan economy exactly as was done by Gen Zia ul Haq. The 'real husband' of Pakistan, the US had no more any use of Pervez Musharraf after he gave up the post of Army chief. Moreover, Gen. Kayani was one who toed American dictates. As in the case of other military rulers, of late, Gen. Musharraf become almost isolated and was ill advised when he targeted independent judiciary and later on imposed Emergency in the country. Since he sided with religious extremists, by and large, barring in the Lal Masjid episode, he could not achieve moderation as he promised and put it in practice in the begining of his rule. He wanted Pakistan to be a progressive model of muslim world and could be compared with that of MA Jinnah in a way. No one can deny that he did try to stabilise relation between India and Pakistan and in a sense even improved them. He could not have used Article 58(2)(b) without the effective backing of the COAS Gen. Ashfaq Pervez Kayani who was unwilling to involve Army in Politics anymore. But at the same time Army could not see its once chief be impeached by 'bloody civilians'. As in known, the Pakistan Army, (Army chief and his formation corps Commanders) remain the main and final arbiter on all political issues, foreign policies. Policy in Kashmir India, nuclear issue, Jihadi groups which are the exclusive domain of Pak army. Now it deals with Afghan policy exclusively. Pressure was mounted on him to quit the post of President. The Coalition finalised impeachment charge against President Musharraf on August 17, 2008 and the following day Pervez Musharraf tendered his resignation. On Aug. 18, 2008 it was an end of era for President Musharraf who claimed that he tendered the resignation 'in the greater national interest'. This eight year rule mixed with good as well as not-so-good actions culminated in his quitting the powers—first as COAS on Nov. 28, 2007 and then on August 18, 2008 as President. Army had also advised Gen. Musharraf that the people voted in the general election of Feb. 2008 for a change and it was right time for him to quit and that they had brokered an understanding with the civilian government that Gen. Musharraf would not be prosecuted after he resigned.

Musharraf assured a delegation of forty members of PML (Q) party led by Marvi Memon, MNA, on August 20 that he wants to continue living in Pakistan. But Aitzaz Ahsan told BBC that Sir Mark Lyall Grant a British diplomat was involved in negotiations to give safe passage to Musharraf. Aitzaz also criticised Grant of undermining his country's rule of law.[7]

A court dismissed a petition on Aug. 22, 2008 filed by Khawaja Khalid Chairman of Defence of Human Rights Society against former President Pervez Musharraf and for killing persons during army action in Lal Masjid. Khalid had also asked the Court in his petition that Musharraf's name should be included in Exit Control List. The Chief Justice of Islamabad High Court Sardar Muhammad Aslam rejected his demand as well stating that the persons named in the petition had not yet been formally charged and could not be stopped from going abroad.

Nawaz Sharif described Musharraf's exit as 'victory for the people of Pakistan. Nisar Ali Khan of PML(N) a close associate of Nawaz said that all political parties, civil Society and lawyers deserved credit for forcing Musharraf to resign. Imran Khan branded the parting speech by Musharraf on Aug. 18 as 'bundle of lies'.

The News (Aug. 19, 2008) reported that it interviewed a number of people, majority of whom were of the opinion that Pervez Musharraf should be tried in court for violating the constitution, killing of hundreds of students of Jamia Hafsa, killing of Baloch Leader Akbar Bugti. Aitzaz Ahsan, President of Supreme Court Bar Association said "President Pervez Musharraf should be tried for his crimes. Ahsan and PML(N) leader Iqbal said "main impediment to Pakistan's growth had gone."

His vision of a modern Islamic Pakistan an Islamic state like Turkey was indeed appreciable. Ambitious as he was, he even forced his way to become chairman of Joint chief of staff committee (JCSC) in early 1999, inspite of his already being COAS and despite being junior to his Air Force and Navy counterparts which resulted in resignation of the Naval Chief. But in October 1999, though ambitious, he was forced to take over the command of the Nation by circumstances and it was at a spur of moment that he decided to overthrow the then Prime Minister Nawaz Sharif. Thereafter he went on consolidating his power. He always consulted his corps commanders and officers of GHQ ensuring unity of command in the Army. He introduced de–weaponisation drive towards curbing terrorism in the country. On June 5, 2001 Gen. Musharraf launched a compaign to flush out millions of illegal weapons meant for sectarian violence and the government announced on June 20 that it would conduct house to house search to detect such weapons. But the initiative was given up after 1,63,000 weapons were seized or surrendered by the end of August 2001. Some 3000 persons were punished under law and 40,000 cases were pending upto July 2002 against those who possessed illegal weapons. The ban on issuance of new arms licences had to be lifted from July 22, 2002. Comprehensive data–base of all licenced weapons was prepared and sent to ISI and IB. Lt. Gen. (Retd.) Haider claimed (July 29, 2002 in Lahore) that as many as 1,65,000 arms reaching from Afghanistan were recovered and claimed that Pakistan is number three in the world as far as recovery of illegal weapons was concerned. US Army also had by July 2002 retrieved 26 missing stinger missiles form various hands of warring factions but claimed that still 200 more stingers were missing. A stringer missle that cost US $ 65,000 was started to be re-purchased through a Pakistani tribesman named Nasir Afridi at a cost of $ 1,20,000 per stringer Rifle.

Improvement in Madarsa education was introduced by him. Gen. Musharraf ordered that alongwith religious teachings, subjects like maths, english and science should also be taught to students. In June 2002 the government made it mandatory for all madaris to register themselves with the government latest by March 23, 2002, disclose their sources of funds. But all these orders simply evaporated. Gen. Musharraf banned Sectarian outfits like LJP and SMP (both Shia organisations) on August 14, 2001. SSP and TJP were also banned in Jan. 2002. This measure became redundant since SSP and LJP by then had already placed their resources with the JeM. Both Harkat-ul-Mujahideen (HM) and Jaish-e-Mohammad (JeM) were also banned since both of them were Jihadi organisation. This measure also proved ineffective since Harkat cadres Joined JeM and JeM itself changed its name to Tehrik-ul-Furqan. In view of an attack on Indian Parliament, JeM was again banned in January 2002. LeT changed its name to Pasban-e-Ahle Hadith before the ban was imposed. The government arrested their leaders viz Maulana Masood Azhar, head of JeM and Hafiz Sayeed, head of LeT. Maulana Abdul Wahid Kashmiri emerged as a new leader of LeT. Hafiz Sayeed was released in April 2002. Gen. Musharraf ordered 2000 workers of these banned organizations, whose total strength was estimated at 2,00,000, to be arrested. But as an after thought, the Religious Affairs Minister Mehmood Ghazi stated that the government imposed a ban on these Jihadi organisation only to prevent them from collecting funds and not for their Jihadi activities necessary for Jihad in Kashmir. On February 12, the government even allowed freedom of these arrested workers on furnishing a personal bond. The government had not banned other Jihadi outfits like Al Badr,

Tehrik-e-Jihad, Tehrik-ul-Mujahideen, Al Qmar, Hizbul Mujahideen, Tehreekul-e-Mujahideen etc. They all attended a conference organised under the aegies of Muttahida Jihad Council (MJC) held in March 2002. Gen. Musharraf announced amendment to Blasphemy law but a gathering of relgious parties at Lahore criticised this action of Gen. Musharraf. On May 16, 2001 Gen. Musharraf himself announced the governments retreat on the Blasphemy law.

He helped US in containing Al Qaida and Taliban militants in Afghanistan, siding with US in its efforts on war against terror. He restricted entry of Afghan refugees into Pakistan. He also extended full co-operation to the US by way of offering facilities at Jacobabad Air base and Karachi Airport. Though American President George W. Bush reached out to his long time ally Gen. Pervez Musharraf on August 21, 2008 and thanked him for his efforts in democratic tradition of the country and his role in the war on terror, it was US only which saw hardly any use of Gen. Musharraf once he handed over the real power base of Pakistan i.e. that of the chief of Army staff on Nov. 28, 2007. Prior to it, on November 21, 2007 after cutting short his visit to Saudi Arabia and returning to Pakistan he promulgated an Ordinance Validating the emergency and the Provisional Constitutional Order (PCO) so that he gets immunity to all actions, under the emergency rule and preventing legal challenges after the emergency was lifted. The power base shifted to the new incumbent Gen. Ashfaq Pervez Kayani and incidently he was also a blue-eyed boy of America. US reinforced the idea of easing Gen. Musharraf out of civilian power particularly after Ms Benazir Bhutto was killed on December 27, 2007 at Rawalpindi. US had desired democracy to be restored and the domestic government to be headed by Ms Benazir Bhutto. It was the US that had initiated the initial raproachment between Gen. Musharraf and Ms. Benazir Bhutto. Saudi Arabia never wanted Benazir in power and for them Nawaz Sharif was suitable and preferable. According to the US journalist Ron Suskind American Communication intercepts showed Gen. Musharraf virtually threatening Benazir a few weeks before her assassination that her life was in his hands and she better behave.[7] Gen Musharraf started becoming unpopular thereafter and America hastened the final outcome. Afterall, Pakistan is governed by three A's–Allah, America and Army.

In what manner America treats Pakistan, a glimpse can be had from the statements of Lt. Gen. (Retd.) Hameed Gul former ISI chief, which appeared in pak urdu newspapers Nawa-e-Waqkt of April 13, 2002 after President clinton's visit. Quote "The way Clinton addressed us was the way one treats the salve nations. We were wrong in thinking that we had a friendly relationship with US. The fact of the matter is that the US agenda is in conflict with Pakistan's existence, security and national prestige. The US wants us to shun our Islamic foundation. We can not accept the order, but at the same time do not want a clash with America. We want a respectable working relationship with America. On the other hand, the US can not afford to leave Pakistan in 'isolation'. Time will prove the truth of this observation." unquote.[8]

Incidently Nawại Waqt, through its editiorial on January 29, 2002 had warned that Gen. Musharraf would be ousted the moment the US found him ineffective. And see how true their assessment was. On November 18, 2007 "when Deputy Secretary of state John Negroponte visited Pakistan, he met once with President Pervez Musharraf for two hours. But before he left town, he held three meetings with a lesser known figure – General Ashfaq Kayani, the Dy. Army Chief. The two shared a Saturday night dinner."[9]

Former DG ISI Lt. Gen. (Retd.) Javed Nasir also wrote an article on US-Pak friendship the Myth and reality[10] "The latest insult that has been inflicted on Pakistan in the 5–hour stopover by US President Clinton during his recent visit of the sub continent. This was a parting kick given to an ally which during the last 50 years fultilled every aspect of its obligations despite repeated US betrayals."

In one of the important opinions expressed by the Chief Justice of Pakistan, the new CJ Abdul Hameed Dogar attributed the military intervention to the failure of lagislatures to function effectively on Nov. 20, 2007 while hearing a petition challenging the Emergency and the PCO issued by President Gen. (Retd.) Pervez Musharraf.

In an another incident which left a bad impression was that the deposed CJ Iftikhar Muhammad Chaudhry was locked in his official residence in November 2007. The main gate of his residence was locked by the police and erected barbed wire barricades parking vehicles outside to prevent him walking out of the residence.

Gen. (Retd.) Pervez Musharraf cemented Sino-Pak relations Further. In the year 2006, during his state visit to Beijing he stated "Friendship between Beijing and Pakistan is deeper than the ocean and higher than the mountain." This is the indicator of closeness between the two countries.

Once Henery Kissinger wrote that it was dangerous to be America's enemy but it can be fatal to be America's friend. Gen. Musharraf also became America's friend. Working exactly on the same lines, Americans worked out on exit strategy for Gen. Musharraf when they found him loosing his acceptability in Pakistan polity. They asked him to lift emergency, quit as Army Chief and free opposition politicians and media men. Of course Gen. Musharraf defended his decision, of imposing Emergency rule on the ground that Pakistans nuclear weapons could fall into the wrong hands if elections led to disturbances. US had spend almost $ 100 million on a highly classified program to help Gen. Pervez Musharraf secure his country's nuclear weapons.[11] Pakistan's anti missile system itself was costing $l 15 milhion estimated. A British Think talk spcei alising on Pakistan's security issues had said that the chances of Islamabad's nuclear assets falling into the hands of tribal militants have increased as most of the arsenals were located in the restive north–western parts of the country. 'The Pakistan Security Research unit in its report 'the Security of Nuclear Weapons in Pakistan' said Islamabad had in place robust measures but each contained some weaknesses and many were being exacerbated by the present political turbulence in the country[12]. However to the Bush Administration, Gen. Pervez Musharraf was a democrat, a visionary and a loyal ally in the war on terror. But Adrain Levy and Catherine Scolt–clark, co authors of 'Pakistan's nuclear proliferation and blackmail trace Musharraf's career in furthering terrorism in Afghanistan India and elsewhere, A California daily referred him as a 'terrorist' San Fansisco Chronicle' headlined an article "Friend or Foe" on him. Michael Krepon of the stimson centre in a commentary wrote" The longer Musharraf stays, the greater the difficulties Washington can expect.[13]

Some of the Pakistanis did loose faith in Gen. Musharraf alleging that he compromised their nation. Terrorism in Pakistan was growing. G–8 nations then led by its Chairman, the Canadian Prime Minister Mr. Jean chretien urged Pakistan on Jan. 27, 2002 to stop terrorist acts. In the month of February 2002. National Movement for the Restoration of Pakistani Sovereignty surfaced with former heads of ISI, including Gen. Mahmood Ahmed who was sacked in October 2001, as its members. This group held anti-American views. US operations in Afghanistan continued. In Jan. 2002 Gen. Musharraf sacked Brig. Abdullah who was heading and looking after Kashmir Division of ISI in order to curb support to militants fighting in J&K[14]." On June 29, 2002 he sidelined Maj. Gen. Ehtesham Zamir, head of political wing of ISI for organising a referendum in April 2000 in his favour, Musharraf was forced to apologise in public after Ballot Boxes were stuffed with 'Yes' votes.[15]

Though Gen. Musharraf sacked Brig. Abdullah, who was overall incharge of carrying on militancy in Kashmir, ISI continued its covert as well as overt support, including financial, to the militants and Hurriyat leaders. ISI kept on giving money through its mission in New Delhi for example on Oct 1, 1993 one Ghulam Nabi was arrested who confessed to have received Rs 60 Lakhs to the then Chairman of Muslim Conference. On June 6, 1999 Ghulam Mohammad Butt, Dy. Director of the institute of Kashmir was given Rs. 10 Lakh when he visited Pakistan High Commission in New Delhi.

On Dec. 27, 1999 Gen. Musharraf issued an statement on Kashmir which said "Let me reiterate. There is a change. I have told everyone, the foreign office also that there is a change in the policy on Kashmir. First we had been telling that with India we will address all the issues. We would like to negotiate on all issues, including Kashmir. The change is and I have told them that we will address the Kashmir issue first and all other issues later. I will maintain this stance everywhere. Wherever I go and wherever I have been to. I have been telling them that Kashmir is the core issue. The maximum we can do is simultaneously we address the Kashmir issue and all other issues. But Kashmir has to be there." This he said while addressing govt. Officers in Muzaffarabad.

Gen. Pervez Musharraf never relented on the issue of Kashmir though he did show a flexible attitude which also met the demands of Pakistan by and large. He came out with a few solutions which indeed were fovourable to Pakistan only in the end. He was prepared to forget the demand of meeting the UN Resolutions on Kashmir. On Jan. 9, 2002 he termed the ISI sponsored and Pakistan trained-and- sent militants in Kashmir as "Freedom Fighter" and the violence in Kashmir was branded by him as a freedom movement. On Jan. 12, 2002 Gen. Musharraf stated that "Kashmir runs in our blood. No Pakistani can afford to sever links with Kashmir. We will continue to extended our moral, political and diplomatic support to Kashmiris. We will never budge from our principal stand to Kashmiris. Kashmir has to be resolved through dialogue in accordance with the wishes of the people of Pakistan and in accordance with the UN resolution.[16] Gen. Musharraf persued Islamist agenda relentlessly on Kashmir issue. Even former DG ISI Gen. Hamid Gul had declared that "the total collapse of the state (read Pakistan) is what we desire because only then by the collapse of the state can a truely Islamic state be implemented"[17] Gen. Musharraf even used Kashmir as a rallying point with his commanders after 9/

11.[17] Gen. Musharraf even wanted to alter the borders or status of LoC irrevocably when he mounted Kargil invasion under 'Operation Badr.' Redrawing of borders was opposed by President clinton who warned Pakistan against "redrawing borders with blood" and added that the stark truth must also be faced that there is no military solution to Kashmir." However his timings of intrusion into Kargil sector were perfect though the whole exercise ultimately ended in a fiasco and a shame for Pakistan. When Indian Army moved to warmer locations during winters from Kargil height and vacated these posts, Gen. Musharraf ordered his army troops from Northern Light Infantry (NLI) to occupy these heights. This was an act of which Indian Army was completely anaware of. When India detected the invasion on May 3, 1999 they were taken aback. Indian Army mounted attacks in which NLI men were killed but Pakistan refused to accept their body bags lest it becomes known to the world that the Kargil invasion was the handiwork of Pakistan Army troops and ISI. After failure of this operation Badr, Gen. Musharraf came out with another solution on October 25, 2004 that the whole of Kashmir – Indian or Pakistan occupied – should be devided into seven regions with Pakistan controlling two and India five regions. Seven (7) regions proposed by Gen. Musharraf were. (*i*) Rajouri Poonch (*ii*) Jammu (*iii*) Ladakh (*iv*) Kashmir valley (*v*) Kargil (*vi*) Pok (*vii*) Northern Areas.

India recognises Five (5) regions only i.e. (1) Jammu (2) Kashmir (3) Laddakh (4) Gilgit (5) Baltistan.

Musharraf proposal would mean giving up Mangla Dam in Pok security. United Jehad Council, Muttahida Majlise Ammal and Jaish-e-Mohammad parties opposed it. Soft borders and joint sovereignity as proposed by him was not acceptable Even to Pakistan Military. His policy of open borders, demilitarisasation, self-governance and Joint Management was also criticsed even by syed Ali Shah Gilani of Kashmir.

ISI used Al Qaeda to train J&K ultras in its camps near

Khost in Afghanistan and maintained direct links with these Islamic fundamentalists and militants fighting in Kashmir. In August 1998 when America bombed the Al Queda's Khost Camp, a number of Kashmiri militants who were being trained there came to notice. ISI continues to maintain a longterm understanding with Al Qaeda. It has close, covert intimate relationship even with Taliban. To keep this relationship under wraps, ISI opposed a trip by President Clinton to Pakistan taking a plea of his safety in October 2001. ISI chief Lt. Gen. Mahmood Ahmed was reluctant to Join US led coalition against Taliban and it was one of the reasons Gen. Musharraf was compelled to ease out the ISI chief to show to the US that he (Gen. Musharraf) is with America in its fight against terrorism. Former DG ISI Lt. Gen. (Retd.) Hamid Gul who opposed the idea of CIA's association with ISI in the war against terror stating 'the ISI is a national Intelligence agency whose potential and output should not be shared or rented out to other countries.[18] Brig. Mohammad Yousuf of Pakistan Army who was head of the Afghan Bureau and stationed in Afghanistan when CIA's collaboration began with ISI in 1984 said that from 1984 to 1987 over 80,000 mujahideen went through these training Camps.[19]

Gen. Musharraf should be credited for making Pakistan's economy stronger. First soon after Sept. 11, 2001 attack on world trade Tower and thereafter from time to time by way of exchanging Al Qaida terrorists with US in lieu of considerable amount of American dollars. Within a short gap of time, Gen. Musharraf kept on handing over Al Qaeda Target and receiving funds. This way he killed two birds with one stone. He not only brought dollars to Pakistan, he also tried to show America in its fight against terrorism that Pakistan is loyal to America under the leadership of Gen. Pervez Musharraf. Thus he tried to enhance his prestige in the eyes of America and kept on playing double game. On one hand he kept Al Qaida and Taliban alive and kicking by extending covert support to them in Afghanistan on the other hand Gen. Musharraf kept on handing over Al Qaeda militants to

America in return of dollars. The first Al Qaeda leader Abu Zubayada captured by Pakistan was handed over to Americans on May 27, 2007. US made a payment of 300 million during Oct.-Dec. 2001, $l 847 million in 2002, $ 753 million in 2003, $ 1221 million in 2004, $ 915 in 2005, $ 1070 in 2006 and between Jan and June 2007 $l 453 to Pakistan, Gen. Musharraf brought a total of $ 11.8 billion form USA alone.

Gen. Musharraf himself had touted as one of his biggest achievements slided down in a tailspin, according to the economists. Though Gen. Musharraf had brought in an economists and banking expert into his Cabinet as Finance Minister, Shaukat Aziz who was later elevated to the position of Prime Minister in Aug. 2004 by him it seems nothing substantial could be done by him to improve the national economic field for the economy to look upwards. At the time of bidding Good bye in Aug. 2008 to the post of the President of Pakistan by Gen. (Retd.) Pervez Musharraf, the foreign Exchange reserves, which had crossed $l 16 billion, were down to less than $ 9 billion, fiscal deficits were almost 5% of the GDP, and the rupee had lost over 10 per cent of its value in the last few months coupled with unprecedented power shortages and a rise in the price of basic utilities, industry had been severely hit, leading to a gloomy outlook in which debt servicing was bound to rise as many of Pakistan's loans rescheduled after 2001 – become due. Inflation over the last 12 months had hit a whopping 25 per cent on average and almost 35 per cent in areas such as food and transport.[20]

But to begin with Gen. Mushrrafs intensions were really good. On economic front he came out with the following guide lines in his maiden speech on Oct. 17, 1999 addressing to the nations were :–

(*i*) rebuilding of investors confidence through stability and consistency in economic policies and economic security. The objective was to encourage the local investors, overseas Pakistanis and foreign investors.

(*ii*) Increase domestic savings

(*iii*) Carry out Pragmatic tax reforms
(*iv*) Turn around the state enterprises towards profitability
(*v*) Boost agriculture and revive industry
(*vi*) Strict austerity measures.

Accountability Cell was set up under newly promoted Lt. Gen. syed Amjad Hussain, Commander Strategic Command HQ in Islamabad mainly to recover the looted public wealth in the form of outstanding public loans of over 250 billion rupees. This cell was given powers to attack defaulters properties and assets like houses, car etc. Out of 5 Lakh defaulting individuals, groups or companies, about 500 defaulters were identified in the begining for recovery of such looted money so that a philip to be given to the sagging economy by way recovering at least 50 billion rupees.

Soon after 9/11, Gen. Musharraf was given $ 800 million cash grant by America on Oct. 20, 2001, in addition to $l 600 million for Afghan refugees. As on Sept. 30, 2001 Pakistan's total foreign debt was to the tune of $ 37 billion which included $ 12.5 billion bilateral and $ 15.4 billion debt of world Bank, IMF, Asian Development Bank and the Islamic Development Bank. Pakistan owed $ 5 billion loan to Japan, $ 3 billion to USA, $ 1 billion to France, $ 1 billion to Germany, $ 318 million to Canada, $ 175 million to Italy, $ 738 million to to Korea,$ 127 million to Sweeden, $ 103 million to Russia and $ 88 million to Netherlands. Gen. Musharraf by way of his cleverly contrived moves, eased this strained financial position of his country.[21]

On nuclear front also he played very cleverly. When united states wanted a few Pakistani nuclear scientists for questioning for alleged links with terrorist organisation Gen. Musharraf quietly requested military leadership of Myanmar to host two Pakistani nuclear experts Mr Suleiman Asad and Mr. Muhammad Ali Mukhtar. These two scientists had long experience at two of Pakistan's clandestine nuclear weapons programme.[22]

With these events, ISI kept on growing and taking shape

of a monster. Benazir Bhutto said that she took over office in 1998 the ISI was a state within a state. However, subsequently, power form ISI passed from the institution to a criteria of retired generals who were in power during the Afghan operation. Under the leadership of the retired generals, during the eightees the ISI received major funding for establishing madarssa. However, in the ninetees the power to manage the madrassas passed from the ISI to private groups. She "further said" the turning point for Pakistan was the Afghanistan operation in the 1980s. 'Suitcases of cash were flown in by C–130s' of US funding for the operation. The money went to the generals and all their children are multi-millionaires today. A group of generals who were active during that phase but have now retired continue to call the shot. Earlier the ISI was the state within the State. Now it is these generals who influence appointments within the ISI, raise private militias and beleive in a theocratic state. It was such generals who sponsored the Jaish-e-Mohammed (JEM). The Harkat-ul-Mujahideen (HuM) and the Lashkar-e-Taiba (LeT) and sent them to Kashmir to spread terror. Ventilating her partys (PPP) views, the spokesman said "the PPP point of view is that one or more Generals on their own initiative sought help of Osama bin Laden to overthrow the PPP government in 1989 and continued to have links with him. It is clarified that Pakistan Army did not want to invade Afghanistan at the time of late President Najibullah. However there was a plan for the Afghan Interim government to announce a confederation with Pakistan and call for the assistance of Pakistani troops which was vetoed by the Prime minister".[23] These elements continue terrorist activities through various 'Tanjeems' of Islamic militants throughout India.

ISI even got involved in heroin smuggling. US result of Federal Bureau of Investigation (FBI) completed a list of at least 30 army and ISI officers – both serving and retired who had allegedly accumulated wealth through heroin smuggling. Resultantly, Pakistani illegal heroin economy has kept it legitimate state economy sustained since 1990 and prevented its collapse. It has also enabled the country to maintain a high level of arms purchases form abroad and finance its 'proxy war' in Kashmir through the Jehadi organisation, the communique issued by FBI stated. The FBI findings say while it is difficult to estimate the money spent by Pakistan on the 'proxy war', it is believed that about 80 percent of its total external debt of $ 38 billion, i.e. about $ 30.4 billion, has been incurred on arms purchases since 1990. This includes its purchases of aircraft and missiles from China, missiles from North Korea, for which payment was made partly in cash and partly in imported US and Australian wheat, Agosta class submarines form France, reconditioned Mirage aircraft from France, Lebanon and Australia and other items from countries such as Ukraine.' The US investigators claimed in their findings that the use of heroin dollars to promote Jehad started after the withdrawal of the Soviet troops from Afghanistan in 1988. In the 1980s, they added, the internal political cell of ISI, headed by Brig. Imtiaz Ahmed (Retd) who worked directly under Lt. Gen. Hameed Gul (Retd) started a special cell for the use of heroin for covert actions." Even the former Prime Minister Nawaz Sharif in an interview to a Pakistan journalist stated that 'the then army chief and the ISI boss had proposed him a detailed blueprint for selling heroin to pay for the countrys covert military operation in 1991.' Brig (Retd) Imtiaz Ahmed later on i.e after leaving ISI joined Intelligence Bureau as its head. He was a close associate of Nawaz Sharif. Brig Imtiaz Ahmed was arrested and convicted by a court on July 31, 2001 and Jailed for eight years. According to evidence produced in the court by the National Accountability Bureau (NAB) Brig. Imtiaz had foreign exchange bearer certificate worth $ 20.08 million, a Pakistani rupee account in the Union Bank with a balance of Rs 2.13 billion, as US dollar account in the Deutseh Bank with a balance of US $l 19.1 million, five residential houses, five commercial units and three shops. The US investigators believe the brigadier accumulated this wealth through heroin smuggling

Inspite of all these practices by ISI, Gen Musharraf defended 'ISI as Pakistan's first line of Defence'. Conspiracies against the ISI are aimed at defaming Pakistan and the spy agency which is a patriotic institution working for the stability of the country, Gen. Musharraf opined[25]

Gen (Retd) Pervez Musharraf's departure may not augur well for India now but in the begining when he overthrew Nawaz Sharif, he did adopt a stiff posture against the Indian state. Since he was the main architect of Kargil operation, he would dismission India's contention and US harping that Pakistan was fomenting violence in Kashmir. Rather, he had encouraged Islamic militants undertaking dare devil attacks in Kashmir in order to invite world attention and keep India 'bleeding'. The main thrust was to keep India engaged in such anti-terrorist operation from which India could not emerge as a regional power. The attack by Pakistan based Islamic militants on Srinagar Secretariat on Oct. 28 and Corps HQ on Nov. 4 were a pointer towards this fact. Incidently, the attack on Corps Hq in Srinagar coincided with the 3–day Congregation of Lashar-e-Toiba in Muridke (near Lahore), Musharraf adopting a hard instance against India concentrated India–experts in his team. Corps Commander-X Corps Lt. Gen. Jamshed Gulzar who was Defence Attache in New Delhi in 1993, Abdul Sattar who was twice High Commission or of Pakistan in New Delhi (He was Director of India desk during, Simla Accord and is a staunch supporter of Kashmirs self determination formula, DGMO Maj. Gen. Shahid Aziz who served as a top analyst of ISI, Chief of General staff Lt Gen Mohammad Amir who ran ISI's external wing for 3 years was Pakistan Armys Kashmir expert etc constituted his team.

But now Gen. Kayani's rule onwards, India would have a tough time dealing with Pakistan is irrespective of any democratic government in power in Islamabad. The future Command of Army is to remain in the hands of those Army officers who were trained by Gen. Zia-ul-Haq and were taught 'hate-India beat India' lessons, who were administered oath of taking revenge form India for 1971 dismemberment of Pakistan. Gen Kayani was ISI chief before taking over as COAS and he had already mounted a number of military operations against India. Now that he himself is chief and all in all, there would be no checks on him of course, barring American dictates. This Trend has already been notice after Gen. (Retd) Musharraf gave up the power. Infiltration cutting off the fences on the border, Jihadi activities inside Kashmir, hosting of Pakistani fiags in Kashmir all prompted by ISI are clearly visible. The Kabul Embassy of India attack on July 7, 2008 by ISI-aided and Taliban–executed is a daring example of what India should expect in future.

Attacks on Gen. Musharraf

(*i*) April 2002 – Suspects included a Rangers Inspector and a Naval Dockyard worker.

(*ii*) April 26, 2003 – Terrorists tried to blow up a car parked on Shatiae Fair at Karachi as his (Gen. Musharrafs) Convoy was passing by. The market vehicle was loaded with explosives. One Kamran @ Atif (28) was arrested in Karachi on May 19, 2004 for this act. He, perhaps, belonged to Harkatul Mujahideen Al Alami.

(*iii*) Dec 14, 2003 – White crossing Jhanda Chichi Bridge near 10 corps HQ shortly after arriving form Karachi. The lapse resulted in the replacement of DGM Maj. Gen. Majid Tariq with President's Military Secretary Maj. Gen. Nadeem Taj on Dec. 18, 2004.

(*iv*) Dec 25, 2003 – Possible involvement of Brigade 313 a Roose alliance of five militant organisation viz Jaish-e-Mohammad, Harkat ul Jehad Al Islami, LeT, Lashkar-e-Jhangvi and Harket ul Mujahideen Al Alami. The two attackers identified were :–

(*i*) Mohammad Jamil. a JeM activist form Azad Kashmir

(*ii*) Hazir Sultan, a JKLF operative form Afghanistan.

Gen. Pervez Musharraf's Rules (An overview)

1998	Oct 7	:	Gen. Musharraf takes over as chief of Army staff Handpicked by Nawaz Sharif inspite of being advised against. Two senior offices superceded resign.
1999	May to July	:	Remained involved in Kargil mischief Indians and Pakistani troops closed at Kargil on May 2 Sharif ovdered Musharraf to withdraw form Kargil.
	Oct 12	:	Staged coup detat. Took over power from PM Nawaz Sharif after Sharif tried to fire him and prevent him from landing in Pakistan on his return form Sri Lanka. Sharif had promoted Gen Ziauddin ISI chief as CoAs. GHQ did not allow him to take over fill Musharraf returned form Sri Lanka.
2000	May 13	:	Supreme Court validated the Coup.
2001	June 20	:	Appointed himself as President before visiting India.
	Sept 12	:	Dropped support for the Taliban and allied Pakistan with the US after 9/11
2002	March 27	:	In Pak Operations, Abu Zubayda an Al Qaida operator captured and handed over to US after Sept 11 attacks.
	April 30	:	Referendum held to extend Presidents

			term. Though controvertial, Musharraf wins.
	Oct 10	:	Pro-Musharraf political Party PML(Q) wins general election.
	Nov 16	:	Musharraf sworn-in for a 5-year term as President.
2003	Dec 14	:	Escapes assassination bid. Explosives week a bridge in Rawalpindi Just after Musharrafs car passes. Days later, Musharraf survived twin suicide car bombing.
2004	Jan 1	:	Gen. Musharraf wins parliamentary vote of confidence
	Jan 6	:	Affirming his unelected rule until 2007.
	Jan 6	:	Commitments made jointly by Pakistan and India regarding Indo-Pak relation
	March 16	:	Pak Army launches first operation against Al Qaida hidents in the North Waziristan.
	Sept 24	:	Joint Statement issued after PM of India and Precident of Pak met in New York. including Gas Pipe line form Pakistan to India.
	Dec 30	:	He reneges on his promise to quit as Army Chief.
2005	April 16 to 18	:	Gen. Musharraf alongwith 45–member team visits Delhi to talk to PM Manmohan Singh. Many CBMs signed. Grade across LoC begins People to people contact enhanced. Reaffirmed the commitments made on Jan 6, 2004 and Sept 24, 2004.
2006	June	:	Musharrafs re-election timetable row erupts.

	Sept 5	:	Peace deal with tribes and militants in the North Wagiristan signed which was criticised by the US,
2007	March 9	:	Musharrafs downfall begins. He sacks chief Justice Iftikhar Muhammad Chaudhry which sparked nation wide protests.
	July 8–10	:	He orders Pakistan Army para troops to storm Red Mosque in Islamabad to flush out Taliban militants. About 100 of them killed in the operation including Abdul Rashid Ghazi. His brother Aziz was arrested while trying to escape wearing a 'Burka'.
	July 27	:	Musharraf meets Ms Benazir Bhutto in Abu Dhabi to discuss her return to Pakistan for power-sharing.
	Aug. 9	:	Gen. Musharraf who had almost decided to impose Emergency relents under US pressure not to do so.
	Sept. 18	:	He assures the nation that he will quit Army if re-elected as President.
	Sept. 20	:	Election Commission fixes poll date on Oct 6, 2007.
	Oct. 6	:	Wins Presidential election in poll with landslide victory. Opposition boycotts. But wait for declaration as winner.
	Nov. 2	:	Supreme Courts meets to decide it Musharraf was eligible to stand for re-election white still Army Chief.
	Nov. 3	:	Imposes state of Emergency, sacks chief Justice Iftikhar Mohd. Chaudhry, suspends Constitution, key opposition members arrested. Some 60 High Court and Supreme Court Judges were sent packing after imposing Emergency Rule.

Nov. 15	:	His 5-year term of Presidential mandate and term of sitting Parliament expires. Senate Chairman Mohammad mian Soomro appointed as a caretaker head to overse elections.
Nov. 22	:	Supreme Court rules Musharrafs presidency legal. The Commonwealth suspends Pakistan for the second time during his tenure.
Nov. 28	:	Gen. Musharraf hands over command of the Army to Gen. Ashtaq Pervez Kayani.
Nov. 29	:	Musharraf sworn in President for second term. Announces plan to lift state of Emergency on Dec. 16, 2007.
Dec. 15	:	Lifts state of Emergency after 42 days.

2008

Jan. 2	:	Elections postponed form Jan. 8 to Feb 18 because of disturbances after Benazirs assassination.
Feb. 18	:	PPP and PML (N) trounce Musharrafs PML (Q) and allies in general election.
Aug. 7	:	Coalition says Musharraf to face impeachments
Aug. 18	:	Musharraf resigns after almost 9-year rule.

Gen. Pervez Musharraf was born at Naharwali Gali, near Golcha Cinema, Daryaguny, Delhi on August 11, 1943. He shifted to Karachi in 1947 after his grandfather Qazi Mushamuddin Musharraf sold his 24 800 sq feet Haveli in 1946 just for Rs. 562.50 only. He remained in Turky (Ankara), with his father form 1949 to 1956 who was serving in Pakistans ministry of Foreign Affairs. He joined Pakistan Army in 1964 after passing out form Pakistan Military Academy at Kakul. During 1993–93 he was Director General Military Operations. While Musharraf was a mere Brigadier in 1987, Gen. Zia picked him up to Command Special Service Group (SSG) at Khapalu in Siachen form where he launched oppressive operations against shais in Glight at the instance of his master Gen. Zia.

US President George W. Bush called up Gen Musharraf on August 23, 2008 and thanked him for his "efforts in the democratic transition" of the country and his role in the war on terror.

2009 Musharraf visited India to take part in a media Seminar after stepping down form power.

2010 Gen. Musharraf denied visa to visit Mumbai and Kolkata to attend a seminar to be organised by YOUNG PRESIDENTS ORGANISATION(YPO) to be held in Delhi on December 5, 2010. His followers had applied for visa in Islamabad to visit multicity.

October 1, 2010 – Making an unprecedented apology to the people of Pakistan, admistting for the first time that some of the decisions he took while in power had 'negative' repurcussions and led to his downfall, Musharraf launched a new political outfits "All Pakistan Muslim League (APML).

October 9, 2010 – Talal Bugti, President of Jamhoori Watan Party made an announcement in Quelta that anyone who kills Gen. Musharraf would get Rs 1 billion ($l 1.1 million).

May 30, 2011 – Rana Nisar Ahmed, Judge in Antiterrorist Court in Rawalpindi declared Musharraf a "proclaimed offender" in Benazir Bhutto murder case.

August 27, 2011 – Anti–Terrorism Court ordered the seizure of Musharrafs property and freezing of all his Bank accounts for waiting to appear before the court in Benazir Bhutto murder case.

During Feb. 25 – March 16, 2009 political turmoil between

President 'Zardari, Lawyers movement and Nawaz Sharifs Joining the Long March, former President Gen (Retd) Musharraf once again tried to rise to prominence. Backing the Army to deal with the crisis he said (March 9) "if I am offered the post of the President and if I can be a useful President then I will want to contribute to this country. It the country faces an internal threat to its integrity it is the responsibility of the Army to protect the country. He said he did not want to be a "useless President."

Advocate Asad filed a petition in the Supreme court on March 20, 2009 on behalf on Akmal Saleemi seeking a direction to the Interior Ministry to put Pervez Musharraf's name in the Exit control List so that "he may not escape from the expected trial and conviction for having committed ottences of murders and high treason."

On March 24, on Zahid Hussain filed a petition in the Supreme Court levelling treason charges claiming that Gen. (Retd) Musharraf violated the constitution twice during his rule form 1999 to 2008.

Musharraf also visited India (March 6–9) at the invitation of India Today to speak on "Challenge of Changes" He spoke at India Today conclave on March 7 where in he said "We have to resolve Kashmir. Kashmir remains key dispute. The resolution of dispute means 'give and take'. There is an emotional involvement of Pakistan people with the people of Kashmir. Therefore, this has given rise to dozens of freelance mujahideen groups and increasing military in Pakistan society. He linked Siachen and Kargil to Kashmir issue and warned of many more Kargils and Siachen if the Kashmir issue was left unresolved. He touched anyother sensitive point. While talking of militancy in Kashmir he said "why did Lashkar-e-Toiba and Jaish-e-Mohammad come into being? However the Rajya Sabha MP Maulana Mahmood Madani told him there are more muslims in India than in Pakistan Indian Muslims have the ability to solve their problems, don't try to alienate them" Musharraf retorting said "If your are happy in your present condition I am most happy. I take my words back" and thus the situation was saved. He wanted LoC to be torn down like the Berlin wall. He blamed India for slowing down the peace process. Musharraf desired to be 'third umpire' between Pakistan and India. He detailed four challenges to Pakistan and India. today: (i) Al–Qaeda (ii) Militant Taliban (iii) Talibanisation in the settled areas of Pakistans Frontier provinces and (iv) extremism in Pakistan society. He desired to head for a solution by India and Pakistan. And to that effect, he said he had given a formula which could for the basis for moving forward and taking it towards a solution. The formula included identifying the zones in Kashmir, going for graduated demilitarisation, especially from the cities, so that the people of Kashmir can heave a sigh of relief, giving maximum self-governance to the people of Kashmir and having some kind of an over–watch on self–governance. He also referred to Siachen and Sir creek disputes. For Siacheen, he suggested the solution as disengaging and demilitarising'. He advised India to initiate confidence building measures without any loss of time end said we must stop unconsidered accusations against each other and also we must stop meddling in each others domestic affairs. He advocated restart of "back-channel diplomacy".[26] One of the important hint he threw when he spoke "But I want to emphasise, if you kill terrorists, whenever anything happens, whether it is Mumbai, Lahore or anywhere, you have plucked leaves of a tree. The leaves will grow again, may be in greater numbers. If you are able to cut off any terrorist organisation, you have chopped off one branch of that tree, the tree will continue to grow. You have to get to the root of threat tree, uproot that tree, then only will you end terrorism and extremism and that the root that I always keep talking been that terrorism is born form the womb of festuring political disputes which need to be resolved.[27]

Gen. (Retd) Musharraf has thrown a very important caution for the concerned Indian authorities He has in clear term, told that there will be many more Kargills and Siachens. India has to take him seriously and prepare its defence forces to rise to the threat. Provide Army with necessary equipment, missiles, Airpower and keep fighting fit troops. Arrousing passion of Indian muslims with intentions (of course inherent and hidden) so that they rise in revolt is another aim of Pakistan and Gen. Musharraf gave vent to Pakistans intentions. But it was certainly great of Mr. Madani that he silenced Musharraf then and there by saying that Indian Muslims do not need any advise form him.

This implies that Pakistan intends to do many more 26/11 and simultaneously help muslim uprising, weaken Indias economy by attacking economic nerve centers and yet to show the world that Pakistan is also a victim of terrorism. The culprit of 26/11 Ajmal Amir Karab has confessed "Kashmir ko azad karne ke liye lodna hai. Ab hame Hindustan par kaise hamle karne hain yeh tai karna hain" (We have to fight to free Kashmir we have to decide how to attack India).[28]

REFERENCE

1. Baluchistan had announced it independence on August 12, 1947 in the wake of Indian Independence Act.
2. The Hindustan Times dated May 24, 2007
3. Outlook December 10, 2007 issue
4. The Hindu did Nov 29, 2007 Musharraf to take oath as President today by Nirupama Subramanian.
5. The Times of India – Times Global section dt Nov 29, 2007. US welcomes Gen's retreat article by Chidanand Rajghatta.
6. Deccan Chronicle, CHENNAI did Jan. 9, 2008 Focus: by John F. Burns.
7. The Hindustan Times Sept. 4, 2008 report by Kamal Siddiqi from Karachi.
8. The Hindustan Times April 1, 2008 report by Kamal Siddiqui from Karachi.
9. The Pioneer did August 21, 2008 Britain accused of striking exit deal for Mush. Repeat by Nandini Jawli from London.
10. The Times of India Aug. 19, 2008 Exit great Dictator Report filed by

chidanand Rajghatta.

11. Nawa-e-Waqkt did April 13, 2000 After Clintons visit Difficulties and possibilities. article by Gen. Hameed Gul.
12. The Indian Express Nov. 22, 2007 US courts likely Musharraf successor by Emily Wax.
13. The Nation did April 21, 2000
14. The Times of India – Times Global section Nov. 19, 2007. Report by David E Sanger o& William J. Broad.
15. The Times of India Times Global section Drd Nov. 23, 2007 Report by PTI.
16. Ibid. Report by Chidanand Rajghatta from Washington.
17. The Hindustan Times June 30, 2002 report by PTI
18. The Hindustan Times June 29, 2002.
19. BBC Jan 12, 2002 Musharrafs speech highlights.
20. The Frontier Post April 30, 2000 Pakistan Moves Ahead under Musharraf – article by Gregory R. Copley.
21. Descent ints Chaos – Ahmed Rashid.
22. The Hindustan Times Oct 30, 2001.
23. The Times of India Sept 25, 2001.
24. India Today Sept 1, 2008 Musharraf is history by Ray Chengappa in Islamabad and Hasan Zaidi in Karachi.
25. DAWN Oct 21, 2001. Islamabad offered $ 800 m immediate cash grant.
26. The HINDU Dec 13, 2001. "Probe Pak Scientists issue"
27. Weekly Independent Dec 6–12, 2001 ISI bugged me as Premier Compiled by Hussain Sajiad.
28. Independent Dec.–6–12,2001 FBI uses ISI heroin hail by Amir Mir.
29. The Times of India Aug 5, 2008. Much defends ISI, lashes out at detractors : Report filed by PTI.
30. For further details of speech and discussion www.indiatodayconclave.in/musharraf.
31. India Today March 23, 2009.
32. The Times of India April 18, 2009 26/11 Proxy war to capture Kashmir report by Swati Deshpande.

10

Chief Justice Iftikhar Mohd. Chaudhary's Rise to Prominence

Between 2000 and 2005 Chaudhary sat on Four(4) pivoted supreme court Benches that validated the military takeover by Musharraf, his refrendum his Legal Framework Order and the 17th constitutional amendment that gave him as President additional powers to continue as Army chief. Pakistan plunged into turmoil after Gen. Musahrraf sacked Chief Justice Chaudhry. From that day onwards the downfall of Musharraf himself began. His action unleased mass anti-government protests across the country. Iftikhar chaudhury was appointed Chief Justice of Pakistan an May 7, 2005 as 20th Chief Justice.

2007

March 9	Gen. Musharraf ousts the Chief Justice. He was asked to resign over misconduct Charges. CJ refused to oblige. Gen Musharraf had vowed to step down as Army Chief if he was re-elected as President and the Emergency came just hours before the SC was to pronounce on the legality of his election.
March 10–12	Lawyers held nation–wide protests.
March 16	Police teargases opposition supporters of Chief Justice.
March 26	PPP and PML hold protest rally jointly for the first time supporting CJ.
March 5–6	CJ Chaudhrys motorcade cheered by thousands from Islamabad to Lahore. CJ

		gives a call "era of dictatorship is over."
March	12–13	CJ prevented from attending rally in Karachi 43 persons killed MQM's virtual dealing of Karachi to prevent deposed CJ's entry into Karachi.
June	4	Gen. Musharraf imposes tough new rules an broadcasters, protest ensued, lifts clamp down three days later.
July	3–11	Pro–Taliban Lal Masjid besieged and stormed by Pak troops More than 105 Islamic militants (Taliban) killed including Ghazi.
July	17	To avenge Lal Masjid action be Govt, a suicide bomber killed 17 at CJ Chaudhrys rally Islamabad.
July	20	Full Bench of Supreme Court, re instates CJ Iftikhar Chaudhry quashing all the charges against him. Held his suspension "unconstitutional."
Aug.	1	Gen. Musharraf who was almost decided to impose Emergency relents under US pressure not to do so.
Oct.	5	Rules polls can be held but result will have to wait Musharraf promulgated the National Reconstruction Ordinance (NRO) dropping corruption charges against Bhutto and Zardari.
Nov.	1	SC says it will not be influenced by threats of Emergency.
Nov.	3	Gen. Musharraf sectors CJ Iftikar Chaudhary. Placed under house arrest and Finally freed in March 2008. Emergency declared. Chaudhury constituted an eight-member bench of SC Judges and quashed the declaration of Emergency.

The deposed Chief Justice of the apex court sated on November 3, 2008 before a large gathering of lawyers in Rawalpindi on the occasion of first anniversary of the imposition of Emergency, that Gen. Musharraf imposed Emergency last year as he feared the supreme court would rule against him contesting polls in uniform after the Judiciary spurned his efforts to influence it. He termed last years Emergency as 'Martial Law' since it was confined to media and judiciary only. He opined that the foundation for the Emergency was laid much earlier as the regime led by Musharraf and shaukat Aziz became upset when the apex court ruled against the privatisation of steel Mills and took the case of political exile of political leaders and late Benazir Bhutto.[1]

The present President Asiaf Ali Zardari also does not want Chief Justice Iftikhar Chaudhry to be restored. Pervez Musharraf who supended the chief Justice twice – first on March 9, 2007 and then on November 7, 2007 is, in fact, likely to face termination of his services and President Zardari is already prevailing upon the government to oust him altogether. Zardari feels that Iftikhar Chaudhary has become involved in politics and questioned as to where was he when he (Zardari) was put in Jail for eight long years and why they did not do justice to him then. Not only the President, even ISI is damn annoyed with the deposed CJ because he repeatedly summoned ISI and questioned them for disappearances of so many citizens who were picked up by them and thereafter they were not seen. Many people who went missing at the hands of ISI were infact handed over to America for their alleged involvement in the militant activities and for this reason even America is silent on the question of restoring chief Justice Chaudhary as CJ of Supreme Court. However, there were efforts afoot to make him the Governor of Baluchistan, the state which he belongs to.

A group of former Pakistani army officers advised Gen. Musharraf to hand over power to sacked chief Justice Iftikhar Chaudhry and appoint another deposed Judge Rana Bhagwandas as Chief Election Commissioner to ensure free and fair polls. But they all wanted Musharraf to step down and the advise was tendered by Jan 31, 2008 itself. The deposed CJ was kept in high esteem by there former military officers led by Air Marshal (Retd) Asghar Khan.

But Gen. Pervez Musharraf had placed Justice Bhagwandas, the only Hindu Judge of Pakistan, under House arrest after he refused to endorese the emergency by him. He refused to take oath under Provincial Constitutional Ordinace. Since he was kept under House arrest in Islamabad, he was not allowed to celebrate Diwali. About a hundred people lit candles and 'Diyas' at the entrance of a coffee shop in Islamaband on November 13, 2007 to show solidarity with Justice Rana Bhagwandas. The silent protesters had displayed placards with words written an them as "Happy Diwali to Justice Rana Bhagwandas." Thank you justice Bhagwandass and six other judges for giving hope to our children. We will always be grateful to you and you will live forever in history."[2]

Pakistan had prepared a 15–Page dossier against deposed Chief Justice in a bid to make the western media aware of the 'real' causes behind the government – Judiciary stand off. The document was given to various journalists in London on Jan 28, 2008 during Gen. Musharrafs 3–day visit to UK on the last leg of his 4–nation European tour[3]

Ms Benazir Bhutto who was forced from one day's detention, desired to meet deposed Chief Justice the following day i.e. on November 10, 2007 but she was restrained by the police from meeting him. Her arrest was made because she wanted Musharraf to restore the Constitution, lift the Emergency and doff his army uniform and also call for elections by mid-January 2008. She was scheduled to go to Lahore the next day to address a Rally there in this connection. Gen. Musharrafs plea in imposing Emergency was that he wanted to fight Islamic extremists and bring peace to the areas in Swat district. The Emergency clamped by Musharraf had annoyed a large number of persons world over and international opinion had gone against him. So much so, even a top US firm Cassidy of Associates that was lobbying for Pakistan for a sum of $ 1.2 million and the agreement was signed in October 2007 shelved its deal. The firm was given a contract to promote Pakistans interests with US as "an important strategic partner."[4]

2008

February 18 : Elections held. PPP and PML(N) form a coalition government with Yusuf Raza Gilani as PM. Coalition promises to restore that deposed Judges. Zardari, dragging his feet on Chaudhury reinstatement can be faced to Zardaris fear that Chaudhury would overturn the NRO.

2008

March 9 : Asif Ali Zardari of PPP and Nawaz Sharif of PML(N) agree to form a coalition government and von to reinstate all the sacked judges including the Chief Justice Chaudhary.

May 12 : Nawaz pulls out his all (nine) minister from the cabinet due to PPP's failure to keep its words on the judges restoration.

2009

March 4 : Pakistan Lawyers announced the schedule for a long march and site in to begin form different ties on March 12 and reach Islamabad on March 16.

March 16 : Prime Minister Yusuf Gilani announced re instatement of Iftikhar Chaudhary as Chief Justice of Pakistan i.e. of March 200, 2009 i.e. after the retirement of CJ abdul Hamid Dogar on March 21.

March 22 : He joins duty though March 22 and 23 were holidays.

March 24 : CJ Iftikhar resumed his duties and visited

supreme court after a gap of 16 months Accorded a Heros welcome by lawyers and staff on arrival in the Supreme Court. A tumultuous welcome and standing ovation was extended to him and his vehicle was showered with rose petals. CJ Choudhary thanked the lawyers and people for their struggle for restoring an independent judiciary. He said he wanted to see the judiciary. "more independent and corruption – free". National and Supreme court flags were hoisted and a function organised because slain PPP leader Benazir Bhutto had once stated that she would hoist the national flags outside Chaudhary's home when he is reinstated. One Israr Shah, a PPP leader who had lost both his legs in a suicide attack on a rally supporting Chaudhary in 2007 was one of those who hoisted the flags. (The Pioner March 23, 2009).

Former P.M Nawaz Sharif had played a significant role in applying final push in the reinstatement of Chief Justice Iftikhar Chaudhury Had there been no order form Supreme Court on February 25, 2009. Banning Sharif brothers from contesting elections and holding public offices, probably the movement would not have gathered momentum. In view of this order of the Supreme Court, Shahbaz Sharifs provincial government in Punjab was removed and Presidents rule was imposed. This infuriated the Sharif brothers and they decided to hold a long March and stage a 'sit-in' in the National Assembly. A chaotic situation was created. CoAs Gen. Kayani gave a caution to the government for proper governance and America also impressed upon the P.M. and President to respect freedom of speech, expression and assembly when the government wated to slap charges of sedition against Nawaz Sharif. Even US secretary of state Mrs. Hillary Clinton had stepped in to defuse the Pak crisis. The government relented not only to reinstate the sacked CJ but to file a writ petition in Supreme Court to review its Judgement/order of Feb. 25, 2009 barring opposition PML(N) leaders Nawaz and Shahbaz Sharif from contesting polls and holding public offices.

Long March from Lahore to Islamabad called off and withdrawn, the crisis defused CJ Iftikhar M. Chaudhary returned to Supreme Court as its top Judge but the unfortunate part of the episode was the top judge was chief justice of Pakistan minus seven(7) districts of the country where his writ would not apply since Sharia courts had started functioning from March 12, 2009 in insurgency hit Swat Valley under an Agreement announced on Feb. 16, 2009 signed between Tehreek-e-Nifaz Shariat Muhammadi (TNSM) a banned organisation and Awami National Party (ANP) led Provincial Government for the imposition of Sharia as demanded by Taliban and Al Qaida in the tribal areas of NWFP. The areas where Qazi courts of Nizam-i-Adl started functioning were (*i*) Matta (*ii*) Khwazakhela (*iii*) Kabal and (*iv*) Bariket all strongholds of Taliban. An Italian news agency (AKI) reported last month (February 2009) that Taliban in Swat valley were paid Rs. 480 million ($ 6 million) in compensation from the special Fund of President Asif Ali Zardari through faudechannal (Repurt published in the times of india of Feb 26, 2009) Prendent Zardari insisted to endorse the deal only after he was satisfied regarding the end of insurgency but Prime Minister Yusuf Raza Gilani who was backed by Pakistan military and ISI was in favour of the deal. Under the agreement the government conceded the demands of TNSM relating to criminal Justice system and in return, Sufi Mohammad agreed to persuade his son-in-law Maulana Fazlullah, the leader of Taliban in Swat valley to give up arms and militancy. Taliban announced a 10–day ceasefire on February 15, 2009 in North Western Swat Valley, released a chinese engineer Mr. Long Xiaower who was abducted by them about six months ago and demanded release of 141

Baloch women detained in the country and tracing of 1109 'missing' persons from Baluchistan. Earlier, a Polish oil worker Mr. Peter Stanezak working for Poland–based Geofizyka Krakow Limited which was exploring natural resources was abducted on Sept. 28, 2008 killing his driver in an ambush alongwith two guards. He was executed on February 7, 2009 after the expiry of given deadline (Feb. 6) (Sunday Pioneer Feb. 8, 2009). Taliban abductors of the Polish engineer had demanded release of several imprisoned militants and had also asked for preventing US drone attacks in the tribal area. Taliban beheaded the Polish hostage on Saturday Feb, 7 2009 in South Waziristan tribal region. Even for his dead body, Taliban demanded $ 2540, (The Times of India Feb. 8, 2009). Taliban handed over his dead body on April 26, 2009. An American national Mr. John Solecki who was head of UN Refugee Agency in Quetta was abducted on Feb. 2, 2009 in Southwestern city of Quetta in Baluchistan after killing his driver. JohnSolecki was abandoned by his captors on 4/5 April 2009 in a southern village. Even a Pakistan Journalist Mr. Musa Khan Khel of Geo Television was abducted and killed on Feb. 18, 2009 in cold blood in Matta area. Imposition of 'Sharia' was seen as a way out of the impass since the deployment of 20 000 troops in Swat area had proved ineffective. About 8 Lakh people out of 18 Lakh inhabitants had slipped out of the area. 3000 Taliban had been operating in the area for about 20 months, claiming move than 1200 lives and these Taliban insurgents were advancing Towards Peshawar and Karachi 'Sharia' had earlier also been imposed in the year 1994 and then in 1999. The peace agreement which was entered with TNSM of Maulana Sufi Mohammad of Malakand in NWFD who formed it in 1992, was called by US defence officials as a negative development and Pakistani Civil Rights activists considered it as a 'surrender to the militants'.

A brief note on Taliban active in swat was mentioned boy way of 'obiter-dicta'. Returning to the topic of Justice Chaudharys reinstatement it can be said that Zardari was avoiding his restoration fearing that once back in saddle, chaudhary could nullify the amnesty granted by Gen. Musharraf to Zardari and Benazir Bhutto against the old charges of corruption. However it is to been seen what way the chief justice would stoer the complex and precarious situation before him. The Lawyers have taken the stand that the C.J. Iftikhar Chaudhary never ceased to be CJ even if removed by Gen Musharraf on November 3, 2007 after imposing emergency which itself was unconstitutional and illegal. It would imply his continuance right form Nov. 3, 2007 itself. In that case the matters decided by CJ Abdual Hameed Dogar would be 'null and void'. It would cause very intricate situation. It seems the doctrine of "Past and closed transactions" would be applied to the decisions of the period of CJ Dogar in the spirit of "forget the past and move on" a call given by President Zardari on March 20, 2009.

At a function on the occasion of Pakistani's National Day on March 23, Zardari invited chief Justice Iftikhar Chaudhary to an award ceremony held at Presidency, but the CJ Chose to stay away. The Supreme Court Registrar Faqir Hussain gave the season that due to preoccupation with preparing for cases, the CJ could not participate. But Zardari in his speech an other Occasion said "the restoration of the deposed Judges has raised the expectations of the people to witness an end to this cycle". He exhorted people to work for national reconsiliation and 'heading of the wounds' in the spirit of "tolerance, mutual accommodation and respect for dissent." He said "Let us dedicate ourselves to upholding the independence of Judiciary in accordance with the Constitution and the guidelines given in the Charter of Democracy." Incidently, on CJ Chaudhry's first day in office after his dramatic reinstatement, a petition was filed in the supreme court seeking the trial of former President Pervez Musharraf who had sacked him on Nov 3, 2007 emergency on treason charges[5]

Kamal Siddiqui, Pakistan correspondent of the Hindustan Times in Karachi in one of his articles published in the said paper wrote that the families of missing persons next of kin of those killed people kidnapped or victimised by powerful mafias, even civil society organisation wanting Karachi buses to work only CNG have all welcomed Justice Chaudhary. One Mannu Bheel, a peasant form Interior Sindh whose nine family members were adducted in 1998 after he fled from the private jail of a landlord calls Justice Chaudhary as "Insaaf ka Devta". In the year 2007 the then chief justice Chaudhary took suo moto notice of Bheel's plight and ordered police to recover the family. Just as the police were to raid the house of the land lord, Justice Chaudhary was removed by President Musharraf and with that all hopes of recovery were dashed. Similarly, Justice Chaudhary was among the first to react, taking suo moto notice to video clipping within hours wherein a 17-year young girl identified as Chaand was shown being flogged for 37 times by Taliban in the Swat district of NWFP for coming out of her house with another man who was not her husband. The media reported that the incident was that of Jan 3, 2009. Though the influence of the Pak Supreme Court in Taliban ruled area is in doubt the chief Justice sent notices to Interior Secretary and the inspector General of police of the Province of NWFP and constituted an eight judge bench to hear the case from April 6, 2009.[6] The reinstatement of Chief Justice Iftikhar Mohammad Chaudhary set in motion action against a High Court Chief Justice over allegation of involvement in murky activities including connections with crime underworld.[7]

The 17 year old Chaand Bibi denied having been flogged by Taliban. She said (April 5, 2009) to the Divisional Commissioner Mr Syed Mohammad Jawed that such an incident never occurred. NWFP Information Minister Mian Iftikhar Hussain told 'The News' that Chand Bibi had made a statement to the two officials who visited her village of Kala killay in Kabal Sub-division on April 5, 2009. The man who filmed the Taliban flogging chaand Bibi, Shaukat, said that the incident occurred two weeks ago. He told 'DAWN' newspaper that the treatment meted cut to the girl was actually a 'punishment' for her refusing a marriage proposal from a militant, The man who proposed to marry Chand Bibi joined the Taliban after the rejection and this was how he took revenge on the girl, Shauket Said.'[8]

A five–member team was appointed by the supreme court to probe the 'flogging' which concluded that no such incident had taken place and as such the video footage was 'take'.[9]

July 31, 2009 Supreme Court ruled that the November 3, 2007 Emergency imposed by Musharraf was illegal and unconstitutional.

REFERENCE

1. PTI Report from Islamabad the Pioneer did Nov 4, 2008.
2. PTI Report. Published in the Statesman did 14.11.2007.
3. PTI Report from Islamabad. published in the Statesman did Feb. 1, 2008
4. The Sunday Times of India did Nov. 11, 2007. Reports filed by Ishtiq Ali Mehkri & Agencies from Karach, Islamabad and Mr Chidannad Rajghatta form Washington.
5. The Indian Express did 24 and 25.3.2009 PTI Reports.
6. The Hindu April 4, 2009 Report by Nirupana Subramanian from Islambad
7. The News, Islamabad, April 3, 2009 reproduced by the Indian Express of April 4, 2009
8. The Indian Express April 7, 2009 report by Režaul H. Laskar from Islamabad.
9. The Times of India April 20, 2009 PTI Report 'Tape of Taliban flogging girl a take : Probe.

11

Return of Ms. Benazir and Nawaz Sharif from Exile

BENAZIR BHUTTO

Benazir Bhutto had exiled herself to London in April 1999 in the face of charges of corruption and political vendatta while Nawaz Sharif was the Prime Minister. Benazir and her husband Asif Ali Zardari were convicted of receiving kick backs worth millions of dollars. National Accountability Bureau (NAB) had put their assets $l 1.5 billion worth. In January 2006 Interpol had issued international notices for arrest of both Benazir and Zardari. Gen Musharraf's earlier stand was also that Ms Benazir did not leave Pakistan of her own but 'ran away' because when was facing prosecution for corruption. If she comes back, she will be taken to court and Justice will take its course. We want educated people in power. And her level of education in unclear to date.[1] 'was the view Gen. Musharraf held for her.'

Benazir Bhutto was married to Asif Ali Zardari on December 18, 1987. Zardari born on July 26, 1955 to a feudal politician of Sindh in Nawabshah was educated in Karachi. He was kept at Karachi Jail from 1996 to 2004 on various charges of corruption and murder. Benazir also faced a murder charge for the June 1996 killing of two Jamaat-e-Islami workers in Rawalpindi. Since marriage of Benazir with Zardari, he remained actively involved in politics. A number of scandals, stories of corruption etc reported in the media against him. Some of the cases levelled against Zardari were :

1. Murtaza Bhutto murder case. He was accused of murdering Benazir's brother Murtaza Bhutto. The trial is still going on.
2. Justice Nizam Ahmed murder case in May 1996. Indicted by the Nawaz Sharif regime for gunning down Sindhi High Court judge Nizam Ahmed and his son, tortured by police and accused of attempting suicide before being given bail in 1999. The case is still pending.
3. Alam Balochi murder case accused of being involved of in the killing of former federal secretary Alam Baloch in 1997.
4. SGS Cotecna case charged with receiving millions of dollars for giving contracts to two swiss companies. He was convicted, then judgement was set aside. Retrial is on.
5. ARY Gold Case charged with receiving kickbacks from a Dubai Company in return for an exclusive licence to import gold into Pakistan.
6. Polish Tractors case allegedly took kickbackes on low–cost tractor imports.
7. Steel Mill Case accused of taking bribes from the former Chairman of Pakistan steel Mill, Sajjad Hussain.[2]

Zardari was jailed in Central Prison Karchi from where he was released in 2004 for treatment in US. He was re arrested for not appearing in the court on due date on Dec 21, 2004 in a murder trial. In August 2004 Zardari admitted ravening a 4.35 million pounds estate in owning Surrey England including a 20–room mansion and two farm on 365 acres of land which the Pakistani authorities allege was bought with the proceeds of corruption.[3] He was finally released from prison after eight years. However, he always maintained that the cases slapped on him were politically motivated. Certain segments of the Pakistan Society were unhappy with Benazir and she was charged with changing policy on Kashmir while she was Prime Minister of the Country. It was alleged that she withdraw support to the struggle for freedom in Kashmir and hoped it would die because of fragmentation and chaotic leadership as Khalistan liberation Movement had. Yet another allegation against her was she revealed Pakistans atomic secrets to USA.[4]

When General Musharraf came under pressure from the United States of America, he dashed to Abu Dhabi on July 27, 2007 to meet Ms Benazir Bhutto to discuss her return to Pakistan. Benazir demanded Musharraf to step down as CoAs. Musharraf relented and a deal was signed on July 27, 2007 itself. It was General Musharraf who once described Benazir as so corrupt that she could never be allowed to plunder Pakistan again. And here he himself rushes to Abu Dhabi, asks her to return to Pakistan, facilitates her return and enters into a deal which culminates in withdrawal of cases against her in Swiss & Spanish Courts instituted by National Accountability Bureau, applied government estoppel in pursuing cases against her in Pakistans Courts, defreezes her foreign bank accounts of $l 1.5 billion and helps withdrawal of Interpol Red Notice. USA played an important behind–the–curtain role in bringing about Benazir Musharraf reconciliation in which Gen. Ashfaq Pervez Kayani, former ISI Chief was also actively associated. Secret parleys were held in September 2007 in London and Dubai in between Musharraf and Benazir representatives initially. Musharraf's side was represented by ISI chief Gen. Kayani who played a very important role in the patch up between them. Benazir, on her part, as a goodwill gesture and who was negotiating her comeback with Gen. Musharraf defended Army action against militants in Lal Masjid on July 10, 2007. A power sharing pact was agreed upon and signed on October 5, 2007. A National Reconciliation Ordinance (NRO) was promulgated granting amnesty to Benazir and Nawaz that he would not hesitate to "kick them". Many others also did not appreciate her return. For example former editor Shaheen Sehbai who exiled himself during Gen. Musharraf's rule said "of course, all she is interested in is getting back her billions, withdrawal of cases against her and Asif Zardari and an amendment in the constitution that would allow her to become Prime Minister for the third time. Party workers have never been her top priority. "Mr Mis Afzal Khan, a confidant of Zulfikar Ali Bhutto and now an unscruplous politician who is ready to throw away the sacrifices of her father a man who had refused to negotiate with the generals even went to the gallows for it.[5]

Consequent upon signing the deal which cleared her of graft charges, Benazir returned to Pakistan on October 18. 2007 after eight years of exile to a tumultuous welcome. The very next day on October 19 she survived an assassination attempt in Karachi in which 136 persons were killed and more than 700 injured. On November 13, Benazir was placed under House arrest for a week in Lahore, hours before she had planned a march against Emergency Rule of General Musharraf and demand for Musharrafs resignation as President. She was assassinated in bomb and gun attack an December 27, 2007 while addressing an election rally in Rawalpindi. Because the disturbances that ensured after the incident, general elections were postponed to Feb 18, 2008 form January 8. PPP and PML(N) trounced Gen. Musharraf's allies in the general election. Benazir Bhutto aide Yousuf Raza Gilani (from Multan) was elected as Prime Minister of the country an March 24, 2008. Her husband Asif Ali Zardari became all-in-all in PPP since her son Bilal had not come up of age by then.

Zardari played a clever game. After he ensured that Army would keep aloof from politics and Musharraf become almost a politician only and US had no more any use of Musharraf since he had already given up the post of chief of Army staff, he offered Nawaz Sharif on August 5, 2008 at Islamabad a proposal to oust Gen. Musharraf from the post of President. and thereafter restore the judges to which Nawaz readily agreed. But Zardari was in fact, reluctant to reinstate the judges sacked by President Pervez Musharraf particularly Chief Justice Iftikhar Mohammad Chaudhry. NRO which granted amnesty was valvd upto Feb 18, 2008 only i.e. upto the date of general elections. Amnesty from corruption charges also benefitted Zardari in the sense that he was allowed to end his exile after assassination of his wrife Mrs. Benazir on Dec 27, 2007. But the NRO itself was under challenge before the Supreme Court and Zardari apprehended is Chief Justice Iftikhar Chaudhary is restored, he might undo the NRO.

Chief Justice Iftikhar Choudhary had introduced far flung changes which no CJ had done so far. He stopped Karachi Steel Mill form being sold to private parties at a throw away price, cancelled allotment of plot in Gwader, ordered ISI to produce hundreads of people it had detained and whose where about were not known after they were picked up by ISI and IB people. All this also annoyed the Pakistan Establishment.

Benazir Bhutto was warned of the danger to her life in Pakistan. Musharraf and some Friendly Muslim Government had warned her of four gangs of 'designated assassins' including the one led by 16 years old son of Osama bin Laden, who wanted to kill her in suicide attacks. These four suicide bomber squads were sent by the Taliban worked Baitullah Mehsud, Hamaza Bin Laden son of Osama Laden, Red Mosque militants and a Karachi based militant group. She stated in her book "when I returned (to Karachi). I knew that the same elements of Pakistani society that had colluded with to destroy my father and end democracy in Pakistan in 1977 were now arrayed against me for the same purpose exactly 30 years later." "Many of the same people who had poll aborated with an earlier military junta in the judicial murder of my father were now entrenched in power in the Musharraf regime and the intelligence apparatus." Beitullah Mehsud, a leader of Tehreck-i-Taliban was named as the mastermind behind the killing of Benazir by President Musharraf. But he denied (The Hindu May 26, 2008) his involvement in Benazir's killing. "Politicians have their own rivalries" he said pointing that her brothers Shahnawaz and Mir Murtaza were also killed but none know who was behind those killings.

Benazir had termed Nov. 3, 2007 as the blackest day which will be remembered in the history of Pakistan. She had also liked a quote from President Bush which he gave to the world in his second inaugural address: "All who live in tyranny and hopelessness can know: the united states will not ignore your oppression, or excuse your oppressors. When you stand for your liberty, we will stand with you."

The deal

Gen. Musharraf ordered closure of all corruption cases against Benazir and in return, she helped the former in the Presidential election in Nov. 2007.

Benazir would be PM and Gen. Musharraf would become civilian President, according to the understanding since military ruler was unpopular in the eyes of world and Benazir carried democratic credentials with her.

Benazir Bhutto

Dec.	1988	Sworn in as first women Prime Minister.
Aug.	1990	Dismissed by President Ghulam Ishaq khan for corruption.
Oct.	1993	Elected PM for the second time.
Nov.	1996	Dismissed by President Farooq Ahmed Leghari for corruption.
April	1999	She and her husband Zardari found guilty of graft charge.
Aug.	2000	Barred form active polities.
March	2005	Her party PPP increases contact with Gen. Musharraf.
Sept. 14,	2007	Holds talks with Musharraf on power Sharing and announces date of her return after ending her self-exile.
Oct. 2	2007	Gen. Musharraf announces to drop graft charges against Bhutto clearing the way for

		her return.
Oct. 2	2007	Corruption Charges dropped.
Oct. 18/19	2007	Benazir returns to Pakistan after 8 years following a power-sharing talks with Musharraf. A suicide bomber kills 139 persons in her welcome rally in Karachi which was actually aimed to kill her. People thought she returned as a part of American Plan.
Nov. 2	2007	Files out of Pakistan.
Nov. 9	2007	Benazir kept under house arrest for a day.
Nov. 12	2007	She rules out further power–sharing talks with Gen Musharraf.
Nov. 13	2007	Placed under House arrest again for a week. She demanded Musharraf must quit as President.
Dec. 27	2007	Benazir Bhutto assassinated in Rawalpindi after delivering a political speech for election.
Dec. 31,	2007	PPP announced her 19–year old son Bilawal Bhutto Zardari studying in Britain to become PPP leader. But his father and husband of Benazir, Asif Ali Zardari takes the leadership of PPP.
Jan. 2	2008	Scheduled parliamentary election postponed to Feb. 18, 2008.
Feb. 18	2008	Resounding victory for her party PPP.
Aug. 22	2008	Presidential election announced for Sept. 6, 2008.
Aug. 23	2008	PPP announces to nominate Zardari for Presidentship.
Sept. 9,	2008	And Zardari becomes 14th President of Pakistan. He was elected President on Sept. 6, 2008.

Nawaz Sharif

Pakistan Muslim League—Nawaz (PML–N) supremo Nawaz Sharif was charged and tried for the October 12, 1999 hijacking case alongwith his associates under sections 402–B(Hijacking), 365 (kidnapping and abduction) and 120 – B (criminal conspiracy) read with section 34 of Pakistan Penal Code and also under section 324 of Qisa and Diyat Ordinance, Sec 7 of Anti–Terrorist Act. The military regime of Gen. Musharraf had also charged him further for waging war against Pakistan, endangering the lives of Gen. Pervez Musharraf and 200 others, hijacking the plane PK-815 on way to Karachi from Sri Lanka and collecting arms. The trial was conducted in a special court of session Judge at karachi and Nawaz Sharif convicted and sentenced to life imprisonment.

But after negotiations by the Royal family of Saudi Arabia, Army granted Nawaz Sharif reprive and he left Pakistan for Riyadh on Dec. 9, 2000 to become the guest of the Saudi Royal family after being pardoned by Military authorities after a deal with Riyadh. He was banned from returning to Pakistan for ten (10) years. Nawaz did attempt to return to the country on Sept. 10, 2007 but was deported from the Air Port itself from Islamabad. Negotiation were held and Nawaz was met by ISI chief Lt. Gen Nadeem Taj in Saudi Arabia, where he was staying in exile for the past 7 years, to facilitate his return to Pakistan. Gen. Musharraf himself visited Saudi Arabia on Nov. 20, 2007 to discuss Nawaz return to Pakistan with the Saudi Rulers king Abdullah crown Prince Sultan bin Abdul Aziz Foreign Minister Saud al-Faisal and intelligence chief Murquin bin Abdul Aziz. Sharifs return to Pakistan from exile in Riyadh was on agenda. And Nawaz returned to Pakistan on November 25, 2007 from exile. His party PML–N participated in the general election held on Feb. 18, 2008 but he himself was not allowed to contest. His party won enough votes but not so enough asto for a PML–N government. Nawaz declared on March 9, 2008 his intentions that he would join Asif Ali Zardari to form a coalition government hostile to General Musharraf but he withdrew PML–N Ministers form the government on May 13, 2008 on the ground that Zardari was not fulfilling his promise of restoring the suspended judges including the chief justice Iftikhar Mohammad Chaudhry fired by Gen. Musharraf on March 7, 2007. Zardari cleverly decided to remove Gen. Musharraf from the seat of power first and he proposed on Aug. 5, 2008 to Nawaz Sharif when he met him and stated that after removing Musharraf they would restore judges. The ruling coalition agreed to a plan to impeach Gen. Musharraf and the agreement was entered into a Aug. 7 and thereafter together they prepared on Aug. 16 impeachment charges against Gen. Musharraf for violation of Constitution and misconduct. Army did not extent support to Gen. Musharraf and on the contrary was advised behind the curtain to save the honour of former chief of Army staff's position as an institution he should give up presidency. Lawyers were already against him. Common man started demanding he be removed forthwith. America who had so far been supportive, switched over to new COAS Gen. Kayani for support in the fight against terror. Forced and unhopeful of support form any corner. Gen. (Retd.) Musharraf quit and resigned from the post of President of Pakistan on Aug. 18 2008. Nawaz finally pulled out of coalition on Aug. 25. When Asif Zardari repeatedly did not come up to his expectations and did not keep his promises of nominating an independent man for Presidentship or restoring the ousted judges inspite of postponing the cut cut off dates.

Nawaz had, naturally and obviously, nurtured a revengeful attitude towards Gen. Musharraf.

Born on December 25, 1949 in Lahore, Nawaz Sharif became Chief Minister of Punjab on April 9, 1985 under Gen. Zia's martial law regime and was elected Prime Minister on Nov. 6, 1990.

Mr. Robert B. Oakley, former US Ambassador wrote in

the Washington Post "Sharif may be the future of Pakistan, an eventuality the United States must prepare for. He Commands a strong following and, most important, has traditionally been strongly supported by the Pakistani Army and Intelligence Services". He predicted Sharif's return, to Pakistan could mark the end of Musharraf's political career.

Events : Nawaz Sharif

Dec. 25, 1949	born in Lahore.
April. 9, 1985	becomes Chief Minister of Punjab under Gen. Mohammad Zia-ul-Haq's. Martial law refine.
Nov. 6, 1990	Elected Prime Minister of Pakistan.
April. 18, 1993	His government dismissed by President Ghulam Ishaq Khan.
Feb. 3, 1997	His party PML(N) wins general election by landslide.
Feb. 17, 1997	Became Prime Minister for the second time.
Dec. 2, 1997	Nawaz remained under investigation and legal battle for the past six months for misuse of power during his first tenures PM ship. President Farooq Leghari who wanted him to be investigated ultimately resigned on Dec. 2, 1997.
Nov. 1997	Accused of Contempt of Court.
Oct. 12, 1999	Overthrown by Gen. Pervez Musharraf in a bloodless coup. Sharif was imprisoned on hijacking charges.
April. 6, 2000	Sentenced to Life imprisonment on hijacking and terrorism charges.
Aug. 2000	Barred form active politics.

Dec. 9, 2000	Goes into exile in Saudi Arbia after pardon form military authorities and a deal with Royal family of Riyadh.
Aug. 23, 2007	Nawaz can return, Supreme Court rules.
Aug. 30, 2007	Sharif announced return on Sept. 10.
Sept. 10, 2007	He returns as announced but sent back from airport itself after 4 hours.
Nov. 25, 2007	Sharif finally returns from exile on second attempt.
Feb. 18, 2008	Resounding victory for his party PML(N).
March. 9, 2008	Sharif says he will join Zardari in coalition hostile to Gen. Musharraf.
Aug. 7, 2008	Ruling coalition agree to a plan to impeach Musharraf.
Aug. 16, 2008	They prepare impeachment charges against Musharraf for violating constitution and misconduct.
Aug. 25, 2008	Nawaj Sharifs PML(N) pulls out of colition and names Saeeduzzaman Siddiqui, former chief Justice of Supreme Court as it candidate for the post of President.

Nawaz Sharif was barred from contesting Feb. 18, 2008 poll on the ground that he was convicted by courts. He was summoned by the Supreme Court to appear before it on Nov. 20, 2008 regarding his eligibility to contest election, but he refused to appear before it saying he does not recognise the present judiciary.

2009

Feb. 25	:	Nawaz Sharif and his brother shahbaz disqualified by the Supreme Court from contesting elections.
Feb. 26	:	Nation wide protests were held in support

		of Sharif. Nawaz urged masses to demand that sacked Judges be reinstated.
March. 9	:	Government threatened Nawaz Sharif with charges of sedition.
March. 15	:	Nawaz was put under House Arrest But Since president Asif Ali Zardari was under tremendous massive pressure from COAS Kayani, Advocates and America, P.M. Yousuf Raza Gilani declared that the government would reinstate Iftikhar Chaudhury, the sacked Chief justice.
March. 16	:	Prime Minister Yousuf Raza Gilani announced that the government would reinstate the sacked CJ Iftikhar Chaudhary w.e. for March 22, 2009 after the current CJ Abdul Hameed Dogar retires on March 21. Nawaz Sharif who was heading to Islamabad to lead an indefinite site-in at Parliament to demand restoration of sacked judges including the CJ, called off the Long March mid way.

A decision by 3–member Supreme Court bench headed by Justice Musa Khan Leghari dismissed all petition (one by the government and others by independents) on February 25, 2009 challenging the Lahore High Court decisions regarding disqualifying Nawaz Sharif from contesting election and also upholding the ban on sharifs from contesting polls. It also declared the election of Shahbaz Sharif as null and void. Weeks later, a detailed verdicts of this bench was issued justifying ban on Sharifs. Apex Court slammed Nawaz Sharif from 'publicly propagating his biased opinion' and acting in a manner 'prejudicial' to the integrity of Judiciary. Sharif had defaulted on loans from several banks and had been convited by an anticorruption Court. SC said Nawaz Sharif was 'not' a sagacious righteous, non-profligate and honest person as he was convicted by an accountability or anti-corruption court.

The order further said "under Article 45 of the Constitution of the Islamic Republic of Pakistan 1973 although sentences were pardoned by the President of Pakistan yet the conviction was still intact and effective and having not been set aside by any competent higher/appellate court, conviction and disqualification would remian in existence." Regarding Shahbaz Sharif, the Order said "Shahbaz was a fugitive from Law" and loans obtained by him and his family were unpaid. It said that Shahbaz had "been and is continuously making well determined and decisively resolute efforts to ridicule, defame, harass, downgrade and humiliate the judiciary since 1997 till date".[6] February 25 short order of the Supreme Court prompted President Zardari to dismiss the Shahbaz's government in Punjab province and impose Governor's Rule for a period of two months within hours. This infuriated Sharif brothers to the extent that Nawaz Sharif described the Apex Court verdict as a 'diktat' and accused President Zardari of hatching a conspiracy against him. He said "this is not a judicial order but a diktat and people know who did this. I want to tell the nation that it should stand up to this lawlessness, to this judgement, to this unconstitutional judgement, to this villanious act by the President of this country, Zardari". Nawaz even accused Zardari of offering him and his brother a "business deal" in return for letting the duo off in the election disqualification case. Nawaz claimed "an emissary came to me and asked me to stop pushing for the reinstatement of the judges. Zardari invited Shahbaz for lunch and said he was offering him a deal under which he could remian CM in return for our help in securing an extension for Chief Justice (Abdul Hameed Dogar)."[7]

The whole episode goes back to February 2008 general elections when the Returning Officers rejected the nomination papers of Sharif brothers for contesting elections. While Nawaz Sharifs papers were rejected on the ground of being a convict of an offence of attempt to hijack the plane in October 1999 which was bringing Gen. Pervez Musharraf form Sri Lanka to Pakistan, his brother Shahbaz was accused in an alleged fake encounter case as well loan default case–both pertaining to his days of Chief Ministership of Punjab. He stood acquitted in the encounter case in mid–2008 but the loan default cases remained. On June 3, 2008, the Election Commission overriding the decision of the returning officers, allowed the Sharif brother to contest the by election. Shahbaz was elected to Punjab Assembly and became Chief Minister of PML (N) led provincial government that had already taken office in March 2008. Nawaz Sharif's march to the National Assembly was abruptly halted by a petition in the Lahore High Court questioning the Election Commission. The High Court decided against Nawaz Sharif. Meanwhile another petition challenged his brothers election too, a decision on which the court held in abeyance The PPP–PML (N) coalition in Islamabad, then at the height of its short-lived honeymoon, went to the Supreme Court in appeal against the High Court decision. The Sharif themselves refused to go in appeal saying that they did not recognise the Musharraf appointed replacements to the judges he dismissed enmass in 2007. On Feb. 25, 2009 He 3–Judge bench led by Justice Moosa Khan Leghari dismissed the government appeal as well as petitions by 'independent' parties known to be close to the Sharif's and the PML (N) against the Lahore High Court decision in Nawaz Sharifs case.[8]

Resultantly, the simmering tensions between Nawaz Sharif and Zardari flared up. Nawaz gave a call to revolt against the Governor's Rule in Punjab and mass protests followed. Nawaz addressed Press meets in the presence of his brother Shahbaz Sharif. PML(N) supporters took to the streets of Lahore on Feb. 25th itself. At Sheikhupura, Nawaz described the SC verdict as 'fraudulent'. He said "the disqualification was a fraud, Governor's Rule in Punjab is a fraud, the decision to impose Governor's rule was also a fraud." He described all decisions of Zardari as 'do number' (fake) and exhorted people to help Shahbaz to reclaim his government in Punjab. In order to cool down in rising political temperature, even British High Commissioner Robert Brinkley met Nawaz Sharif on Feb. 28. On March 1, Nawaz accused Zardari of acting on

US dictates like Gen. Musharraf. Awami National Party and the Jamiat-e-ulema Islami also made some moves to make peace with PML (N) through a meeting between PPP Chief Minister of Baluchistan Nawab Aslam Raisani and Shahbaz Sharif.[9] Nawaz announced on March 1 that PML(N) would join the Long March of Lawyers to Islamabad. On March 4 he reconfirmed his decision and stated that PML (N) would fully participate in the long March. He addressed a press conference on March 9 in Islamabad. Mr. Rehman Malik, the head of Interior Ministry termed Sharifs utterances as 'seditious' and appealed to the political parties not to make statements creating a law and order situation and "dont create a situation like 1971." Major confrontation was sparked between PPP and PML(N) in general and Zardari and Nawaz Sharif in particular. On March 12, Nawaz Sharif told 'the Guardian' newspaper accusing the government of plotting to kill him. He said "threats to my life come from high ranking government officials, certain topmost people in the government officials, my sources say". But the government raised his personal security level to the equal footing with that of the President and Prime Minister. i.e. of VVIP level. In order to bridge government-opposition rift even US Ambassador Anne Paterson met Sharif on March 12 amid Pakistan's crackdown on opposition activists and ban on rallies. Acting spokesman of US state department Mr. Robert wood said that political parties should rftrain from violence but Islamabad must respect freedom of speech, expression and Assembly.9 Anti-government protest was held at Karachi on March 12 by lawyers and others. Long March started from Quetta, Karachi and Lahore etc. which rocked Pakistan on March 12 itself Gen. Kayani chief of Army Staff never wanted to muddle in politics directly and had decided to pull out the Army of politics unless of course it is forced to intervene. But Gen. Kyani did call an PM Yousuf Gilani asking him to prevail upon Zardari to be reasonable and sensible. Army was not willing to side with Nawaz Sharif in his spat with Zardari though it had no special corner for Zardari either. The United States also kept itself aloof of Sharif since he was considered as close to militant religious outfits and was opposed to US efforts on war on terrorism. In the estimation of US, he pressed for Islamic laws for Pakistan prompted in testing nuclear bomb inspite of US advise against it and once stormed the supreme Court Nawaz Sharif Joined Lawyers movement to demand Zardari fulfill his promise to reinstate the sacked judges. Pak authorities blocked all roads to Islamabad to which Nawaz opined "that by resisting the popular will, I dont think he (Zardari) will be able to complete his 5–year tenure." Police tought pitched battle with stone pelting anti-government protesters on March 15 as authorities tried to detain Nawaz Sharif in his house only. Meanwhile Shahbaz Sharif went into hiding. Before police could serve orders for his house arrest Shahbaz gave a slip to the police and had gone to the home of PML(N) leader Chaudhary Tanveer Khan in Rawalpindi on March 12 itself.[10]

While Nawaz Sharif was in Gujranwala on March 16 en route to Islamabad, Prime Minister Yousuf Raza Gilani addressed the nation announcing restoration of chief Justice Iftikhar Chaudhary from March 22, 2009. The Long March was immediately called off. US Welcomed the announcement to reinstate CJ Chaudhary describing it as 'statement-like decision and a 'substantial step tawards national reconcilation.[11] United States which so far avoided Nawaz Sharif changed its opinion. In the words of Mr Robert Oakley, former US Ambassador to Pakistan 'we and all sensible Pakistanis, need the support of Saudi Arabia and the more moderate Islamist parties, particularly Jamaat-e-Islami. If we are ever going to fame the Jehadis Nawaz's good standing with them is very important."[12]

But all this left its scars on Gilani. Zardari developed strained relations with his Prime Minister Yusuf Gilani. He became unhappy with the "deepening relationship "between Gilani and Nawaz Sharif and his brother after the PM became as peace maker and acquired the role of a sane advisor to the President in the stand off on the deposed Judges.[13] PM Gilani desired to implement the charter of democracy signed in between Nawaz Sharif and Benazir Bhutto in the year 2006. 'The News' even reported that Gilani could be the first victim of Zardari's extreme anger and vengenance.[14] Nawaz Sharif at a Press Conference on March 18, 2009 demanded that the government should scrap the 17th amendment to the Constitution that gives President the sweeping powers to dismiss Prime Minister and dissolve the Parliament.

A growing rift exist between President Zardari and PM Gilani on various counts. Zardari was looking forward 'to punish' PM Gilani by way of depriving him of Prime Minister's Post. For this Zardari finalised strategy during a secret meeting with Chaudhary Shujat Hussain, Chaudhary Parvez Elahi and Moonis Elahi all from PML(Q) formed during Gen. Musharraf's rule.[15]

Meanwhile Pak government on March 19, 2009 filed two petitions in the supreme court seeking review of its verdict of Feb. 25 disqualifying the Sharif brothers from contesting election and holding public offices[16].

Addressing a farewell function on Feb. 21 for bidding good bye to the outgoing chief Justice Abdul Hamid Dogar. Zardari observed that the "restoration of sacked judges should be seen as another step in the evolutionary process of strengthening institutions. It is time to look forward and build on what has been achieved. It is time to forget the past. It is time to move on."

US UK and Pakistan Army chief Gen. Kayani had put pressure on Zardari to defuse the tension by way of acceding to the demand of Nawaz Sharif to restore the top judge which Zardari happily did. On March 30, 2009 Zardari lifted the Central Rule in Punjab allowing PML(N) to re-install its government. The following day a five member bench of the supreme court headed by Justice Tassaduq Hussain suspended the Feb. 25 verdict of the Apex court against Sharif brothers which forbade them from participating in electoral politics. Shabbaz Sharif was re-installed as Chief Minister of Punjab on March 31 itself.[17]

US seem to be realising slowly the growing importance and influence of Nawaz Sharif particularly during the long march (March 14–16, 2009) the News (March 3) editorial said "western allies are said to be looking at Sharifs with a new eye and perhaps conscious of this, Mian Nawaz Sharif has emphatically denied that he or his party has any links with extremists." Nawaz, of course did oppose current US Policy of fighting terror on Pakistan but never proposed so far as to how to tackle terrorism. But during the whole episode Nawaz exhibited his battle and political acumenship and presented himself as a mature politician in the sense that no sooner Prime Minister Yousuf Gilani announced the decision of reinstating the sacked chief justice, Nawaz who was in Gujaranwala that day immediately called off the long March without even consulting religious hardlines. He did not bother even to inform them directly Hyam before such an announcement on March (16 at 5.4/9 am. Pakistan Standard Time) by PM Gilani" It is not that Nawaz has become a 'pious' politician. He simply wanted to down and belittle Gen. Musharaf by getting CJ Chaudhary, who was sacked by the former, back to his seet in the Apex Court so that he could claim victory over his old enemy Gen. Musharraf and he won the battle. Nawaz was lucky this time in the sense that he got a chief of Army staff Gen. Kayani who kept his army away from politics and incidently, was not against the reinstatement of the sacked Chief Justice either.

All is not well and over in Pakistan. A lot many more tougher battles lie ahead including the battle of the survival of Pakistan itself. There in no doubt, effective in Punjab politics but it is doubtful if Nawaz could contain the extremists and Talibans in Pakistan. Should he come to power he would sway with them proving the us assessment that he would contain religious extremists and militants, wrong. It anybody can do that it is Pakistan Army and it is not willing to fight them in border areas of Afghan-Pak border. The only solution is more and more drone attacks but only after making sure that the area is inhibited by Taliban and militants. No innocent citizens should be droned by US. Pak Army says they will not fight muslims in muslim land. The Drone attacks by US inside Pakistan territory has been described by Nawaz Sharif as an affront to national sovereignity.

REFERENCE

1. The Hindu May 8, 2002 I will crush extremism Musharraf.' Report filed by B. Murlidhar Reddy.
2. India Today January 28, 2008 issue The Man who could Rule Pakistan. Report by Raj Chengappa and Hasan Zaidi in Pakistan.
3. India Today January 28, 2008 issue The Man who could Rule Pakistan. Report by Faj Chengappa and Hasan Zaidi in Pakistan.
4. The Indian Express Sept. 10, 2008. Report by Rezaul H. Laskar.
5. The Frontier Post Dec. 29, 1999.
6. Outlook dt 27 Aug 2007 Et Tu, Mohtarma? Report by Mariana Baabar from Islamabad.
6. The Times of India March 23, 2009 Report by PTI from Islamabad.
7. The Times of India Feb. 26, 2009 Report by TI from Islamabad.
8. The Hindu Feb. 26, 2009 Report by Nirupana Subramanian.
9. The Hindu March 3, 2009
10. The Hindus Times Dtd. March 13, 2009 report form Shri Lalit K. Jha from Washington.
11. The Times of India dated March 16, 2009 PTI report.
12. The Hindu March 17, 2009
13. The Times of India Did March 26, 2009 Report by Jane Pervez.
14. The Pioneer March 20, 2009
15. Ibid
16. The Indian Express Did March 20, 2009. Report by Rauj Klasra
17. Ibid

12

Aftermath of Gen. (Retd.) Musharraf's Resignation

Pakistan Muslim League—Nawaz (PML–N) withdrew from ruling coalition on Aug. 25, 2008 on the question of restoration of sixty Supreme Court Judges including Chief Justice Iftikhar Mohammad Chaudhry and forty four other High Court Judges. On Aug. 25 itself Asif Ali Zardari, PPP Chairperson and an aspirant for the post of President on behalf of PPP apologized to Nawaz Sharif stating that "I seek to apologies to Mian Nawaz Sharif Saheb. I admit his feelings have been hurt." But he maintained his stand not to reinstate sacked CJ Iftikhar Mohammad Chaudhry and said "perhaps I can not reveal the whole truth to the nation." PML(N) in its reply to apology stated that there is no looking back for it anymore. And Nawaz Sharif nominated former Chief Justice Saeed-uz-zaman for Presidential contest on behalf of PML(N) who filed his nomination papers on Sept. 6. The contest for Presidential election was to take place on Aug. 28, 2008.

Eight judges of Sindh High Court out of sixty sacked by former President Gen. (Retd.) Musharraf on Nov. 3, 2007 were re-appointed on Aug. 27, 2008 to their position as an Nov. 2, 2007. Anwar Zaheer Zamali was appointed new CJ of Sindh High Court and the strength of judges was increased from twenty eight to forty. On Aug. 6, 2008 only President Musharraf had signed a notification to reinstate eight judges of Sindh high court but the move was put off following a protest from PML (N). Even at time, the deposed Chief Justice of Sindh High Court Shabihuddin Ahmed, a critic of Gen. Musharraf was not among the judges who were restored. Yet, another 4 sacked judges were restored on Aug 30. All these four were from Lahore High Court and were administered oath by Lahore H.C. Chief Justice Syed Zahid Hussain Bukhari. Three judges were restored on Sept. 5. It was decided in principle that the former Chief Justice of Supreme Court Iftikhar Chaudhry will not be reinstated to his previous post . He could Join in case he is prepared to work under chief Justice Abdul Hamid Dogar, as per version of Zardari.

Soon after president Musharraf's departure form the presidency on Aug. 18, 2008, militant outfits which were banned by him started re-surfacing and becoming active again by reopening their offices in Karachi. Lashkar-e-Taiba (LeT) which was renamed Jamaat-ud-Dawa(JuD) had an office at Salman Terrace, Gulshan-e-Iqbal near the National Stadium, was closed after the government banned LeT or LT. However, the LeT re-opened a temporary office at the Jamia Darasat al Islamia, opposite Safari Park in Gulshan-e-Iqbal and after Musharraf's departure the office at Salman Terrace was re opened. LeT not only reappeared, its chief Hafiz Saeed addressed a rally in the third week of September 2008 in Karachi on behalf of JUD and advised the government of Pakistan that "this was not the time for friendship with India but the time to take revenge for the Kashmir people". The other banned Jihadi organization Jaish-e-Muhammad (JeM) or JM also re-opened its office in Manghophir on Aug. 20, 2008. Before it was banned, the JM had its Office in Nazimabad and that office remained closed. Sipah-e-Sahaba Pakistan (SSP) now known as Ahle Sunnat waali Jamaat Pakistan (ASWJP) had its Karachi Hqrs. at Masjid Siddique-e-Akbar near Nagan Chowrangi, north Karachi and after the ban it stayed active form the same area. Though the office had remained closed, ASWJP leaders have been conducting meetings from this office from the past few days after Gen. Musharrafs departure form the post of President of Pakistan.

Central leaders of SSP Maulana Ghafoor Nadeem stated (Aug. 20, 2008) that the ban an all religious parties including the SSP was a part of the 'American' agenda. "The ban created hatred and anger amongst our supporters as the SSP is patriotic and its leaders were chosen by the people to be members of Parliament" Nadeem stated and desired that Gen. Musharraf should not be provided a safe exit as he was responsible for the killings of thousands of innocent muslims. "He is a national offender and only the nation can forgive him. If the government lets him got without facing trial, it will be considered as an accomplice of the former President" he said.[1]

Soon after Gen. (Retd.) Musharraf tendered his resignation on Aug. 18, 2008 there were two suicide attacks. Taliban suicide bomber struck at a hospital in North-Western City of Dera Ismail Khan. On Aug 21, 65 people were killed when two suicide bombers allow themselves outside the main gates of Pakistan Ordnance Factories at Wah Cantt. In the year 2006 there were 5 suicide bomb blasts. They increased to 50 in the year 2007 and till Aug. 22, 2008 the number of such suicide attacks had reached 23. Though Gen. Musharraf got terrorists militants etc. Flushed out from Lal Masjid but nearly 70 new unauthorized masjids had sprung up by Sept. 18, 2008 in Islambad itself soon after Gen. Musharraf left ruling the country.

Gen. Kayani would not rein in ISI. On the contrary he would quietly allow it to continue its support to militancy in Kashmir and its efforts in Afghanistan to make it pro-Pakistan. And it is not for nothing that soon after the departure of President Musharraf from the corridors of powers, Gen. Kayani COAS rushed to Afghanistan on August 19, 2008 the day after Musharraf resigned Presidency. At home front, Gen. Kayani certainly wants to de–politicise the army so as to restore its credibility.

Asif Ali Zardari and Nawaz Sharif could not pull on together beyond a certain point and a very short spell of time. They were unnatural allies and had been on strained terms with each other's party. PPP and PML(N) never saw each other with an accommodating eye. Zardari had clearly committed to restoring the sacked Judges by Musharraf on

Nov. 3, 20C7 with in 24 hours of Musharraf's resignation or his impeachment but avoided their restoration and then surprised the Nation by having himself unilaterally nominated for the Presidency. The coalition was formed After 18, 2008 general election but fell apart on the question of restoration of judges. Initially, Zardari had agreed that they would Jointly nominate a neutral candidate for President. But Zardari ultimately backtracked from every promise he made and every assurance he gave to PML(N) supremo Nawaz Shairf. It seemed Zardari hobnobbing together was aimed at ousting Musharraf only But Nawaz Sharif sincerely wanted to reinstall the ousted Judges as well which Zaradari did not agree though agreed to initially and as late as a August 7, 2008 even when the last agreement was signed between them through which Zardari was clearly committed to restoring of Judges. But Zardari had different plans and he repeatedly avoided the agreed dates by which the judges were to be restored. Zardari respectely failed keep his oath to Nawaz Sharif. Defected, Nawaz Shairf declared his decision on Aug. 25 that he was withdrawing and now would sit on the opposition benches since Zardari was reneging on Written agreements. Though Zardari apologized to Sharif on Aug 25 itself but stuck to his stance on the reinstatement of judges and hinted that perhaps he cannot reverl the whole truth. On Aug. 31, Zardari came out with a statement that the establishment (read Army) was with him in his Presidential Poll of Sept 6. He also simultaneously staged that since the media was very vacuously against him in view of reports in western newspapers about his mental health, he felt tremendously under pressure and shifted to the Prime Ministers House annexe for security seasons. In March 2007, New York psychologist Steven Reich concluded that Zardari was chronically anxious and apprehensive and had thoughts a suicide that he has not acted on them. According to the Financial Times, a New York Psychiatrist, phillp Saltiel found that Zardari's long imprisonment in Pakistan while facing corruption probes had left him with "emotional instability" as well as memory and concentrational problems.[2] The US had serious reservation about Zardari having command over Nuclear arsenal of Pakistan in case his becoming the President Zardari was diagnosed with mental problems including dementia, depression and post-traumatic stress disorder last year by doctors hired by Zardari.

The ruling coalition ally Nawaz Sharif was confronted with re-opening of (1) money laundering and (ii) loan defaults, (iii) accumulation of wealth beyond known sources of income etc all graft cases by National Accountability Bureau were started on Sept. 2, 2008 but adjourned till Oct 7, 2008 for hearings. All this was to divert his mind to fighting the cases of graft against him and his brother Shahbag Sharif.

Regarding Zardaris stand on Taliban i.e Pakistani Taliban, he stated on Aug 25, 2008 when he nominated himself for the contest of presidentship that Taliban had ganiend upper hand in the Northern Areas of the country, that the country was losing the war on terror. But the very next day he banned Tehreek-e-Taliban outfits, Prime Minister Yousuf Raza Gilani who Taliban said was responsible for the an going offensive against militants in the northwest of Pakistan, was made a target by militants on Aug 2, 2008. But since he had received a tip off he changed his travel plans and thus escaped the Taliban bullet. Later on Sept 4, Tehreek-e-Taliban claimed that they had done it i.e. they had fired shots at his car.

On Sept. 6, 2008 result of Presidential elections were declared and Asif Ali Zardari stood elected with thumping majority. He polled 481 votes out of a total of 702 far more than the required 352 in the National Assembly, the senate and all the for four Provincial Assemblies. His Score was 69% in 3–way contest. He won in NWFP Baluchistan and Sindh. But in Punjab he lost because of the influence of Sharifs in their home state. The electoral college comprises of National Assembly, Senate and four Provincial Assemblies. In Parliament itself. Zardari secured 281 votes out of 436 votes cart. PML(N) nominee Saeeduzzaman bagged 111 votes and

Syed Mushahid Husain secured 34 votes only. Nawaz Sharif termed Zardari victory as 'triumph of democracy' and hoped Zardari would rise above his party loyalty to represent the Federation of Pakistan Zardari was sworn sworn in as 14th President Pakistan on September 9, 2008.

In a survey conducted by Gallup Pakistan the results show that 34% of the respondents opined that they wanted a non–party President. 44% of Pakistan rejected all the three candidates for the countrys Presidential polls.[3]

The departure of Gen. Musharraf from the position of Chief of Army Staff first and thereafter from Presidentship have started making many people feel the vacuum. Even Teresita Shaffer of Center for strategic and international studies in Washington has opined that India–Pakistan relations were a success story in the past four years. Opponents of peace with India, including Pakistan intelligence services may seek to fish in troubled waters. Ominously, major firing incidents are threatening India–Pakistan cease-fire. [4] Infiltration the indo Pak border and firing there at has increased any told. Indian Army says there have been around 150 attempts by Pak-based terrorists to cross into J&K in 2008 alone so far fill July. To Facilitate these infiltrators, Pak army broke the ceasefire as many as filtering (30) times since January 2008 till Aug. Major infiltration and attacks in 2008 (till August) were on May 11 when terrorists killed 6 people after sneaking into Samba in India; on July 2 when eight terrorists and a soldier was killed as Army foiled infiltration bid in Kupwara; on July 28 when Pak troops crossed the LoC at Nawgam and killed an Indian Soldier; On Aug 15 when Pak troops fired mortar and rockets at Indian Army and BSF position at R S Pura in Jammusector and Mandi in Poonch Sector; on Aug 16 when an armyman was killed as Pak troops opened fire at an Indian post along LoC at uri; on Aug 21 when Pak troops attacked Indian posts along LoC at Nowshera in Rajouri district; on Aug 22 when army foiled infiltration bid, killed two terrorists at keran in north

Kashmirs Kupwaras, 12 terrorists and 3 soldiers were killed after a 2–day long encounter along LoC in Kupwara was carried out; and on Aug 26 when terrorists crossed the LoC under covering fire form Pakistani troops and they simulataneously attempted to push terrorists into India form Sabzian area of Poonch. Four BSF men on our side were wounded.

Zardari became accidental beneficiary of the National Reconciliation Order mooted by Gen. Mushrraf to facilitate Benazir's return to Pakistan and Benazir benefitted Zardari and ultimately he rose to become the President. He was on bail in the murder charge of his brother in law Murtaza Bhutto who was killed in 1996. The NRO which absolved politicians , bankers and Joureaucrats resulted in dismissal of 5 cases in March 2008 which included his having received $ 10 million in Kickbacks form a gold importing Company, taking bribe from ARY gold bullion dealership based in Dubai in pieu of awarding him a license for import of gold worth $ 500 million in 1994.

Zardari had earlier served as MNA during 1990–93 and then in 1993–96. Benazir made him Federal Minister of the Environment during 1993–96 and Minister of Investment during 1993–96. He was also a senator during 1997–1999. He was famous as Mr. 10% which meant that he would do someone's work only after charging commission @ of ten present.

The initial stage of the Presidentship did not prove smooth for President Zardari. A 10–member terrorist group of LeT/ JUD origination form Pakistan attacked Mumbai on November 26, 2008 (know as 26/11) which included Mohammad Ajmal Amir Qasab who was luckily caught alive. There was clear involvem of ISI backed militant outfits in the attack and as such India demanded arrest and handing over of those persons to try them. In a small way this incident was responsible in distancing Zardari from his Prime Minister Yusuf Raja Gilani and Pak Army chief Gen. Kayani. Pak Army became unhappy with Zardari when he promised India to send his ISI chief to New Delhi to help investigate the 26/11 attack. But soon after he had to backtrack under pressure from ISI. On the issue of Mumbai investigation regarding 26/11 attack, Zardari developed a rift with his prime minister Yousuf Raja Gilani in the sense that the former wanted Pakistan to do its time bound part whereas the latter, supported and suggested by ISI and Pak Army wanted to go slow over the matter. On the incident of alleged intrusion into Pak Air space by Indian Aircraft, President Zardari took it lightly saying that such 'Technical faults' do take place and they should not be taken any strong notice of. But ISI and Pak Army did not agree with Zardari when he said "Democracies do not go to war", "there is a bit of India in every Pakistani and vice versa or "India does not pose a threat to Pakistan" or 'militants in Kashmir are terrorists' were seen by Pak authorities as Zardari's capituatiero to India- leveraged by US pressure The fact the last year (2007) Zardari, soon after becoming President chose to dash to US Enjoarry in Pakistan for consultation with American Ambass-aders was also not liked by these men. Similary after 26/11 attack also in Mumbai, Zardari post visit to US Embassy in Islamabad which was again, disliked by ISI and Army.

The Lawyers movement and subsequent participation of Nawaz Sharif and his political outfits PML(N) certainly lowered Zardari's place in people's estimation simply because of his obduracy, tactleess and inept handling and his inability to grasp the peoples mood. Zardari had reneged on his promise qrestoring ( ) gfti khan Nawaz attributed supreme courts decision of Feb 25, 2009 against him and his brother Shahbaz Sharif to Zardari only. The folly on Zardari part was no soon the Apex Court gave it decision gainst Shahbaz holding the political office as chief Minister of Punjab province, Zardari dismissed the provincial government and imposed Governor's Rule. This really infuriated Sharif brother and it proved to be the last straw which culminated in Long March and Chaotic conditions Consequent upon the Supreme Court order against Shairf brothers, Nawaz decided to participate in the Long March, Gen. Kayani Chief of Army Staff had in clear term warned that he would keep aloof from politics. Zardari brand of politics was devoid of morality and keeping to commitments. Had he been fulfilling his promise to reinstate the chief justice Chaudhary and other judges, there would not have been any problems for him. On the contrary perhaps he could have tightened his grip over the administration. A leading journalist Zhaid Hussain says that during meeting at presidents House, he (Zardari) called information minister Sherry Rehman witch, bitch and 'Jadoogarni' (soreeress) "He called Benzair Bhuttos close confidant Raza Rabbani, 'Khasi' or impotent. Both sherry and Rabbani resigned from their posts, fanning speculation that the old guard of the PPP could join hands to wrest the party out of Zardari's control.[5] On Sherry Rehmans resignation, Zardari cited a urdu couplet: 'go ki zara si baat per barson be yaaraane gaye', lekin itna hua ki kuch log pehacane gaye!

Sidelining PPP's Senator Raza Rabbani, a staunch and old Bhutto loyalist, Zardari chose to nominate his own loyalist Farooq Nyek as Senate Chairman. Different personalities gave trained remarks on Zardari. Lt. Gen (Retd) Talat Massod said "the president has been highly weakened by the latest developments. His actions were untenable and were rejected by the people and even his own party.[6] Former ISI chief Lt. Gen. (Retd) Hamid Gul felt "if Zardari does not mend his approach to the problem, then he would have to say good bye to the President's house "very soon".[7] Hamid Gul told to an Indian TV channel "He (Zardari is a very weak politician who does not understand the mood and the temperature of the people. He tried to run the affairs of the state by gimmickry rather than the principles and that is where he has gone wrong'.[8] Political analyst Harris Khalique said Zardari had been misd by aides who believed Sharif would not be able to organise a major protest and todays developments should serve as a 'reality check' for the President."[9] Karachi-based political commentator Agha Masood said "before he become President, Zardari called about dialogue with the militants and hinted at peace deal. That has not happened in Swat." He Further says "Zardari has two big flaws. He is not, capable of independent thinking, having lived under Benazirs shadow all his public life and he does not enjoy popular support. But he thinks highly of himself and tries to push his agenda. And he is playing his own game by trying to get the army on his side. With him its always, one step forward, two steps backward".[10] Political commentator and member of parliament Ayaz Amir called Zardari on American puppet, "their karzai in Islamabad someone who was supposed to fight the Taliban better than the discredited Pervez Musharraf. But by proving to be an all-round disaster, he is undermining everything

Because of his inept and reckless handling of long march, US secretary of state Hilary Chinton had to intervene in defusing a dangerous political power keg in Pakistan, forcing its warring political parties and it ever present military to back down from a growing controntation and arrive at a compromise for now at least."[12] Even the 'Foreign policy' magazine listed Zardari as 5th biggest looser in the world.[13]

But whatever way Zardari might have decided to deal with the long march, once the storm was over it seem Zardari realised the lapses on his part in inept handling of the situation and later on spoke few soothing and soft sentences both for Chief Justice Chaudhary and Nawaz Sharif. Zardari ordered reinstement of CJ Chaudhary and Shahbaz Sharif after so much disturbances which he could have avoided showing a little farsightendess and proper assessment of the situation. It is only because of his factless handling that Gen. Ashfaq Kayani had to deliver a stern message to the Prime Minister Yousuf Raza Gilani Saying "that he must play his constitutional and legal role in calming down in situation." Zardari seems to have been lucky to have COAS like Gen. Kayani. Had there been Generals like Ayub or Zia or Musharraf, the political repercussions of such situation would have once again be different than what they are. The political rule again would have been reverted to Army. Zardari was looser on other front also. His information minister Ms Sherry Rehman broke from him on the question of blocking Geo television network without consulting her. Her resignation was accepted on March 14, 2009. Benazir's loyalist Ms Naheed Khan broke from him on the tssue. Her resignation was accepted on March 14, 2009. Benazirs loyalist Ms Naheen khan and safdar Abbasi also came out openly against him. Benazir Bhuttos sister Sanam also got annoyed with Zardari America is developing a soft corner for Sharif mainly because of proximity with religious militant parties. Zardari is aiming at his Prime Minister Gilani now and in busy hob nobbing with PML Q to see the ouster of his prime minister.

Taking all of a sudden a U-turn Zardari in an interview to "the independent' said he is willing to cut down Presidents sweeping power. He stated that the package of constitutional reforms will be introduced and they shall return to the basic structure of 1973 constitution.[13]

Prime Minister Yusuf Raja Gilani invited (April 12, 2004) PML (N) to re-join the PPP-lied federal government to help steer the country out of the challenges it was facing more especiially when one of the precondition of restoration of judges has already been fulfilled. But PML(N) chief Nawaz Sharif who was in Dubai declined the offer saying than they would support the government in its struggle to fight militancy and revive economy. Prior to it on April 10 the National Assembly had passed a resolution unanimously to form a committee to implement the charter of Democracy and repealing the 17th Constitutional Amendment.

REFERENCE

1. Daily Times August 21, 2008 'Banned Outfits rear their heads in Karachi post resignation. by Fareed Farooqui.
2. The Times of India Sept 2, 2008 US worried about unstable Zardari finger an N-button report by chidanand Rajghatta.
3. PTI News in the Times of India Sept. 7. 2008

4. The Pioneer at Sept 3, 2008 'US Policy after Musharraf' by teresita Schatter.
5. Outlook (weekly magazine) 30 March 2009. Article by Mariana Boabar from Islamabad.
6. The Times of India March 17, 2009 PTI Report
7. Ibid.
8. Ibid.
9. Ibid
10. The Times of India March 15, 2009 Report by Chidanand Rajghatta form Washington.
11. The Hindustan Times March 24, 2009.
12. The Indian Express April 9, 2009. PTI report from London.

13

Secrets are Made to be Found out with Time

—Charles Sanford

A large chunk of ISI personnel remain engaged in anti India and anti Indian activities. ISI, which is a sprawling organisation, mainly stassed by Pakistan Army men, is divided into eight (8) main Divisions. One of the Division known as Joint Intelligence North (JIN) is entirely and exclusively devoted to Kashmir affairs only. It is responsible for infiltration and extiltration of militants or even Pak Army personnel in disguise, their deployment at selected targets inside Kashmir assigning them the tasks, targets, training them, providing them with necessary required arms and ammunition, funds and guidance. Another Directorate called joint intelligence Bureau (JIB) posts Defence Attaches to India and other countries of the world. The defence Attache posted by JIB in Delhi is in most of the cases Station incharge of ISI. He collects intelligence on Defence matters of Inida and keeps a liaison with Army offices in India. But there is no bar on him on collecting intelligence on other fields should an opportunity come to him on that score. He keeps a tab on all movements of Indian Army. His men posted in the Mission keep on collecting TAC numbers and then the collation and analysis is done in ISI Hqrs regarding movements and spread of Indian army locations. He keeps a track of the Indian Defence Attache's to be posted to Islamaband of course, with the aim of developing 'friendly' relations with him. A large section of this Directorate deals exclusively with India and carries out 'operations' detrimental to Indias security. Yet another big directorate of ISI is known by the name of Joint

Counter Intelligence Bureau (JCIB). It is this Directrate that keeps an eye on Indian Mission staff and Diplomats posted in Pakistan, terrorising, threatening and abusing them and their families. Keeping them under constant threats and constraints is the main job, prerogative and privilege of this Directorate. Bumper-to-bumper surveillance, constant close. shave-Static watch at the residence or when the mission member goes shopping etc is its responsibility. Still another Directorate known as Joint Intelligence Miscellaneous (JIM) functions as ISI's Ambassador-at-large. Staff posted under JIM can do any operation, anywhere, anytime. They can do espionage, recruit special agents to accomplish a particular assigned job by their master. Commit theft, steal, print and carry take currency employ people who will help carry the take currency in the target country to dischevelle its economy or make arrangements to send/supply drugs. Certain trained employees of this Directorate also carry out disturbances as in Indias northeast region. Then there is a Signal Directorate which is known as Joint Signal Intelligence Bureau (JSIB) whose main job in Indian context is to monitor all incoming and outgoing calls to and trothe country. So far as India is concerned, monitoring office is located at Malir Cantt. in Karachi. All telephone calls originating from Pakistan to India first go to Malir Cantt. exchange and from there only calls are transferred to forward locations. Each and every Telephonic call is intercepted and monitored. A Technical Directorate also exists with ISI which is known as Joint Intelligence Technical (JIT) which handles all electronic gadgets used for bugging the houses of foreign mission members their telephone are intercepted round the clock, get the staff clandestinely photographed, implant listening devices etc.

Besides ISI, Intelligence Bureau's different sections also keep an eye on Indian Mission and its members including the High commissioner. Military Intelligence, special Branch of Police, F/A all inclusive seven or eight intelligence outfits of Pakistan cover them. Not only that, the sentries and guards engaged by others residing nearly the residence of Indian mission staff are also tasked by IB and ISI to keep a watch on the visitors of the Indian occupant of the house.

Pakistan all-out efforts right from 194 tfill date are aimed at westing Kashmir from India by hook or crook. Its leadership is not prepared to listen to what tough leaders like Lal Denga of Mizo Insurgency fame said that nobody no in suregent outfits can win by waging war with the government of India. Pakistans ISI would not listen to their own man even Gulbuddin Hematyar of Afghanistan who had in July 2004 said that Kashmir Jehad can not break up India. This was the opinion of the one who was leader of Hizbe Islami and who ran Al Badar I, Al Badar II and Al Badar III camps in khost (Afghanistan) for training Kashmiris, Pakistanis and foreign Islamic militants to be sent to J & K for carrying out Low intensity conflict (LIC), terror and mayhem. In Pakistan ISI and IB had mainly and exclusively been concentrating on individuals on Indian Mission members directly. Their targets are persons posted in Islamabad and Karach from India in Indian Mission. *For example* 151 fargeted indianNaval Attache in Islamabad from 1990 to 1991 to obtain information about Indian Navy. During the decade of ninetees and thereafter, Pakistan hankered for information on Indian Navy. Incidently, in the then Naval Attache Commander Sridharan, ISI found a man falling for sex. They threw a girl on him who was given a cover of a 'lady working' with the Military Nursing Service of Pakistan Army. She was in fact, an agent of ISI and Sridharan fell in the trap compromising pictures of the two at a specially rigged hotel room the Karachi were taken by ISI which were shown to him later on to force him to work as a 'spy' for Pakistan Intelligence. Sridharan dateron claimed that he had given only some bits of inconsequential information and that to wriggle out of the situation he had agreed to work for the Pakistanis at Rs 15000 per month as per report in the media.

ISI, IB or MI etc would not spare any effort to put Indian individuals in trouble thinking, perhaps, if a diplomat posted in Islamabad is harassed, probably India would give Kashmir to Pakistan on a platter. Taking a cue from the basic cause of division of the country in 1942 on religious basis which was also named as two-nation theory, ISI decided to play religious cared in J&K as well knowing fully well that it was a muslim majority area. They, with the help of some fundamentalist religious parties like Jamaat-e-Islami etc propogated religious fundamentalism in Kashmir and all Kashmiri muslims were administered lessons on the facts that they are separate than India which is that of Hindus. They dont consider Kashmir as India's part. ISI and its aided, instigated and supported Pakistani fundamentalist and militant parties trained, indoctrinated, selected muslims leaders from Kashmir, gave them money, arms and ammunition, took them to Pakistan and Afghanistan to impart training in 'Jihad' in militant comps like Al Badar etc. They were directed to create militants so as to create disturbances and anarchism in J&K on their return. They were tasked to keep Indian security forces engaged. ISI conducts operations inside Kashmir absolutely independently and defies all controls from political bosses. In fact, it has no political bosses at all. ISI works in kashmir according to an agreed and given policy to achieve certain target and purses its own goals and agenda considering itself supreme and saviour of the country. A rogue organization, always a law unto itself, ISI is omnipotent, omnipresent and omniscient all over Pakistan. As such, the aim of ISI for India is hit whomsoever you can with what so ever means you can at whatever level you can in whatever way you can without bothering for consequences or world opinion. This rogue agency has no regards for manners, decency, humanity or even the diplomatic immunity under Geneva Convention. It is mainly staed by Punjabis and one has to know the Punjabi mind before mixing army culture and hatred towards India and Hindus in it. ISI at times runs amok. The middle and lower ranking ISI operative are errant and act according to their religious beliefs. In March 1996 Sajjad Hyder, a 25 year old Sunni muslim resident of Faisalabad, a front ranking Hizbul

Mujahideen militant, during interrogation after his arrest disclosed that ISI had successfully used the issue of religion in India to stregther its network.[1] Sajjads disclosure can be vouched with the fact and example that syed Ali Shah Gilani, leader of Tehreek-i-Harriyat in Kashmir gave a call on Oct 26, 2007 to the people of state at a rally in Srinagar where he asked them "to use their religious duty and raise their voice against India's aggression". On May 26, 2008 he blamed the Indian government stating that "after turning Kashmiri muslims into a minority. it will either massacre Muslims also it did in Jammu in 1947 or carry out a genocide as a was done in Gujarat".[2] JUP chief Maulana Shah Ahmad Noorani had said that 'Jehed' had become 'farz' (compulsory duty) under Islam against India and added that atom bomb was not a decoration piece but was made to be thrown over India, therefore there should be no delay in launching it. He further said that it is no time to shakehands with India but it is no time to shake hands with India but it was time to throw the bomb.[3] ISI, a state within a state, has immense capacity and capability to carry out 'jehad' against India ensuring to implement a thousands year 'Jihad' as per a call given by Z.A. Bhutto. ISI has been executing the goal set by Bhutto. What sort of idea Pakistan keeps about India, a small glimpse can be seen from the following paragraph. Quote is on the even of its outbreak (Bengladesh war of Dec 1971), one of Z A Bhutto's confidants in President Yahya Khans office informed him in a secret message: "Any day now you should become the Prime Minister to our great delight" and that "once the back of Indian Forces in broken in the East, Pakistan should occupy the whole of eastern India and make it a permanent part of East Pakistan. This will also provide a physical link with China. Kashmir should be taken at any price, even the Sikh Punjab and turned into Khalistan." Bhuttos inimitable voice lent authenticity to the text." Let us not forget the whole background and history of India compared to our own. In the remotest of our village the humlest of our people possess a self-confidence, a ready willingness to march forward into

India—a spirit the equivalent of which cannot be found on the other side. Great and terrible scourges have come to India from this side...every invasion from this side has defeated India."[4] unquote. ISI is like unbridled horse. It is does not like any taming so for India and Indians are concerned. If the political leadership of the country tries to install it own man at the top most position of DG ISI, it was observed that it has not proved to be helpful at all. It rather backried. When Ms Benazir Bhutto brought a retired Liut. Gen. Kallue to head ISI, ISI engineered her own ouster from the position of Prime Ministership of the country. So, the message was touch ISI and get ready for consequences. Pakistan's in general are terribly afraid of ISI. They live in constant fear of ISI. ISI can pick up anybody, anywhere anytime. When ISI started picking up people who were not traceable after their custody by ISI and they approached chief justice Chaudhary who in turn asked the ISI to product these men chief justice himself was removed from his post. The case of one of the most honourable man of immense importance, eminence and a learned Journalist Mr. Najm Sethi of the Friday Times, Lahore in already on the record. ISI's jurisdiction is infinity and immeasurable, its grip binding even on Pakistan Army from whom its cadres are drawn. The whole Pakistani nation including all government officials Senior or Junior alike ordinary citizens, politicians and even Army itself feels its throttling and squeezing hold.

A few hours after Prime Minister Yousuf Raza Gilani left for Washington on July 26, 2008, Pakistan government issued a notification placing the ISI alongwith the Intelligence Bureau under the control of Interior Minister Mr. Rehman Malik with immediate effect. But just a few hours after the said notification, it had to be withdrawn by way of issuing a humiliating clarification, that to at the unearthly hour of 3 am, saying its notification had just been 'misinterpreted' and that the ISI would continue to report to the Prime Minister.[5] ISI must have scolded the authority that issued the order and must have asked him whether he wants to continue to live his life. But all this was done to hoodwins America and its President Mr George Bush who is so much mesmerised by Pakistan. American never understood the Pakistani game. It simply never tried to Pakistan is interested in American dollars only. It started from Lyndon Johnson the then vice President who visited Islamabad in early sixties and who was given a camle-ride. He was so impressed that from that day onwards till date America countinues to be dictated by Pakistan. ISI has never been answerable to any PM even in reality. It has never been answerable to anybody except its own Army Chief on whose hands remain the power of posting, promotions and removal. It in COAS who can post retired Army officers or even in-service officers on important position. Whatever reports ISI thinks suitable sends it to the Prime Minister which are normally of political nature or where international community comes into the picture. Operation against India or Afghanistan are no told to the PM in full. The Kargil episode where PM Nawaz Sharif claimed that he was not told complete things about intruding into Kargil heights is one of the examples yes, when ISI chief is a man who is pro–P.M. for example Gen. Zia uddin then definitely yes he must have reported to the Prime Minister besides keeping the chief of Army staff informed. But Gen Ziauddin did not inform the ouster of COAS Gen. Musharraf which was proposed by Nawaz Sharif thus, the substance is that nothing substantial and conclusively can be said whether ISI gives all reports to PM and. Experience says they have acted differently at different times. COAS has either not attached any importance to even the DG ISI as incase of Retired Gen. Kallue who was treated as 'persona non grate' by Gen. Aslam Beg or Gen Zia uddin who was kept away from many important development and decisions. It is the CoAs and the group of then corps commanders which at times, includes GHQ officers also, who run the country behind the curtain. On matters India and the Indians, the middle ranking and lower ranking ISI operatives act of their own often. Not always, in an over enthusiastic manner acting and behaving recklessly, in an inappropriate manner as a ruffian. It is not clear so far whether the attack on Indian Parliament by JeM on Dec 13, 2001 was carried out after obtaining OK form DG ISI or whether DG ISI, in turn, discussed with chief of Army Staff Gen. Musharraf. There is no mention of this attacks details by Gen. Musharraf in his book in the line of Fire" though he mentions other events in detail. Gen. Musharraf privately told US Ambassador in Pakistan at the time that it was a very 'dirty' business but never clarified what that meant. Did the ISI not tell him about the plan to attack the Parliament? Or did the ISI's client operate outside its control for someone else.[6] After the attack on Parliament, when the then foreign minister Jaswant Singh pointed out finger towards JeM plus ISI, Pakistan spokesman suggested it was a put-up job by India but later, Gen (Retd) Javed Ashraf Qazi, former head of ISI admitted that the JeM was responsible for the attack.[7] Thus a deliberate confusion is left asto who controls ISI. Even US President was put on confusion and he asked Pakistani Prime Minister on July 31, 2008 as to who controls ISI while expressing concern and some annoyance over leaking of intelligence, shared by Washington, to militants by ISI.

The aim of ISI for India is let whomsoever your can with whatever means you can at whatever level you can and whenever you can in whatever way you can. So far as India is concerned, ISI can abduct a diplomat with impunity. Administer electric shocks to him to obtain information from him, can cause theft in his house or steal house hold effects can cause, stage and involve him in motor car accident with a view to make him infirm or even kill him. Terrify the Insurance Company to either delay or not pay compensation at all for causing damage to his motor car. Intimidate, thereafter or abuse him using filithy language coming from one who has no civilized existence. They are simply devoid any regard towards Geneva Convention, culture, humanity, courtesy and dignity. It is this ISI which has brought a bad name for Pakistan and was a cause to get Pakistan declared a terrorist sponsoring state. United States has also stated that ISI has been an issue historically and there are signs that it remains so.[8]

ISI, though browbeats political bosses, but uses them to issue denials of involvement of ISI in an incident. Only July 7, 2008 Indian Mission was attacked in Afghanistan where in two diplomates and about 60 persons including many innocent Afghan nationals were killed. When National Security Advisor (NSA) of India Mr. MK Narayanan pointed finger towards ISI on July 12, forthwith came denial form Pakistans Foreign Minsiter Shah Mehmood Qureshi on July 12 itself. The denial was so prompt that it seemed as if he was waiting to issue denial should the accusations come from India for ISI's involvement in bombing of Indian Mission in Kabul on July 7. The Deputy Director of CIA Mr Stephen R. Kappes travelled to Islamaband on July 28 to tell the Pakistani authorities of ISI's involvement with Taliban militants in Afghanistan and its complicity in the incident of bombing of Indian Mission. Pakistans Defence Minister Chaudhury Ahmed Mukhtar also came to the rescue of Pakistan spy Agency ISI and stated that it was 'inappropriate' of India to make such an allegation without any proof adding a soothing sentence that it would not have any effect on the India-Pakistan peace process."[9] But proof of ISI's involvement was given by Washington when US showed US Intelligence intercepted Communication between Pakistani spies and terrorists, as per the New York Times report. Pakistan kept mum, no substantial results came in CIA chief Mr. Michael V. Hayden had met Prime Minister of Pakistan Mr. Yousuf Raza Gilani on July 28 in Washington at a dinner where the former handed over a 'chargesheet' to the latter regarding Pakistani Intelligences linkes to militant activities and was told to 'reign in the ISI' the PM of Pakistan kept mum. Nothing happened. No concrete results came in.

The fact is that it is no point in asking the civilian government in Pakistan to control or rein in ISI. The civilian government in simply unable to impose its will on the powerful inter service Intelligence. Since early 1990 successive Prime Minister of Pakistan have had no control over ISI and no other choice but to comply with ISI's policies in India and Afghanistan.[10] In an interview broadcast on July 29, 2008 on the PBS programme "The News Hour" with Jim. Lehrer", Mr Gilani said he rejects as "not believable" any assertions of ISI's links to the militants we would not allow that he said.[11] Mr Gilani might have had honest intentious in not allowing such activities but he can do that only when ISI seeks his permission for doing such and such act:

A firm determination to return them in the same coin is the answer. Indias NSA spoke in clear terms" I think we need to pay back in the same coin and we are quite clear in our mind.[12] Such resolute statements from authorities have rarely come out. But the real action under India system of the government lies in the hands of the Prime Minister of the country. Almost all the Prime Minister in Indian wanted to have good relations with Pakistan ignoring such distractedly acts. They have been very mild and accommodating. Even United States was also doing the same. It had been ignoring ISI's contacts with militant outfits and the mayhem and killings these outfits have been doing. But now it is for the first time US has started ignoring the protests of Pakistan and assisting itself in conducting raids inside Pakistan without prior permission of the country. US soldiers started in the month of September 2008 striking against Al Qaida-Taliban targets inside Pakistan near Pak-Afghan border. Probably Jehadi infrastructure can not be eradicated root and branch from Pakistan for many more years to come. It would rather grow by leaps and bounds.

These Jihadi outfits of Pakistan or Taliban in Afghanistan are aided, supplemented and directed by Pakistan 'authorities' in Kashmir and Afghanistan respectively. Maulana Masood Azhar of Jaish-e-Mohammd (JeM) claimed (Dec 23, 2001) that he had been asked by the 'authorities' 'to go slow' on his activities.[13] In the aftermath of 9/11 all militant outfits who were made to operate in Kashmir were noticed changing their names. Lashkar-e-Taiba (LeT) changed its name to Pasban-e-Ahle-Hadith. The Herald, a monthly english magazine published form Karachi, a monthly journal of DAWN group described Let as Pakistan's largest so called "Jihadi organisation". It was projected as Pak based organization giving Telephone and fax number in Pakistan. Mr. Amanullah Khan Pok based JKLF Chairman, in a letter to President Bush with a copy to the secretary of state Gen. Colin Powell took exception to the description of LeT as Kashmir based group. Khan said LeT is based in Muridke (near Lahore and Muzafarrabad. LeT trains it militants in mobile training camps.[14] LeT assumed a new name Jamaat-ud-Dawa on Dec 24 2001 so that India does not increase problems for Pakistan Prof. Sayeed LeT chief also announced (Dec. 24 2001) the appointment of Maulana Abdual Wahid Kashmiri as new head of the militants outfit Saeed said "this is not the result of giving in to Indian, American or Pakistan pressure This was only a strategic decision

These Pakistani 'authorities' adopted the same policies towards Afghanistan in promoting Taliban avoiding and directing to achieve strategic depth. They helped Taliban by way of leaking CIA provided strategic intelligence and later joined even in firing at US Military posts during first fortnight of September 2008. Pak troops fired to turn back US choppers on Sept 19 to Afghanistan when they were advancing towards tribal region of South Waziristan. So far Gen. Musharraf was playing a very clever game with American President George Bush Even Gen. Kayani attempted to make America perplexed by saying that American reckless action will only help the militants and further fuel the militancy in the rea. Meanwhile America possible became tied up after receiving CIA reports that Pakistan ISI's help to Taliban is not allowing American operations puccessful against Taliban . US President George Bush approved in July 2008 orders for the first time allowing us special operation forces to carry out ground assaults inside Pakistan without prior approval of Islamabad. Americans had also got fed up and called President Bush policy of 'engaging' Pakistan into question. Presidential candidate Barrack Obama was scathing in his criticism of Pakistans failure to tackle the

'Jehadis' inspite of so much of financial aid given to it by America. He even said whatever financial a id US is giving to Pakistan to fight Taliban in Pak-Afghan border or in tribal areas, Pakistan is diverting the funds to prepare itself for war against India. Democratic Presidential candidates verbatim was 'we are providing them with military aid without enough strings attached. So they are using the military aid preparing for a war against India."[17] Earlier New York Times had published a report on Sept 7, 2008 that American Officials confirmed the involvement of ISI with fighters of Jalaluddin Haqqani to bomb the Indian Embassy in Kabut on July 7, 2008. Haqqani himself was not seen or heard since the year 2001. All this culminated in America taking a tough stand against Pakistan and changing its strategy against its "staunch ally in fighting a war on terror." US Joint Chiefs of staff admiral Mike Mullen asserted Washingtons Plan to launch military operations to eliminate militant sanctuaries in Pakistan. Gen. Musharrf did no quite deliver on his promises to play a role of staunch ally in US led war on terror though Lt. Gen. (Retd) Shahid Aziz who served as Chief of General staff form October 2001 to December 2003 has alleged that GHQ did not know most of the Pakistani nationals apprehended by Pakistan Army and handed over to ISI for interrogation were completely in dark about the most controversial thing Gen. Musharraf did in handing over Pakistani nationals to American which caused a lot of resentment in the top echelons of the army."[18] US top military officers met Gen. Kayani aboard the Aircraft Carrier USS Abraham Linclon on August 27, 2008 where he claims to have impressed upon them that military action alone can not solve the problem. He also impressed upon US officers that the security Forces of Pakistan have made sacrifices in this war and it is the presence of army which has denied the freedom of movement and operation to Al Qaida and (their) affiliates.[19] Now US troops have started operating of its won on Pakistan's soil. COAS Gen. Kayani have come out with a statement that "the Sovereignty and territorial integrity of the country will be defended at all costs and no external forces is allowed to conduct operation inside Pakistan."[20] Inspite of Gen. Kayani's caution to America, US choppers had started coming inside Pakistan territory to carry out missle attacks on choosen targets in Waziistan (north) only so far. Pakistan tribesman had retorted by saying that if America does not stop attacks in tribal areas, we will prepare a Lashkar (Army) to attack US forces in Afghanistan.' The statement was delivered by tribal chief Malik Nassrullah in Miran shah in Waziristan on Sept 13, 2008.[21]

'Terrorism' is what Chairman Mao called the death of a thousand cuts.' It hurts the morale of people and eventually saps the will of people to resist. Terror groups are not normally opposed to the 'Core states' which surfers to democracies with market economics aligned with the US and the west.[22] ISI seems to be taking a cue from this saying of Mao when it gets terrorism spread in India causing bomb blast and creating panic among masses. But it should also take notice of what its own renowned scientist (nuclear scientist) had to say. Pervez Hoodbhoy, a learned teacher in Qaida Azam University Islamabad opined that even if American retreats which is unlikely Pakistan is now unable to escape the terrible consequences of a weapon developed to bleed India and to secure Afghanistan for strategic depth."[23] It is realy strange that inspite of US and Pakistan forces stood face to face on the Afghan-Pak border, the Bush Administration urged US congress on Sept. 16, 2008 to release more than $ 250 million to arm Pakistan with upgraded F–16 fighters jets. Mr. Haroun Mir, co founder of Afghanistan centre for Research and policy studies blamed Pakistan stating the "Pakistan can hardly be a part of the solution. It is the problem. Mir also stated that ISI had devastated Afghanistan right from, the point when it created the Taliban and that Afghanistans people would continue paying the price for decades to came. Afghanistans President Hamid Karachi himself had blamed Pakistan for creating troubles in Afghanistan during the past several years. During soviet occupations of Afghanistan, US had given a number of stingers to Pak Army for their use in supplying then to mujahideen. A few of them were given to Mujahideen and rest were stored in Ojhri camp for the use of Pak Army. Similarly Pakistan is asking for F–16 on the pretext that it has to ferry in tribal areas to fight Taliban and Bush gets convinced that yes Pakistan need them. Because Bush wants immediate results before he demits office. He wants Osama caught dead or alive. In that desire he is not able to see the game Pakistan has been playing. Even in July 2008, Bush Administration had proposed shifting $ 226.5 million in US Counter terrorism aid to Pakistan to upgrade Pakistani F–16 fighters. And that too, when the Presidential aspirant Mr Barack Obama has openly declared that this arms aid is being utilized to prepare Pakistan for war against India. India centric military preparations and preparing 'Jihadis' giving them the cover of home grown militants is what Pakistan is busy with. Right from 1971 it had stepped up its efforts in this direction. How ISI and Pakistan Army helped Mizo insurgents was already known. But the facts have been corroborated By Brg (Retd) Z.A. Khan of Pakistan Army who has confirmed the Mizo insurgents were supplied food by the Government of Pakistan just across the border from Assam. Mizos were led by 'President of Mizoram, Laldenga' whose 'government' consists of various ministers and commander in chief of the Army. One of them [who] identified himself as Paulian, the Foreign Minister of Mizoram, met Brig. Khan and informed him there were about 2000 men and 3000 non-combatant civilians living in the Pakistani territory and their food supplied had stopped. I returned to chittagong and informed Paulian that the Mizos could start coming to Rangamati, we would supply food for their army and the non-combatants, they would have to place their army under my command. Paulin was satisfied and left immediately to inform his government."[24] America is decided by a player in the affairs of Pakistan. Pakistan always served western interests in general and that of Americans in particular. But it always asked for cost for such services which Americans paid for in billion and billions of dollars. Yet the

US National Intelligence council and the CIA combire forecasts a Yugoslavia-like face for Pakistan in a decade with the country riven by civil war, bloodshed and inter provincial rivalries as recently seen in Baluchistan. By 2015 Pakistan, according to NIC-CIA is stated to become a failed state as it would be effected by civil war, complete Talibanisation and struggle for control of it nuclear weapons.[25] The mujahideen, Jihadis or militants of Taliban Pakistan has trained over the years either of fighting soviets in Afghanistan or for continuing the militant activities in Kashmir are bound to become nightmare for Pakistan itself. Once they were trained, ISI did not have full control of them. Gen. Musharraf did try to exercise some control after major incidents but a faction in ISI was always there to nullify and negate his orders. US Ambass-ssador to Pakistan Nancy Powell, had called upon Gen. Pervex Musharraf to end to use of Pakistan as plateform for terrorism, sate Department official Mr. Richard Heas had confessed that washington had been unable to persuade Pakistan to stop cross border terrorism and Mr. Michael Evanoff, a US embassy official in Islamabad called Pakistan the epicenter of terrorism.[26] The earlier and the sooner Pakistan listens to these statesman and behaves like a 'state', the better in would be for its bright future.

Pakistanis living in the country side are not very well of people. One of the cartoon that truely depicts the real state of economic status appeared in the News International Lahore edition on May 21, 1999 wherin a little boy of hardly any age asks his father, who had committed suicide by handing himself because of poverty, that he will not ask for toys and 'Roti' is really touching and heartrending. Some of the Pakistanis who migrated to Pakistan in 1947 keep on thronging Indian Embassy seeking visa to visit their near and dear ones still living in India. Most of the visa seekers have to spend the night close to the visa section of the Indian Mission, in open since their number stands far beyond the handling capacity of Embassy staff. Early in the morning they have to form a queue in order to obtain a token number to deposit their visa form.

Intelligence men form ISI/IB/ local police keep round the clock vigil on these visa seekes. Consequently they also have to spend the night in a pitched tent for themselves where they exploit the misery and helplessness of young female visa seekes while others battle cold. On one such occasions when these ISI/IB people where enjoying and exploiting the womenfolk, one sincere and honest Incharge visited them during night checking duty, and to his horror he found them sleeping with girls in their tents. He ordered all these ISI/IB men back to lines. Next morning a new team was detailed.

VISA SEEKERS BATTLE COLD

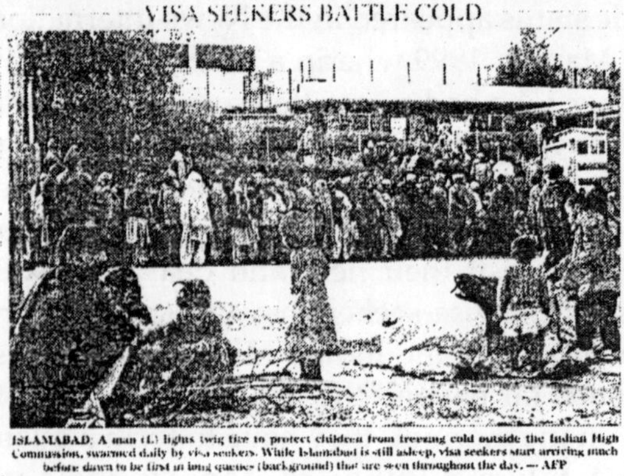

ISLAMABAD: A man (L) lights twig fire to protect children from freezing cold outside the Indian High Commission, swarmed daily by visa seekers. While Islamabad is still asleep, visa seekers start arriving much before dawn to be first in long queues (background) that are seen throughout the day. — AFP

1. The Hindustan Times March 25, 1996.
2. The Hindu Sept 10, 2008 article by Shri Praveen Swami
3. The Friday Times Jan 25-31, 2002 Page of 'Comments'.
4. The Pioneer Sept. 13, 2008 As in Bengladesh, so in Georgia article by premen Addy.
5. The Hindu July 20, 2008 An ISI story by Nirupana Subramanian.
6. The Hindustan Times Sept. 11, 2008. It carried an article adapted from a book "the search for Al Qaeda: Its leadership, ideology and future" by Bruce Riedel, a senior fellow at the Brooking Institute.
7. Ibid
8. The Pioneer Aug 7, 2008 Report by S. Rajgopalan form washington.
9. The Hindu July 14, 2008
10. The Times of India July 2, 2008 The long Arm of Pakistan by Haroun Mir. (He was special assistant to Afghanistani former defence minister Ahmad shah Massoud.)
11. The Indian Express did July 31, 2008
12. Sunday Pioneer July 13, 2008
13. Ausaf Pakistans newspaper. Report by Hamid Mir Editor. Story Carried by The Hindu dt Dec 26, 2001.
14. The Hindu Dec 24, 2001
15. The Hindu Dec 25, 2001
16. The times of India Dec 25, 2001
17. The Times of India Sept 6, 2007
18. The Indian Express did Sept 15, 2008 report filed by PTI form Islamabad which was picked up form the News Daily.
19. The Indian Express September 12, 2008.
20. The Hindustan Times Sept. 12, 2008
21. The Hindustan Times Sept 16, 2008
22. The Nation Pakistan July 31, 2000 Indian anti-Christan cult seeks A Bomb. Report form Humayun Akhtar.
23. The Times of India March 12, 2008
24. The way it was Inside the Pakistan Army Page 293–94 by Brig. (Retd) Z.A. Khan of Pakistan Army.
25. Quoted by former Pakistan High Commissioner to UK Wajid Shamsul Hasan, The Indian of India, Feb 13, 2005.
26. The Hindu July 13, 2004 Misleading Patterns by Ajay Shani.

14

Talibanisation of Pakistan

More than one hundred years ago, in the year 1908 Lord Curzon said in London "if the Central Asia Society exists and is meeting in 50 or 100 years hence, Afghanistan will be as vital and important a question as it is now." In today's context how farsighted analysis was done by Lord Curzon and how vital the issue of Afghanistan has become after almost one hundred years. Had there been no problems in Afghanistan, possibly there would not be Taliban and all the militancy.

Soviet entry into Afghanistan in 1979 gave rise to a number of warlords. One of such a warlord once got two girls abducted for the use of his troops which was objected to by Pakhtoon youngsters. They organised a small group wearing black turbans, stormed warlord's base, rescued both the girls and punished the warlords by hanging him. The story began from this incident and Pakistan took a cue to create 'Taliban' to protect its trade interest which later on turned into further greed and went all out to have Taliban rule all over the country. Taliban were youngsters from Madarsas, to begin with. The invasion of soviets caused annoyance and anger to USA which pressed its CIA to launch operation to oust soviets from Afghanistan CIA, in turn, approached and tasked Pakistan's ISI to do the job for it. Gen. Zia told the CIA in clear cut terms that everything would be decided and done by ISI and they should only keep on pouring dollars and arms. America had no choice but to accede to the dictates of Gen. Zia and the operation began. All powerful spy agency ISI covertly created about 8000 mujahideen, organised, financed, trained armed and supervised them. They fought so well that Soviet occupation forces were forced to withdraw from Afghansitan 1989. During this period a number of Afghans and Pakhtoons escaped their country and sought refuge in camps in Pakistan, growing up with hate, anger and revenge. ISI fuelled this rage with funds form Saudi Arabia and its own sinister ideas of having Pakistan's influence or covert rule in Afghanistan which they later on called "Strategic depth". Saudi Arabia poured funds to prepare Jihadis in Madarsas in order to send them to Afghanistan to fight soviets, spread Islamic fundamentalism and create Pakistan's influence over Afghanistan. Since these Jihadis were students (Talibs) in madarsas, they came to be known as Talib, plural of which is Taliban. Jihad happens to be an important component of Islam and 'Taliban' carry on the Jihad on behalf of radical Islam and certain countries like Pakistan "Jihad is the only way to re-establish and re-enhance the power and the glory of Islam. Each and every Muslim should do his utmost to accomplish this precept, having recourse to force if necessary".[1]

The withdrawal of Soviet forces form Afghanistan created a vacuum for Jihadis for they had nothing to do thereafter. They were accustomed to fighting and now there was none to fight with. In 1989 itself these Jihadis, then sifted their activities in Swat when on June 28, 1989 Sufi Muhammad launched : Tehrik-e-Niaz-e-Shariat-e-Muhammadi (TNSM) outfit and tried to implement Sharia in Swat area replacing tribal customs. This outfits also made efforts towards removal of Benazir Bhutto government in 1994-95 by carrying out low-intensity war which re-emerged in 2006. The Awami National Party (ANP) government did try to negotiate peace with cleric Maulana Sufi Muhammad in vain. Since sufi Muhammad was a radical and fanatic Islamist he dared to declare in 2009 that Islam and democracy can not co-exist and were at cross-purposes. He also desired that women should not be allowed to leave home not even for medical treatment except for Haj. So much so, ultimately the Pakistan Army had to move in to crush TNSM insurgency in May 2009. Three military operations launched earlier op. Rah.-e-Haq I in October 2007, Rah-e-Haq-

II in July 2008 and Rah-e-Haq in January 2009 resulted in fasco. However Sharia Courts have started functioning in Swat valley form March 12, 2009.

After Soviets departure, America almost abandoned these Jihadis and duped Pakistan. Its rulers thought that when they can oust the world power from afghan soil with the help of Pak-controlled Jihadis, they can as well take control of Afghanistan itself and started harbouring the desire to gain 'strategic depth' in Afghanistan so that in case of war with India, Pakistan would retreat, to Afghanistan and then attack Indian forces with more vengeance. Pakistan chose Engineer Gulbaddin Hekmatiyar of Hizbe Islami outfit to have effective hold on Afghanistan. With the fall of Soviet occupation, various existing Islamic militant outfits started vieing with each other to have control of larger areas in Afghanistan. Many militant groups came to Afghansitan to get training in arms and military crafts.

Meanwhile on August 20, 1998 America bombed two Al Qaida training Camps near Khost and Jalalabad in retaliation of bombing of their embassies in African countries. On August 22, 1998 Maulana Fazlur Rehman Khalil denied that Osama bin Laden was involved in terrorism. On August 25, 1998 Khalid said "the US has proved itself to be the world's biggest terrorist by carrying out terrorist attacks on Afghanistan and Sudan. I want to convey to the American leadership that we will take revenge for this attack". Then on September 1, Khalid said "the American's have struck us with Tomahawk cruise Missiles only two places, but we will hit back at them everywhere in the world, whereever we find them. We have started a holy war against the US and they will hardly find free to take shelter beneath it." Thus plotting against America began with more resoluteness.

With the fall of Dr. Nazibullah government in 1992 Kabul fell to the Jihadis. Bitter fighting took place between Gulbaddin Hykmatiyar and President Burhanuddin Rabbani in 1993. Next year Gulbuddin and Dostum attacked Kabul. In

September 1994 various war lords started ruling their specified areas. Some of them used to levy taxes or even loot the goods under transportation to Central Asian Countries. In September 1994 itself Benazir Bhutto and her Interior Minister Major General (Retired) Naseerullah Babar raised a band of 80 young Islamic students drawn from Madarsas of Akora Khattack (Peshawar) and Binori Madarsa (Karachi). They were given training by SSG and MI (not ISI). This band of young Talibs of Kandahar to free a convoy of 30 Pakistani trucks full of export goods on way to CAR countries which was attacked by war lords near kandahar on November 4, 1994. Babar even created an Afghan Trade Development Cell within his interior ministry with the main aim of coordinating efforts to facilitate a trade route to central Asia. But the hidden aim was to provide logistics backing to the Taliban escorting the export goods. The trained Taliban freed the convoy and secured the land route for Pakistani goods passing through Quetta to Kandhahar in Afghanistan and then onwards to Herat to Ashgabad in Turkmenistan in Central Asia. These Talibans were considered to be a great 'strategic assets' for Pakistan by Benazir and her interior minister. Success of this mission led Pakistan to recruit create more and more Taliban drawn mainly from religious seminaries in NWFP and Baluchistan run by Maulana Fazlur Rehman of Jammat-e-ul-ulema Islamic (JUI) and Samiul Haq. another JUI leader, Darul-ul-uloom at Akora Khattack, Binori Madarsa consisting of extremists of Sunni sect. Darul uloom began as Maktab (School) founded by Maulana Muhammad Qasim at Deoband. The first graduate of this school, in 1877 was Mehmood-ul-Hassan who founded Samratul Tarbiyat, a quasimilitary body whose volunteers known as 'Fidayeen' were thought to prepare themselves for armed jehad. Pakistan's permanent enjoy to the UN Mr. Abdullah Hussain Haroon has openly blamed the clerics of Darul uloom at Deoband for being the fountain of extremist mischief in the sub continent.

Taliban captured Kandahar in 1994 and occupied Kabul in September 1996 in which about 2000 regular Pakistan Army men also participated forcing President Burhanuddin Rabbani government flee is Kabul. In 1995 Maj. Gen(R) Naseerullah Babar mixed Afghan and Pakistan Tele networks to facilitate direct dialing to Afghanistan from any place in Pakistan. Mazar-e-Sharif was captured by Taliban in August 1998 with the active help of Pakistan Air Force pilots who did aerial bombarding of Bamyan, Kunduz and Mazar-e-Sheriff air fields. They took off from airfields in Pakistan. Pakistani Jihadis and militants form Jordan, Saudi Arabia and Bangladesh who participated in Afghan war were captured by Northern Alliance in September 1997 and their names with identifying particulars were sent to the united Nations. The Taliban militia consisting of Pakistanis in majority, Myanmarese, Chinese and Arabs who owned allegiance to Harkatul Ansar and Harkatul Jehad wee even paid by Pakistan government. It paid Rs 300 million on June 20, 1996 towards salary of Taliban at Kabul. During 1997-98 Pakistan provided US $ 30 million in aid in the form of food, PoL,, arms and ammunition, defense spare parts and equipment for the Taliban Air Force. Afghanistan virtually came under the influence of Pakistan through Taliban except a portion of the country ruled by Northern Alliance led by Ahmad Shah Masood. Taliban fully an finally captured Kabul in 1999 declaring it Islamic caliphate of Afghanistan headed by Mullah Mohammad Umer. Islamic fundamentalism of worst form grew during this period till 9/11 took pace. Taliban tried to sell king Zahir Shah's car FORD Model To which belonged to Amanullah wali who ruled form 1919 to 1929 and was forced to flee Kabul in 1929, dating from the begining of the centuary (Incidently, it was the first motor car in Afghanistan) to Pakistan in December 2001 but was refused entry at the border. Then Taliban disfiguard and dismanteled statues of Lord Buddha in Bamiyan. All sorts of strange things were done by them. All sofrts of Jihadis has stationed themselves in Afghanistan. Even Al Qaeda was formed there. On August 7, 1998 suicide bomber (Fidayeen) of Al Qaeda targeted the U.S. Embassies in Kenya and Tanzania. 213 people including 12

Americans and 34 local embassy staff died in Nairobi bombing. Another 11 died in the Tanzania blast. America retalidated by bombing two training facilities near khost and Jalalabad of Al Qaeda on August 20, 1998.

Taliban, in Pakistan, also took its shape. Jamaat-e-Islami, Hizbul Mujahideen, Harkat-ul-Mujahideen, Lashkar-e-Toiba, Jamaat-ud-Dawa adopted global Jihad ideology and started operating inside Pakistan and Indian part of Jammu & Kashmir.

After the fall of the Taliban government, a combination of Jehadi outfits was launched in Afghanistan in 2001 known as Brigade 313 created and prompted by Illiash Kashmiris with the help of ISI. Its members were HUJI, JeM, LeT, LeJ.

It had attempted to kill Prime Minister Shaukat Aziz and President Gen. Pervez Musharraf. The first attack in Islamabad was made by militants in Nov. 1995 when a truck load of explosive was rammed into the Embassy of Egypt in Diplomatic Area. On May 8, 2002 in a suicide bomb attack by HUJI outside Karachi Sheraton Hotel eleven french engineers working in a sub marine project were killed. In December 2003 twin attacks on Gen. Pervez Musharraf were made by Amjad Hussain Farooqi, a key operator of HUJI who was killed in Nawab Shah (Sindh) on September 26, 2004. In 2004 Qari Saifullah Akhtar, a close associate of Mullah Muhammad Omar, a graduate of Jamia Binoria (Karachi) was arrested. Because of all this militancy by Pakistan Taliban, Maj. Gen. Safdar Hussain corps commander entered in an agreement with NeK Muhammad of Al Qaeda.

Fazlullah who had links with Baitullah's TTP set up his HQ in Iman Dhehri in 2002. Afghan writer Fazal Wahab was assassinated in Swat for writing against Al Qaeda in 2003. Fazlullah set up over 30 illegal FM Radio stations in 2004 to spread fear among the populace of the valley and attacked schools and Music shops. [An enquiry into a Royal Mess by Kamran Shafi appeared in Deccan Chronicle, Bengalure on June 24, 2009.]

In the year 2007 extremist outfits in FATA formed a joint front under the banner of Tehrik-e-Taliban Pakistan (TTP) led by Baitullah Mehsud and supported by Maulana Fazlullah of Swat. TTP is largely dominated by Pakhtoons who make up almost 15.4% of Pakistan's population. Nearly 70% are Sunni Muslims and 20% are Shias, rest 5% are Hindu and Christians etc. 44.6% are Punjabi, 14.1% Sindhi, 3.5% Baloch 7.5% Mohajir, 8.3% Sairakis and 6.2% others exist in Pakistan. ISI supported Afghan warlord Sirajuddin Haqqani started playing his role in Afghanistan as well as in Pak-Afghan border areas adjoining Khurram. In North Waziristan Dawar tribe raised its own Islamic Insurgent Taliban force. Pro-Taliban legislators Maulana Merajuddin Qureshi and Maulana Malik Wazir made peace agreement with Nek Mohammad in North Waziristan in April 2004 which in known as Shakai Agreement carrying the understanding that if Pak Army troops called off their offensive against Jihadis, they will not attack Pakistan and allow foreign militants live in peace in Pakistan. Soon after say within seven weeks or so the peace agreement fell to pieces and even Nek Muhammad was killed in a missile attack giving filip to Islamic militancy in Waziristan on June 19, 2004 by US Predator drone.

In South Waziristan, Baitullah Mehsud, Jihaadi Commander from Shabikhel sub-tribe cropped up commanding 35 to 40 thousands fighters. He owed loyalty to Mullah Muhammad Qmar. Militant activities rose to such a level that the corps Commander of XI corps Lt. Gen Safdar Hussain had to sign a Peace Agreement with him on February 7, 2005 at Sararogoha near WANA which is known as Sararogoha Peace Deal. Under this deal Bailtullah agreed to oust foreign militants form Waziristan. Baitullah used this peace deal to make his Jihadist outfit stronger and re grouped.

Sararogha peace deal of February 2005 also remained ineffective as Shakai one. On August 30, 2007 Baitullah's forces captured 200 Pakistan Army Soldiers and on September 5, 2007 demanded withdrawal of security forces form Waziristan or else he would kill them. He actually beheaded three soliders during next three days which forced Gen. Musharraf to release 25 hardcore undertrial militants charged with terrorism. On October 18, 2007 a murderous attack was made on Benazir Bhutto in Karachi on her return form abroad. On November 13, 2007 she told journalist Amir Mir (Dy editor of The News Lahore) that Karachi could not have been possible without the 'blessings' of Gen. Pervez Musharraf. Ultimately she was killed on December 27, 2007 in Rawalpindi. Gen. Musharraf blamed the murder on Baitullah Mehsud. But Amir Mir who had interviewed Bẹnazir just before she was assassinated does no accept that Baitullah had killed her. She herself had described the Taliban as "my children". It was she who brought Mullah Omar into the limelight by way of giving him the task of controlling Taliban and bring Kabul into the fold of Islamabad. In the first week of November 2007 these Pak Army soliders were set free by Baitullah Mehsud and started fighting again. All this contributed in Gen. Musharraf's declaration of Emergency although he had other scores also to settle through his proclamation of Emergency Order. He sacked almost 50 judges of Superior Courts including the Chief Justice of Pakistan. Military authorities refused to release 5 of the 25 Mehsud's men which resulted in a serious of suicided attacks against Pak Security forces. In retaliation, government launched military action in South Waziristan. By this time another Taliban leader Nazir Ahmed appeared on the scene. He had declared closeness with Al Qaeda at operation-al level in May 2011 and said "we might have different strategies but at the policy level we are one and the same."

Quote. "well known Pakistani writer Zahid Hussain pointed out the cost to Pakistan during an India Pakistan Afghanistan editor's meet. He said: "I think 2007 was the turning point for Pakistan when almost a dozen militant leaders got together and formed the Tehrik-i-Taliban Pakistan (TTP). This group had a distinctive agenda of enforcing a so called sharia rule in the style of the Afghan Taliban before that the focus of the Pakistani militants had largely been on fighting the US coalition forces across the border. That also changed the perception of how the Taliban and the Afghan Taliban are tied together. It is not only the nexus between the TTP and al-Qaeda, there is also a growing nexus between the banned militant groups and the Taliban, and a new form of al-Qaeda that has emerged. I think probably al Qaeda has taken a different form, which the Americans have failed to understand. The new al-Qaeda is largely Pakistani. Further, there is also distinction between al-Qaeda and the Taliban: TTP provides the recruits or suicide bombers, but al-Qaida largely attracts educated Pakistanis who have no been a part of other militant organisations". Unquote. article by Shri A.S. Pannearselvan "Time to bury the idea of strategic asset" appeared in the HINDU May 10, 2011.

Pakistan Army signed a third Peace Deal with Uthmanzuai wazirs of North Waziristan in the year 2006 to ward off low level attacks by Jihadis. But both the sides were at war within less than a years time. The insurgency re-erupted once again with full force.

Meanwhile an important development took place on December 12, 2007 when a council of 40 senior militants met in Peshawar and formed Tehrik-e-Taliban Pakistan which together commanded around 40,000 militants. Baitullah Mehsud was appointed 'amir' Maulana Hafiz Gul Bahadur as 'naib amir' and Maulana Faqir Muhammad of Bajaur Agency was made Third-in-Command with the sole aim of uniting Pakistani Taliban under the umbrella of TTP to fight the NATO forces in Afghanistan and bordering Pak-Afghanistan. It also admitted to fight Pak security forces who were conducting military operation in FATA and NWFP. The combination closely co-ordinated with Afghan Taliban to carry on Jihad against Pakistan Army and it Intelligence Agencies mainly with suicide bombing techniques/tactics. Baitullah, on December 13, 2007 described the main objective of launching the TTP was to unite the Pakistan Taliban and set up a centralised organization against NATO forces in Afghansitan, besides waging a 'defensive jehad' against the Pakistani forces, carrying out military operation against innocent civilian in the FATA and NWFP.

On January 16, 2008 Baitullah's fighters captured Sararogoha Fort which was under the occupation of Frontier Corps (FC) and demolished it killing some of the FC men and capturing some of them. The confrontation continued for almost a full month till the new Prime Minsiter Yousuf Raza Gilani (after general elections on February 18, 2008) declared his willingness to talk to all those who were prepared to give up arms for the sake of peace. "Let me make it clear that our government will prefer negotiating with the militants as a strategy to counter the rising terrorism and extremism to ensure peace" he said.

Baitullah, on January 28, 2008 in an interview will Al Zazeera said "the main object of the coalition of militants is waging a defensive jehad. The Pakistan Army is deploying its soliders under orders form Bush. The Army is bombarding our houses and fighting with us. Therefore we have formed the coalition to guarantee the safety of civilian and this war which the army launched in tribal areas in an American war. We never feel sad about Pakistan's soldiers death. They are actually implementing the orders of the west and the United States and they are destroying our houses. And I do pray that Allah guide them back to the right path because they are Muslims and this is an Islamic country. But when the Army soliders come to this area to kill us we will definitely be killing them." "Our main aim is to finish Britain and United States and to crush the pride of non-muslins. We pray to god to give us the ability to destroy the white House, New York and London. And we have trust is God. Very soon we will be witnessing Jehands miracles". Musharraf is no more than a follower of his masters. He started attacking mosques, killing women, children and the elderly inside the mosque. (The reference was about the Lal Masjid action by Gen. Musharraf). What was pushing him to do all this was to satisfy George Bush."

Once again an understanding took place between Baitullah Mehsud and the government side on May 15, 2008 on 15 points to enter into yet another Peace Agreement under which Army would withdraw form the area under his Command and, in turn, he would not indulge in provocative acts or violence. Incidently, on May 24, 2008 Baitullah Mehsud addressed reporters in Waziristan where he confessed "yes, we are helping the Taliban in the Jehad against America. We send our people to fight against America and God willing we will evict these Americans from Afghanistan the same way the Russians were driven out from there." The admission of Baitullah that he was sending Taliban to Afghanistan to fight against America, alarmed America and it pressed Pakistan not to sign the proposed 15-point peace deal and stopped further talks with the government on June 1 and threatened on August 6, 2008 Country wide suicide attacks. Baitullah warned "if the military operations continue people will see Sindh and Punjab turn into furnances." Maulana Fazlullah chief of TNSM at Swat added fire to the fuel on August 7 and declared support to Baitullah's plan. Baitullah, true to his promise, got two suicide bombers explode themselves outside Arms Factory at Taxila on August 21 killing 80 people and injuring 150. TTP Spokesman Maulvi Omar accepted the responsibility for the twin attacks stating that it was in revenge for Pak military operation in Bajaur Agency and Swat. On August 25, 2008 the government banned TTP under Anti Terrorism Act. Baitullah Mehsud was killed on August 5, 2009 in drone attacks.

According to a study done by Pakistan Institute for Peace Studies, Islamabad, 5000 youths (between 15 and 22 years) have been trained to become suicide bombers.[2] They were shown videos of the killing of Muslim by non-muslims in Afghanistan and the Middle-East. Their instructors constantly told them that a war was being waged against Islam. The 2007 storming of Lal Masjid was used as a powerful indoctrination tool. Teens are kept in isolation. Only three to four people are allowed to meet them. The theological brainwashing convinces bombers of the virtuousness of their mission. They believe that by taking part in Jihad and killing infidels they will find a place in paradise in the company of 72 virgins. In May 2008 Pakistan Army division that overran Spinkai, a small town in south Waziristan, found a TTP suicide bombing school there. Pakistan Taliban have three (3) secret camps in South and North Waziristan close to the Afghan border to train over 1000 potential suicide bombers. "We have three facilities exclusively for fidayeen (suicide bombers). Each one has more than 350 men being trained in it "said Shakirullah Shakir, a spokes person for the little known Fidayeen-e-Islam group of Taliban while speaking to Journalist in May 2011. Over 300 would be suicide bombers have been arrested in the last two years.

Terrorist forced a 8–year old girl Suhana a student of class III to wear a suicide vest to blow herself at a police chekpost in Balambat area of lower Dir in Khyber Pakhtoon Khwa in the third week of June 2011. However she raised an alarm and surrendered herself to the very police she was supposed to attack. On April 3, 2011 when a 14-year old would be suicide bomber was nabbed before he could detonate himself told the police that around 350 Taliban Sleeper cells were being trained at a mosque in Mir Ali region of North Waziristan Agency.[3] 325 Sleeper cells of Taliban trained at Bannu mosque in Bannu district (NWFP) were asked to lie low and go to safer places and wait for further directions to carry out terror activities in their respective areas.[4]

A theory of 'Good Taliban' and 'bad Taliban' emerged Even former Law Minister of Pakistan Iqbal Haider ridiculed it on March 5, 2009 stating there is only one Taliban that believed in terrorism and wanted to impose its brand of Islam in Pakistan. President Asif Ali Zardari described Taliban as murderous thugs and militants who pose a danger to Pakistan, the US and India. But Z-A Bhutto had said "Islam is the solution the Islamic bomb is the means." However ISI maintained links with all the Taliban, good or bad. Jalaluddin Haqqani based in Miram Shah (North Waziristan) and his son Sirajuddin Haqqani were Taliban Mujahideen who were very closely linked with ISI. Islamisation of the country was the main aim that began with Gen. Zia-ul-Haq. It continues with the help of Taliban now. Even Pakistan Supreme Court banned the charging of interest on loans deciding it was not Islamic—a step towards Islamisation. Both Islamaisation and Talbanisation is going on in Pakistan at a fast speed. Pakistan can not see other relgious exist in that country what to talk of their growing. They want only Sunnis to exist and inhabit Pakistan. It is deadly against Christians, Jews, Hindus and even Shias. It has gone to the extent of demolishing 'Shamshan Ghat (cremation ground) in Rawalpindi on July 19, 2010 used by Hindus and Sikhs to perform last rites. Pervez hoodbhoy, a prominent Pakistani Scholar says "Islamisation of Pakistan's school began in 1976 when an Act of Parliament required all government and private schools (except those teaching the British O-levels from Grade 9) to follow a curriculum for Grade 5 Social studies class that includes topics. Such as "Acknowledge and identify forces that may be working against Pakistan," "make speeches on Jehad" and "Indian's evil designs against Pakistan."

At the initial stages of Gen. Pervez Musharraf's rule, on January 12, 2002, he of course outwardly, in a TV broadcast, denounced religious extremism, pledged to reform Islamic schools in Pakistan, announced a formal ban on five(5) Jihadi groups." Kashmir runs in our blood" he said and pledged to continue moral, political and diplomatic support for Kashmir's liberation but he for the first time condemned the attack on Indian Parliament as a 'terrorist attack' and said no organisation will be allowed to indulge in terrorism in the name of Kashmir.

Afghan Taliban militants and Pakistani Taliban militants are aiding each other and working in concert. On June 16, 2011, two hundred Afghan Taliban aided by Pakistan Taliban stormed and targeted Mamoond village in Bajour (near the border with Kunar Province of Afghanistan) killing 5 person. It the month of April 2011 also they had made similar incursions in Shalotal area of upper Dir district in Khyber

Pakhtoonkhwa province killing 27 security personnel and 7 civilians.

Not only that, Taliban had been mounting concerted attacks on nuclear sites of Pakistan :–

1. November 2, 2007 : Eight Pakistan Air Force Officers were killed in a suicide attack on Sargodha Air base the largest of Pakistans Air bases which also stores M–11 nuclear missiles.
2. August 21, 2008 : Pakistans Ordnance Factory, War was attacked by twin suicide bombs killing 70 people in one of ever deadliest attacks on a military site. Wah also stores nuclear weapons.
3. October 10, 2009 : Ten Pakistan Taliban militants wearing army uniform attacked the General Head Quarters in Rawalpindi killing six (6) army personnel including a Brigadier and a Lt. Col.
4. October 24, 2009 : Eight people were killed in a suicide attack on the Pakistan Air Weapons Complex Kamra. It also stores Air-dropped nuclear weapons.
5. May 24, 2011 : Militant Gunmen over ran Mehran Naval Air base and destroyed two P3C Orion (American made) in a siege lasting 17 hours. Mehran and Masroor also are suspected to store some nuclear weapons.

So much so, even a Radical Pakistans Army Brigadiel Alikyeda any facing court martial was repoted to here planned b bomjb GHQ uith F-16 jet during a copence of top Conmarders, according to a PTI Report.

In Haripur, Pakistan has stored some of its nuclear weapons and Taliban had an eye on them. After Mehran, Head of Tehreek-e-Taliban Pakistan (TTP) in South Waziristan, had stated that they would carry out nine (9) more attacks on key installations in Pakistan to avenge the killing of Osama bin Laden on May 2, 2011 in Abbottabad by Americans. The Deputy Chief of the Pakistani Navy and an Air Vice Marshal told the Standing Committee on Defence of the National Assembly that the finding of an internal enquiry committee indicate that the terrorist attack in which 10 security personnel were killed and two maritime surveillance aircraft destroyed was carried out by 'inside support'.

6. July 11, 2011 : Three blasts ripped through a facility linked close Pakistans nuclear programme Pak Army arms depot at SIHALA located 20 km away form Rawalpindi.

On the question of safety of nuclear weapons in Pakistan, consider what Pervez a Hoodboy, a Ph. D. form MIT who teaches nuclear physics in Islamabad's government run Qasid-e-Azam university said in an interview to the Indian Express newspaper in Islamabad. Quote "It does not matter whether Pakistans chief of army staff Ashfaq Parvez Kayani wears on the Quran that he will make sure that nuclear weapons will be safe. The question is does he have the power to do that ? 'It seems to me that the Pakistan Army is playing with fire. It knows that these nuclear weapons are ultimately in the hands of their own people and their own people have been effected by decades of radicalisation. They may claim that they have personnel reliability tests, but I do not believe that answering questions on a form may indicate his intentions. Now Rehman Malik (Pakistan's Interior Minsiter) must be a genius to have come up with the figure of 200 per cent. How he arrives at that we have no idea but that is what the Pakistan military wants us to believe and to unquestionably accept that the nuclear weapons have been provided security in Pakistan. Which personally I do not believe. 'So to come up with wild figures, I do not beleive there is source of any reassurance to the people of Pakistan or to the thinking people. We have seen the infiltration of radicals into the ranks of the Army. Very recently, a brigadier and four majors have been arrested. And our brigadiers are in charge of missile regiments too. So where things could go, I do not know. 'Ultimately, it is the people who handle the nuclear weapons, just as the people are responsible for the defence of the Army, Air Force and Navy bases. 'So the worry that something similar may happen with the nuclear weapons crosses everybodys mind. Therefore, even if the strategic plans division says everthing is fine, that does not reassue every body. 'Pakistan is building as many nuclear weapons as it can. They have very little utility they provide a cover under which (there is) yet another spurt of nuclear weapons production." unquote.[6] Brigadier Ali Khan serving in Regulation Directorate of the General Headquarters for two years was ordered by chief of Army staff kayani to be detained for his links with Islamic militants of Hizb-ut-Tehrir. He had no teturned home since June 21 2011 indicating his possible arrest. Shortly after the US raid that killed Osama bin Laden in Abbotabed on May 2 (2011), the Hiz-ut-Tehrir distributed pamphlets in military cantonments that called on army officers to establish an Islamic Caliphate.[7]

However, the nuclear scientist of Pakistan A.Q. Khan states that the location of nuclear arsenals in Pakistan is known to a few persons. They are not stored in one place. The weapons are lying in tunnels and safe houses where no one can access them, except very few relevant people.

A Pakistani journalist, Salim Sehzad (40) who wrote articles over the last several years that illuminated the relationship between the militants and the military was abducted from the capital (Islamabad) (on May 29, 2011) three days after the publication of his article that said the al Qaida was responsible for an audacious 16–hour commando attack on Pakistans main Naval base in Karachi on May 22, 2011. The attack was a reprisal for the Navy's arresting upto 10 naval personnel who had belonged to a al Qaida cell, shehzad said. The article published by Asia Times Online, detailed how the attackers were guided by maps and logical information provided from personnel inside the base. Shehzad gave details of an October 17 meeting at ISI Headquarters where tow senior officials in the press section wanted to discuss an article he had written about the release of an interrogated Afghan Taliban Commander Abdul Ghani Baradar. The discussion Salim Shehzad had with Rear Admiral Adnan Nazir, Head of press section of ISI led Shehzad to understand and believe that it was veiled death threat which in turn, he immediately after the meeting conveyed to three eminent journalists of Pakistan stating that if any harm comes to him in the form of his death, ISI should be blamed for it. A senior US Official also said there was enough other intelligence and indicators immediately after Shehzad's death for the Americans to conclude that ISI had ordered him killed. Shehzad was the 37th journalist killed in Pakistan since 9/11 attacks, according to the Committee to protect journalists.

(The Hindu of July 6, 2011 article by Eric Schmidt and Jane Ferlez "ISI tied to slaying of journalist")

The other ISI officer of the Press section was commodore Khalid Pervez, Deputy to ISI media using Director General Rear Admiral Adnan Nazir.

Sunday Mirror had reported that it was Mullah Barador who leaked the where bouts of al Qaida chief Osama bin Laden to US investigators. There was yet another report that Pakistani Doctor helped the Americans crackdown Osama bin Laden before he was killed in May 2011. The Doctor was taken into custody by ISI and CIA was trying to negotiate his release when the exposure about ISI undercover official Muhammed Tasleem an attache in Pakistani Mission in New York in posing and taking himself as FBI agent was noticed and FBI took action against him. Tasleem's job was to keep a watch on Pakistani diaspore in the US and he was quietly posted out of US when FBI noticed his activities. FBI had arrested Ghulam Nabi Fai Chairman of Kashmir American Council on July 19, 2011 for being ISI man ISI had paid millions to influence US and Kashmir. Fai got turo yeas's jail for illegally morling for 151. The routenee of imprieonment was announced on march 30, 2012 by judse liam O'grady of a court in Alexandria (Virsinia) USA.

Attermath of ObL's death on May 2, 2011

March 13, 2011	:	Frontier Constabulary (FC) training centre at Shabqadar near Peshawar attacked killing 80 persons.
May 16	:	Militants killed 2 persons accused of spying for US in Dattakhel region of North Waziristan.
May 16	:	A Saudi consular officer shot dead by 4 motor cycle born militants in Karachi.
May 18	:	A police checkpost attacked in Peshawar by 100 militants in which to security personnel and 20 militants were killed.
May 21	:	NATO Oil Tanker blown up in Landi Kotal (Khyber). 15 persons killed
May 22–23	:	Mehran Naval Base attacked by militants. The News (Pakistani daily) reported on May 31, 2011 that a former Pakistan Navy Commando Kamran Ahmed had been arrested in the DNS Mehran case alongwith his brother Zaman Ahmed and three friends for allegedly providing maps of the base to the attackers. Kamran was also picked up by the Agencies after the 2008 attack on the Naval was college in Lahore (The Indian Express June 4, 2011)

It is indeed strange that inspite of Taliban militant's attack on Pakistani targets, ISI is still close with them and had been tipping them off about any intelligence passed on by the US to ISI for action against Taliban.

Because of the Taliban Terror threat, Pakistan Navy moved any its main battle ships form Karachi to Ormara in Baluchistan as a 'precautionary measure'. The Commando style gun and rocket propelled grenade attacks on Mehran on May 22, 2011 that resulted in the destruction of two P3C ORION airplanes and the killing of to security personnel really shook the Pak Navy. Commodore Raja Tahir, the former Commader of PNS Mehran airbase, the naval aviation Commander and the security officer of the airbase are to face court martial according to the internal inquiry conducted by Rear Admiral Tehsinullah Khan.[9]

Pakistan Army tipped off militants about bomb building factories in tribal areas

Action plan on Osama Bin Ladens capture or death was kept totally secret form Pak forces yet to test Pak's sincerity once again, US provided information to Pak force on two (2) more bomb making sites by militants for attacking and destroying them. US kept an eye on these Camps and movements therein by their unmanned drones. But to their surprise they found militants moving away within 24 hours taking any weapon or bomb making material with them just as militant had done the first two times. A total of four (4) bomb making sites the US shares with Pakistan only to have the terrorist suspects flee before military arrived. (The Indian Express June 20, 2011) Pakistan Taliban Dy leader Wali-ur-Rehman, in a video tape aired on Al Arabia, threatened attacks against US and NATO Countries. Fazal Saeed Haqqani, a senior Commander of Pakistan Taliban in the Khurram Tribal area said on June 27, 2011 that he is splitting from the group and forming his own "Tehrik-e-Taliban Islami" to protest attacks on civilian in suicide attacks and bomb blasts in mosques and to focus on fighting NATO troops in Afghanistan. Pakistan Taliban are different than Tehrik-e-Taliban Pakistan (TTP). Hours after the reports of split, gunmen in a car killed Taliban Commander Shakirullah Sahkir near Mehram Shah, who helped train over 1000 suicide bombers in North Waziristan.[10] TTP is led by Hakmullah Mehsud.

Fazal Said parted with 500 men. He said on June 28 "we abhor killing innocent people though suicide attacks and bomb blasts, attacks on our own army and destruction of social infrastructure. The new organisation will not attack our own security forces" and condemned "suicide attacks at mosques markets and other civilian targets."

But Tehrik-e-Taliban Pakistan (TTP) leader Maulana Faquir Mohammd says his group would launch more large-scale attacks against Pakistani security forces like PNS Mehran and border checkposts etc. He also stated that "India is ruled by non-muslims and they have always consigned India an enemy country".

US is working towards the goal of separating Al Qaida from Taliban on the line of thinking that Al Qaida and Taliban belong to two different fields of action. Al Qaida in operating globally whereas Taliban are engaged to take control of Afghanistan to a considerable extent of Pakistan and then of course carry on militancy in Indian part of Jammu & Kashmir. But US mainly concerned about Talibans Afghan Centric activities for it has to withdraw its forces and that of NATO by 2014. To meet this end CIA has even started to have direct links with various militant outfits in Pakistan. United Nations Security council has agreed to remove Taliban from the purview of UNSE resolution 1267 that defines the Al Qaida and Taliban sanctions regime. Afghanistan government is also working on reconciliation policy towards the Taliban.

NATO forces began exit of all foregin forces on July 17, 2011 form Afghanistan which is to be completed by the end of the year 2014. There are around 1, 50,000 foreign troops in Afghanistan and nearly 1, 00,000 of it are from United States of American itself. Taliban militancy killed President Karzai's half brother on July 12 in Kandahar. Afghan Taliban sensed victory and July 18 showed a video showing fighters executing 16 Pakistani tribal policemen in a hail of gunfire. One June 1, 2011 hundred Taliban fighters had entered Pakistan upper Dir from Eastern Kunar province of Afghanistan. Pakistan Army spokesman Maj. Gen. Athar-Abase stated that the video is genuine and the Taliban fighters who executed the Policemen come form SWAT Valley.

On February 20, 2003 Musharraf Ali Mir, Air Force Chief of Pakistan died in Air Crash. In 1996 he had entered into pact with leader Abu Zubaya promising him supply of arms. Three Saudi Prince associated with Mirs deal in 1996 with Al Qaida died in similar mysterious circumstances shortly thereafter. Both Mushaf Ali Mir and all the three Saudi Princes were responsible for increased influence of Al Qaida in Pakistan and Saudi Arabia which was not liked by Gen. Musharraf and Saudi Monarch.

An interesting write up by Ms. Meeran Karim of Lahore notes: Quote "A majority of Pakistan's 180 million people follow the Barelivi School of Islamic jurisprudence. Founded by Ahmed Raza Khan Fazil-e-Barelivi. Its followers defended the supposedly unorthodox beliefs and practices of South Asia's Muslims, greatly influenced by regions sufi saints, against the more conservative school of thought. Many sufi practices are also followed by Barelvis, including qawwalis and large ceremonial processions outside the shrines of their leaders. Consequently, this version of Islam popular amongst Pakistanis and their south Asian counterparts is known to be distinct from the highly orthodox Wahabi School followed most notably in monarchical Saudi Arabia. However, this may not be the case anymore. Metal detectors and government sponsored security guards now inhibit the celebratory atmosphere of increasingly vulnerable Sufi Shrines. Security Checkpoints decorate Lahores walled city. Beggars Shiver in fear, as their hardened hands reach out for the food distributed to devotees at shrines an a daily basis. Musical performers who previously attracted thousands, now play to the pleasure of installed security cameras. CD-Shops carrying qawwali music sung by the countrys leading artists are now the target of unabashed violence. According to one estimate, more than 70 suicide blasts have left hundreds of followers injured dead since 2005 in the country. Tehrik-i-Taliban, the Pakistani branch of the Taliban, has come out with a vengeance against Pakistan's progressive Politicians too, eager to gain votes for upcoming elections, are cutting off their personal ties with all main testations of subcontinental culture. And with this, Pakistans secularist brigade is increasingly under siege, to the disappointment of many of its peace loving citizens. unquote.[11]

Nexus of ISI with Terror Groups

Heavily dominated by Military officers, headed by a Lt. Gen. of Pakistan Army, with outdated and dangerous mindset, most of them with Islamic fundamentalist bent of mind, they consider themselves as President's true guardians and savior-faire. ISI, a complex outfits with mythic reputation controls everything in Pakistan from a fly to an ant, form human rights to their inhuman behaviour in carrying out hundreds of disappearances, particularly in Baluchistan, managing and rigging election, taking to task those Pakistanis who directly or indirectly want and support peace and good relations with India. Arrogant because of huge accumulated American dollars and Chinese friendship, ISI controls niddle to thread. Anti India stance that was adopted by ISI after creation of Pakistan, continues with more vehemence and vengeance with each passing day. The Civilian leadership exists and works under the directions of ISI. After developing nuclear weapons, ISI had become more arrogant. It can do anything in Pakistan none can stop it no law, no parliament. ISI maintains links with Islamic militants both religious and radicals. It started growing from Gen. Zia's time when Americans wanted Pakistan to fight their war to oust Russians from Afghanistan and poured dollars billions and billions Since then ISI grew and grew. So much so even with Osama bin

Laden it maintained links for 25 long years till his death on May 2, 2011 in Abbottabad and kept on denying any knowledge of his whereabouts to America. It is a pastmaster of creating intrigues, lies, producing religious militants, double speak and double dealing, creating unrest world over, begging dollars from America for its survival and at the same time stabbing it at its back. It is strange of American that inspite of reports of their CIA on all these aspects of ISI, America relied on ISI and kept on giving American aid, arms, and F–16s etc. Shuan Gregory of Pakistan Security Research unit wrote in his Research Paper on January 24, 2008 "the ISI and the war on terrorism" "it was the ISI that facilitated Ladens initial meetings with the Taliban which were successful enough to see him move to Kandahar as the winter of 1996 closed in. Under the protection of the ISI and the Taliban leader began to expand the activities of al-Qaida for global Jehad. Focussed on its regional agenda Kashmir, the support of the Taliban and a growing determination to sate a strong hand in the it rich southern caucus the ISI collided with Bin Laden to establish further training camps inside Afghanistan and to faciliate the spread of Ladens influence in existing camps on both the sides of the border, in order to host, indoctrinate and train foreign fighters for waging Jehad in both Jammu and Kashmir and Afghanistan." Hussain Haqqani Pakistan's Ambassador to Washington wrote in one of his article in 2007 instead of just protecting Pakistan from enemies identified by a lawful government, which is than an intelligence or security service is supposed to do the ISI defines what is or is not good for Pakistan. "The ISI is convinced that India is Paksitan's eternal enemy, Kashmir can be won by weakening Indian resolve to hold on to it through unconventional warfare and Afghanistan should be the backyard of Pakistan in every way. Instead of implementing the state policy, the ISI virtually makes it own policy for the states. Historically, intelligence agencies that have grown so large, so powerful and so unaccountable, as the ISI, eventually causes problems for the state they control. Instead of ISI controlling Pakistan, the

Pakistani should be controlling the ISI. Otherwise, convert terrorist operations abroad will continue to undermine the Pakistani democracy and keep the country engaged in conflicts with Afghanistan and India".

The Researcher Shaun Gregory maintains that the ISI manipulates intelligence for it own internal and geo political reasons and misdirects American and British Intelligence.[12]

All these militant outfits religious or radical are creation of ISI. They have raised them, trained them, financed them and ultimately tasked them to create unrest in India, Afghanistan and other countries of the world including America and UK. If Pakistan is not contained and saddled today, tomorrow it would be very late.

Of India, Pakistan is so concerned that once Tariq Fatemi, a former Pakistani envoy to US said "if American walks away (from Afghansitan), Pakistan is very worried that it will have India on it eastern border and India on its western border." in Afghanistan".

But the Taliban (TTP and others) including Al Qaieda elements are enraged with Pakistan Army because in their estimation they (Pakistan Army) has sided with US in its "war on terror and under its instruction/directions it is mounting operation against them in Waziristan and other FATA areas.

Lal Masjid, Islamabad Episode (July 687, 2007)

Fast growing religious extremism was openly sthibited when Maulana Abdul Rashid Ghazi, a fanatic cleric of Red Mosque (Lal Masjid) in Islamabad threw a direct challenge to the government of Gen. Pervez Musharraf. The General was compelled to launch 'operation silence' against Ghazi's misdeeds and misadventures. It all started with the demolition of quite a few illegally constructed mosque by Capital Development Authority (CDA) in Islamabad. Lal Masjid clerics demanded their restoration to which the government agreed. Realising that the government is amenable and agreeable to their demands, the clerics raised new demands like imposition of sharia all over Pakistan and started indulging in acts of grave provocation, kidnapping policemen, occupying public library building and issuing religious decrees etc. in which both male and female occupants of Jamia Hafsa (for girls) and Jamia Fareedia (for boys) actively indulged and participated. Lal Masjid had been utilised to vomit Venom against India on Kashmir issue and played a significant role in recruiting militants to fight Russia in Afghanistan during 1979–1989. On June 22, 2007 militants inhabitants of Lal Masjid abducted some chinese national is engaged in acupuncture profession. Beijing asked Gen. Musharraf to take quick and stern action against the abductors. Compelled by such a demand from Beijing, Gen. Musharraf decided to launch operation silence which took thirty (30) hours of 111 Brigade of Pakistan Army to destroy the underground bunkers inside Lal Masjid compound on July 3, 2007 leaving 10 people dead and 150 injured, on July 4, Maulana Abdul Aziz was caught by Army while trying to escape wearing 'Burqa'. He had threatened action by a Brigade of militants present inside Lal Masjid. In the gun battle that ensued on July 6 and 7, about 80 people including 10 SSG Commandos died. Another Cleric Maulana Abdul Rashid Ghazi was killed on July 10 after he refused to surrender. His father Maulana Abdul Rashid Ghazi was killed on July 10 after he refused to surrender. His father Maulana Abdullah had personal relations and special ties with Osama bin Laden. He was also close to Lashkar-e-Jhangi and Sipah-e-Sahaba Pakistan. Lal Masjid was being used as the recruitment Centre of the Harkat-ul-Mujahideen.

The Mosque was re-opened on July 27, 2007 under a new Maulana. This episode, infact, increased and hastened the Talibanisation of Pakistan and made Taliban angry with the Islamabad government. About 45 suicide attacks took place after Lal Masjid action. On November 4, 2007 a bus carrying ISI personnel was attacked killing 20 of them. A second attack on them was mounted on November 24 killing 15 personnel.

February 25, 2008 : Lt. Gen Mushtaq Baig Director

		General of AMC was killed in Rawalpindi in a suicide attack.
March	4	: Twin Suicide attack on Naval war college in Lahore killed 10 people.
March	11	: Federal Investigation Agency (FIA)'s provincial Head Quarter was attacked billing 30 people using human bomb.
March	15	: Terrorist targeted a restaurant in Islamabad.
July	6	: 20 people were killed by a suicide bomber in Melody market in Islamabad on the 1st anniversary of Lal Masjid Operation.
August	22	: Two human bombs exploded outside wah Ordnance Factory.
September	20	: an explosive laden truck was rammed into main entrance of Marriott Hotel in Islamabad killing 80 people and injuring over 200.

In January 2002 Gen Musharraf has promised certain measure to be taken to tackle terrorism including bringing the madarsas into the main stream so that their misuse for preaching political and religious intolerance could be stopped. This statement was issued in the wake of 9/11 attack in New York and Dec. 13, 2001 attack on India Parliament. In January 2004, International crisis Group (ICG) in its report "unfulfilled promises". Pakistans failure to tackle Extremism" stated Gen. Musharraf promise to derive extremium away from Madersas remains unfulfilled today, two years after he had promised his sweeping reforms, the Jehadi madarsa remain the key breeding grounds for radical Islamist ideology and the recruitment centre for terrorist Jehadi networks. The government inaction continues to pose a serious threat to domestic, regional and international security. Gen Musharraf's priority has never been eradicating Islamic extremism but rather the legitimisation and consolidation of his dictatorial rule. And for that he depends on the religious rights. The failure to curb rising extremism in Pakistan stems directly for the military governments own unwillingness to act against its political allies among the religious groups. Having co-opted the religious parties to gain constitutional cover for his military rule. Musharraf is highly reliant on the religious right for his regime's survival. It the US and others continue to restrict their pressure on Musharraf of verbal warnings, the rise of extremism in Pakistan will continue unchecked." And events took place exactly as assessed by ICG. On March 28, 2007 ICG released yet another report "Religious Pakistan: Karachi's Madarsas and Violet Extremism "by which they criticised the sectarian groups being supported by the network of madarsas. Even July 2005 suicide attacks on London by British born Islamist of Pakistan origin including Shehzad Tanweer and Siddique Khan had met with Osama Nazir of JeM at a small madarsa known as Jamia Fatahul Raheem in Faisalabad. It seems they were trained there in use of explosives. Osama Nazir was nabbed from the said madarsa in Faisalabad in November 2004.

ISI's 'S' wing which directs intelligence operations in Afghanistan has been supporting Mullah Muhammad Omar and his Quetha based Taliban followers. Engineer Gulbuddin Hekmatyars militant network based in Afghanistan itself and Jalaluddin Haqqanis group are important Jihadi outfits on which ISI/Pakistan depends and considers them as strategic assets for Pakistan to gain strategic depth in Afghanistan. In any event and at any cost Pakistan would not let Afghanistan slip out of its full and complete control.

The religious Islamic extremists to fight in India are chosen by ISI from various militant outfits depending upon the type of militant activity to be undertaken amongst whom is LeT and JeM. These religious militants from the very begining are taught in madarsas in the following manner:– Alif for Allah, 'Bay' for Bandook (Gun), 'Tay' for Takrao (Collusion), 'Jay' for Jehad, 'Khay' for Khanjer (dagger) and that India is their enemy Number 1.

Even Chinese were trained in Pakistani Jihadi Training Camps. Mr. Praveen Swami in his article "Begins increasing Jihadist challenge" which appearsed in the HINDU of August 4, 2011. Writes quote in 2008 startting evidence emerged during the trial of Malika el-Around the life of the assassin of the Anti Taliban Afghan warlord Ahmad Shah Masood and her new husband, Moez Garsallaoui-In 2008 in proceedings in a Belgian Court, a witness identified, for legal reasons, only by the initials 'wo'–stated that the largest group of Jihadists in Pakistan's north west was form China "unquote.

November 26, 2008 Mumbai episode

ISI through LeT hand picked Ten–member terror squad out of a team of 32 trainees to do the 26/11 mayhem in Mumbai which continued for two-days i.e. on Nov. 26 and 27, 2008. 10 member team was divided into 5 groups consisting of two each. They were equipped with 8 grenades, 1 AK-47 Assault Rifle, 200 Cart ridges two magazines and one cell phone and dispatched to India via Karachi and Arabian sea. Zakiur Rehman Lakhvi was overall operation incharge 10-member team consisted of :–

1. Ismail Khan He was the leader. Hails form Dera Ismail Khan in NWFP, Pakistan
2. Ajmal Amir Kasab He is from Okara, Pakistan He alongwith Ismall Khan formed one team and attacked CST. Metro junction, Nariman point, Girgaum Chowpatty. He was the only militant who was caught alive out of the whole lot of 10 Pakistani terrorists.
3. Abdul Rehman from Multan, Pakistan
4. Abu Ali form Okara, Pakistan
5. Abu Shoaib from Sialkot, Pakistan

6. Abu Umer from Faisalabad, Pakistan
7. Abdul Rehman from Multan Pakistan
8. Fahad Ullah from Okara, Pakistan (Both of them i.e. Sr. no. 7 and 8 were attackers of Trident Hotel,) Mumbai)
9. Abu Aksha from Multan, Pakistan
10. Abu Umar from Faisalabad, Pakistan (Both of them attacked Nariman House, Mumbai).

LeT trained them before assigning them to do the Mumbai terror. They were trained for twenty one days basic training course known as 'Daur-e-Aam'. Kasab and others were trained in the art of swimming and acclimatised to the lite at sea. Thereafter they under went another 3–months training course known as 'Daour-e-Khas' which trained them in specialization in dismanting and re assembling assault ritles, using maps including GPS system. They were also imparted training in raids, ambushes, escape to the jungle, and merge into the crowd after carrying out attack. Most of them were trained in river crossing and handling of explosives which is known as 'Baitul Rizwan'. They were also taught Intelligence collection methods, handling of those who impart the intelligence to them and sabotage. This training is known as 'Daur-e-Ribat'.

The 10–member terrorist squad left Karachi on November 23, 2008. They wee originally scheduled to sail for Mumbai on September 27. They hijacked Gujarat registered boat MV Kuber after being dropped from the Pakistani vessel Al Hussaini and sailed towards Mumbai. A 'Thuraya' satellite phone was later on found in MV Kuber from which calls were made to Lahore and Karachi in Pakistan as also to Jalalabad in Afghanistan. All of them were trained by retired military commandos of Pakistan Army. Chairman US Joint Chief of staff admiral Mike Mullen flew to Islamabad and told Pakistani officers on December 3, 2008 that Washington has enough evidence to establish a Pakistani hand in 26/11 attack in Mumbai.

Pakistan repeatedly denied that Ajmal Kasab hails from Pakistan and refused to accept the evidence even. It was Dawn TV network that quoted a high ranking official had declared "sadly it has been established that Kasab is a Pakistani citizen. He is the son of Amir Kasab and Mrs. Noor Illahi of Faridkot." The high official, though not named by Dawn TV, was Pakistan National Security Advisor Mehmud Ali Durrani who was soon after sacked by Prime Minsiter Yusuf Gilani for not keeping him on board before admitting the Pakistani nationality of Ajmal Kasab. Jasab. Jamaat-ul-Dawas (JuD) urdu language mouthpiece "Ghazva" termed the Mumbai attack "A historic victory". It said "it was a historic victory for the Muslim warriors who had actually avenged the grave atrocities being committed by the Indian establishment against Muslim minority in several parts of India and in the state of Jammu & Kashmir".

Mumbai mayhern left 126 people 98 civilians, 14 policemen and 14 foreigners dead and 327 injured.

Mounting concrete evidence came to hand regarding active involvement of ISI in planning, generating, training financing and executing the Mumbai strike. Revelation to this effect also came, apart from quite independent of the confession of Ajmal Kasab form co-conspirators of 26/11 namely Tahawwar Hussain Rana, a Pakistani-Canadian and David coleman Headley a ka Dawood Gilani. Rana told the US District Court that he worked on behalf of Pakistans ISI and that the ISI had the authority to act in India to protect Pakistan's interests and that he carried out espionage for the ISI in Mumbai. Rana's trial in Illinois began on May 16, 2011 attacks. In June 2010 Headly told the National Investigation Agency (NIA) that 26/11 attacks were possible only with the "complete support" of the ISI that the major Lashkar operation was supervised by the ISI and his reconnaissance of five targets made the Mumbai operation successful. He had set up an Immigration service office in Mumbai under the name of First world immigration Services for which money was provided by Major Iqbal of ISI who also handled him (Headley) alongwith Major Samir Ali. Rana owned an immigration business in Chicago and it provided a perfect cover to him for his Mumbai operation. He also revealed that after the attack was over, ISI chief Lt. Gen. Shuja Pasha had met Lakhvi to discuss the operation. He had made a total of 9 trips to India since 2006 and kept on returning to Pakistan to brief senior LeT Operatives each time. Five days before 26/11 also Headley flew to Bombay. He was arrested by FBI on October 3, 2009. The Court case in New York which was filed last November by the kin of Rabbi Gavriel Noah Holtzberg and his wife Rivka who have been killed by the terrorists at Nariman House during the attacks, he summoned ISI chief Shuja Pasha and LeT chief hatiz saeed. The Court had also summoned former ISI chief Lt. Gen. Nadeem Taj, Major Iqbal, Major Ali and Azam Cheema of LeT. In Mumbai, Headly did recce of the targets, posed as tourist and used fishing boats. Hafiz Mohammed Saeed of the University of Engineering and Technology, Lahore established Markaz-al-Dawa-wal-Irshad in 1986 to fight soviets in Afghanistan. Lashkar-e-Toiba is its military wing whose over all incharge in Zakiur Rehman Lakhiv. LeT is secretive and selective being indirectly under control of ISI. It is mainly India-centric but of late it has started doing militant activities in other countries as well the directions of ISI. In order to destroy India, Pakistan would even destory itself. Under Zakir-ur-Rehman, the following important functionaries work :–

(*i*) HM Ashraf (Caters to financial needs and raises funds)

(*ii*) Abual Kama (oversees all Kashmir operations on behalf of ISI)

(*iii*) Azam Cheema (Launching Commander for infiltrating militants in India)

(*iv*) MMA Bahazir (LeT propoganda master mind)

(*v*) Abu Muzammer (Controls operation in India)

Tahawwur Hussain Rana, a Chicago businessman accused

of providing financial and logistical support to 26/11 Mahen in Mumbai was put to trial and David coleman Headley was main witness.

Major (Retd) Haroon Rasheed alias Abu Khattab, sought retirement from army in 2003 and joined LeT became advisor to Lakhvi and also served as trainer and made improvised mortars. He was involved in kidnap of Karachi–based filmmaker Satish Anand (uncle of actress Juhi Chawala) in late 2008. He was freed after taking a ransom of Rs. 16 million. Rasheed had also killed Maj. Gen. (Retd) Amir Faisal Alivi a former chief of SSG and brother-in-law of V.S. Naipaul, author, on November 18, 2008, according of media reports. Alvi was killed because earlier he commanded operations against Taliban/Al Qaida.

MARKAT-UL-ANSAR (HJA) (Movement of Friends)

As part of Pakistan's Jihadi net work to fight Russians in Afghanistan, Jamiat ulema-e-Islam (JUI) and Tableeghi Jammat (TJ) had established Harkat ul Jihad-e-Islami (HUJI) in 1980 whose founding father was Maulana Irshad Ahmed. It split in 1985. One group retaining its original name of HUJI and the other adopting the name of Harkat-ul-Ansar founded by Maulana Fazlur Rehman Khalil in 1993. He was signatory to the Osama bin Ladens 'fatwa' declaring war against the United States of America. HUJI merged in Harkat-ul-Ansar in October 1993. HUJI and HUA were designated as Foreign Terroist Organisation in October 1997. Harkat ul Ansar has turned into Harkatul Mujahideen (HUM) in 1997 and ultimately became Jamiatul Ansar (JUA) after Gen. Pervez Musharraf banned HUM in January 15 2002.

It represents Deobandi school of Islamic Though/sect. HUJI offered Co operation with Afghan Jihadi groups led by Yunus Khalis of Hizab-e-Islamic On February 25, 1980 Pak Jihadis went to Afghanistan to join Jihad. On June 25, 1985 Maulana Irshad Ahmed died during Afghan Jihad itself and a power struggle ensured soon after. Maulana Fazlur Rehman

Khalil formed Harkat ul Mujahideen (HUM) after splitting with Qari Saifullah Akhtar who remained with HUJI. Fazlur Rehman Khalil took active part in Kargil operation at the prompting of Lt Gen Mohammad Aziz Khan of Pakistan Army After withdrawal of Soviet troops from Afghanistan HUM militants went to Kashmir in 1991 under Sajjad Shahids leadership and started operating in Baramula, Poonch and Anantnag.

On October 13, 1993 Harkatul Jehadul Islami, Harkat ul Mujahideen and Jamiatul Mujahideen merged resulting in formation of a new outfit known as Harkatul Ansar. In April 1994 Al Farhan surfaced in Kashmir. HUA's amir became Maulana Fazlur Rehman Khalil. On August 22, 1998 he declared that ObL was not indulging in terrorism and warned USA on September 1, 1998 that "the Americans have struck us with Tomhawak Cruise Missiles at only two places, but we will hit back at them every where in the world wherever we find them. We have started a holy war against the US and they will hardly find a tree to take shelter beneath it." On August 25, 1998 Khalid declared that only nine HUM members died in three camps in the US attacks.

HUM fights for the global supremacy of Islam, liberate areas with a muslim majority, protect muslims in non-muslim areas. With the aim to liberate Kashmir it also operates from Bengladesh, Myanmar and Tajikistan. After Osama bin Laden was killed in US operation in Abbottabad on May 2, 2011 alongwith his Courier, the examination of ObL's phone and other material revaluated that Al Qaida was in close contact with Harkat ul Mujahideen.

For the benefit of esteemed reader, I am re producing what an eminent journalist Mr Khalid Ahmed wrote in Lahore weekly "Friday Times". (August 18-24, 2000)

Writing in the *Friday Times* (August 18-24, 2000) of Lahore, Khalid Ahmed, the well-known Pakistani analyst, said: "The Harkat-ul-Mujahideen formally announced itself as a new organisation in June 1996 in Muzaffarabad. In January 2000, Massod Azhar of Harkat-ul-Mujahideen was sprung form an Indian jail after the Kathmandu hijack. Masood Indian jail after the Kathmandu hijack. Masood Azhar had gone into India through 'proper channels,' as a journalist endorsed by Islamabad (that is, the ISI). He was a follower of Maulana Haq Nawaz Jhangvi, the founder of the anti-Iran and anti-Shia organisation Sipha-e-Sahaba, who was killed in 1990.

"After his release, Masood Azhar wished to revive the legacy of his master. By this time Harkat had become a major Deobandi organisation in Pakistan. Its main strength remained the militants of Punjab who not long ago had been the militants of Sipah-e-Sahaba.

"His return, therefore, caused an upheaval which climaxed in a grand split in the Harkat. The split was soon followed by the assassination of Maulana Yusuf Ludhianvi, a key figure in the Deobandi movement because of his status as a spiritual guide to two important Deobandi leaders his Khalifas: Maulana Fazlur Rehman of JUI and Maulana Azam Tariq of Sipha-e-Sahaba.

"The split in Harkat-ul-Mujahideen was caused by the militants in Punjab. Masood Azhar and his Punjabi following isolated the Harkat Azhar and his Punjabi following isolated the Harkat leader Fazlur Rehman Khali. The formation of Jaish-e-Muhammad as a new organisation was announced, but Masood Azhar and Fazlur Rehman Khalil began to fight over the Harkat assets.

On 19 March 2000, the two submitted to a *hakam* (arbitration of their elders. Harkat was represented by Muhammad Farooq Kashmiri and Jaish was represented by Maulana Abdul Jabbar (a key figure in the Kathmandu hijack) on the pledge given that they would abide by the *hakam*. The verdict was given by three elders: Mufti Rasheed Ahmed of Ahmed of Zarb-i-Momin Jihadi militia, Mufti Nizamuddin Shamzai of the Binori Town complex and Sher Ali Shah of Waziristan. The decision was that all offices of the Harket, occupied by Jaish in Punjab, would be returned to the Harkat, which in turn would pay the Jaish Rs. 40 lakh as its share of the division of assets.

"The implementation of the *hakam*, however, was not so smooth. The vehicles and offices returned by Jaish to Harkat were in such bad repair that Harkat refused to accept them and thus also refused to pay the stipulated 40 lakhs.

"In Pakistan the Jaish emerged as the more radical and more sectarian part of the Harkat because of its Sipah-e-Sahaba background. Maulana Yusuf Ludhianvi, it is said, inclined to their creed more than to Harkat's moderate view. Mufti Shamzai seemed to vacillate between the two splitter groups, thus allowing the Harkat's overall leader Fazlur Rehman Khalil to be eclipsed.

"Finding himself thus isolated, Khalil is said to have gone to Osama bin Laden and made up some of his losses by getting form him 12 new double-cabin pickup trucks to replace those reined by the Jaish in Punjab."

TEHRIK-e-NIFAZ-e-SHARIAT-e-MOHAMMADI (TNSM) (The Movement for the Enforcement of Islamic Laws)

The group was formed on June 28, 1989 by Maulana Sufi Mohammad, a cleric form Lal Quila (Dir district) after sidelining Jamaat-e-Islami. He belonged to Wahabi School of thought and associated himself with Afghan war (1980–88). The motto of TNSM was "Sharia or Shahadat'. 'Jehad fi Sabilillah' (holy war in the name of Allah) and he wanted enforcement of Islamic Judicial system in Pakistan in its Tolality. On March 30, 2002 he was jailed on charges of terrorism and released on May 16, 2008 as per Peace Deal with the government. TNSM was banned on January 15, 2002. On October 30/31, 2006 a missile attack in the Bajaur Agency which killed Maulana Liaqat and 80 others was revenged by Liaqats elder brother by carrying out suicide bombing on November 8, 2006 in Punjab Regimental Centre Training School at Dargai killing 45 army recruits. Ultimately a six-point agreement was made with Maulana Sufi Muhammad on April 20, 2008. His son-in-law Maulana Fazlullah (real name Fazl Hayat) also participated in the leadership of TNSM. Fazlullah had thousands of Islamic armed extremist elements under his command in NWFP and FATA regions and ran a FM Radio Station.

After Lal Masjid operation in Islamabad on July 13, 2007, Gen. Musharraf had ordered action in Swat also. As such on October 22, 2007 Pak Army launched operation to dismantle Mullah Fazlullah militant network whose followers were known as "Black Turbans." Fazlullah joined hands with Baitullah Mehsud, leader of Tehrik-e-Taliban Pakistan. The Government signed a peace deal with him on May 21, 2008.

The best book on this topic is written by Syed Saleem Sehzad who was reportedly killed by ISI. It gives a vivid account of rise of Al Qaida and Taliban in Afghanistan and Pakistan. The book "Inside Al-Qaida and the Taliban Beyond Bin Laden and 9/11" was written a few months before he was abducted and killed in May 2011 by ISI in Pakistan.

On May 10, 2009 President Asif Ali Zardari had publicly said "India was not a threat to Pakistan" and thus became the first Pakistan President to say so. But Gen. (Retd) Musharraf openly confessed and accepted the fact that it was Pakistan which tanned terror in Kashmir. In an interview to German magazine Der Spiegel, Gen. Musharraf said "yes, we formed and trained Militant groups to fight India. It is the right of any country to promote its own interest when India is not prepared to discuss Kashmir. (The Pioneer October 6, 2010). Then an October 9, 2010 he states in an interview to NDTV that Pakistan regarded terror groups such as Lashkar-e-Toiba (LeT) as 'mujahideen' fighting for the rights of Kashmiris and there is great public support in Pakistan for groups like the LeT and anyone fighting in your part of Kashmir was a 'mujahideen' for Pakistan. He also contested that LeT and Hizbul Mujahideen Came into being in 1989 after the freedom struggle started in Kashmir. (The Pioneer October 10, 2010).

However, just opposite of President Zardaris true opinion of May 10, 2009, Pen poll (A Pew Research Centre poll) says three out of four people have unfavorable opinion of India, up form 50 per out five years ago 57% of Pakistanis feel India a bigger threat than Al-Qaida. (The Indian Express, June 23 2011). This state of affairs is there when Pakistan Security forces are, every off and on, attacking by way of firing on our border check posts, trying to infiltrate their militants and their won people counter that Pakistan is preparing for a final war with India in the year 2012.

On the part of India, please consider what India has done for Pakistan right from 1947. Shri Satish Chandra, former High Commissioner of India in Pakistan, has brilliantly given certain facts in his article "PM bails out Pakistan." The Pioneer.

REFERENCE

1. The Search for Al Qaida by Bruce Riedel (Its leadership, ideology and future) Chapter The Thinker Zawahiri. Page 19. It originally appeased inteh book Emmanuel Sivan "Radical Islam: Medieval Theology and Modern Politics."
2. Qaswar Abbas in Islamabad India Today June 20, 2011 issue
3. The Indian Express April 9, 2011
4. Deccan Chronicle Bengluru July 8, 2009.
5. Indian Today May 30, 2011. "Soft target in Pakistan"
6. The Indian Express June 27, 2011. "Pak not capable of keeping n-arms safe top nuclear physicist" by Shubhaf it Roy.
7. The Indian Express June 22, 2011. PTI Report
8. The Indian Express June 28, 2011.
9. The Indian Express did July 25, 2011. "A perfect stranger Recollections of Lahore at Delhi's Chadani Chowk is express @ express @ india.com.
10. Page 288 to 290 of the book "The Fluttering Flag of Jehad" by Amir Mir.

15

The Latest Till Date

The ISI also seems as if it is being made a target by Taliban and Al Qaeda elements. On Sept. 4, 2007 a suicide attacker blew himself up after boarding a bus carrying ISI employees killing 25 of them. Another suicide attack was done on Nov. 24, 2007 outside Army Hqrs. in which 35 persons were killed. Para military soldiers were deserting the Frontier Corps. In the year during September to November, atleast 300 members out of a total of 40,000 serving the tribal area had deserted and the reasons were: (1) horrified parents saw a beheading video and begged his son to quit the force (ii) lack of food and ammunition at the front and (iii) watching wounded comrades languish for days awaiting medical attention.[1] In the year 2008 (till September 20) there had been atleast 7 major suicide blasts viz. on Jan. 10, Feb. 2, March 2, March 11, June 2, Aug. 21 and Sept. 20. On Feb. 29, 2008 suicide bombers killed Lt. Gen. Mushataq Beg, Chief of Army Medical Services. Suicide bombers had struck 116 times till October 9, 2008 since 1st incident of its kind in March 2002 at an Islamabad Church. The September 20, 2008 blast by a suicide bomber in Marriott Hotel in Islamabad with 600 kg of explosion and a blast at Police Headquarters in Islamabad on October 9, 2008 were, indeed, alarming. The Taliban suicide squads desire withdrawal of Us-Red forces from Afghanistan. Pakistan and its ISI, Pak Army inclusive, want the Taliban to takeover the government in Afghanistan so that Pakistan's aim of achieving strategic depth is achieved and its writ is run. Nawaz Sharif, former Prime Minister, who himself is a product of ISI and Pak Army (Particularly Gen. Hamid Gul) is busy in negotiations between Taliban and Afghan governments in conjunction with Saudi Arabia. Nawaz who has excellent relations with all sort of hues of Taliban was in Saudi Arabia for about two weeks during Sept. & Oct. 2008 facilitating a deal among Taliban, Afghanistan President Karzai and Saudi Arabia. India should expect hard times for itself in Afghanistan should that happen. The first thing the Taliban would do would be to oust all Indias from Afghanistan, stop all the welfare projects they are doing for the benefit of Afghans and then deal with US led forces. The Islamic militants fighting in Pak-Afghan border at present would be deployed on Pak Indo border and in Kashmir. President Zardari promises that the ISI will be handled, that in their problem (Sept. 29, 2008) but Pak Army Chief vows to eliminate militants from Pak. Afghan border (Sept. 29). Whatever they may say their efforts would be to keep on weakening Afghanistan and have full control over it. Whatever efforts NATO forces had put in under the leadership of America were negated by Pakistan's taliban. Taliban is a creation of Benazir Bhutto and Nasirullah Babar and they were raised for having control over Afghanistan. Pakistan's anti-Americanism in Afghanistan would pay.

President Zardari's branding Islamic militants fighting in Kashmir as 'terrorist' also does not carry much importance on the ground. Moreover the statement has immediately been retracted. What Pak Army says matters in Pakistan. Civilian leadership has not grown that strong so as to do any thing of its own and to the disliking of ISI, Army i.e. Crops Commanders and COAS in matters concerning India with a band of 'Zia-Bharti' Army Officers takes over the command of Pak Army after 4-5 years (they have already come up of age) India should expect a lot more troubles. The livers of control would remain with America for sometime to come thereafter china is the future of the world and A strong China means a strong Pakistan' would be followed leaving America aside.

Taliban and Al Queda elements inspite of likelihood of taking over the government or participating in the government of Afghanistan are not likely to sit quiet. Their aim would continue to take over the civilian administration in Pakistan as well. They would not like to stop at anything less than that. In facts, they have already made in roads in Pakistan.

ISI is trying to revive militancy in Indian Punjab. In violence-affected Udalguri district of Guwahati (Assam) miscreants hoisted a Pakistani flag on Oct. 4, 2008 in Sonaripara, village by Bangladeshi immigrant. Why Pakistani flag when the miscreants were Bangladeshi? They could have at the most gone for the flag of their motherland. It indicates ISI's hand in disturbances in that area.

Opening new trade routes etc. would hardly help. Though India opened Srinagar-Muzaffarbaad Bus Service in April 2005 and it was agreed upon by Pakistan since it suited them. All sorts of people under disguise and incognito could walk in Srinagar. But as far as India is concerned, Pakistan does not permit Indians to enter POK. In the wake of Oct. 8, 2005 earthquake that was devastating in POK, when India wanted to help and sought permission, Pakistan said no. Pakistan never wanted India to step in their soil even at such a time of calamity. Again when India proposed Kargil-Skardu road in June 2005, Pakistan did not agree. But for the trade route on Srinagar-Muzaffarabad and Poonch-Rawalakot on Oct. 21, 2008 Pakistan readily agreed because it provides them an opportunity to sent 'all sorts of men' in Kashmir. Recently, it was revealed by Britishers that a Taliban Commander killed by British Commandos in Afghanistan last year was a Pakistani Military Officer and that the Commander killed by them in a compound in the sangin valley in Helmand province had Pakistani military ID on his body.[2] Similar incident could happen among the Islamic militants fighting in Kashmir. Who knows?

Pakistan has voiced concern over Siachen but never speaks of frequent violation by its forces of Indo Pak border to cause infiltration. Indian army had reported 50 incidents of ceasefire violation till Oct. 14, 2008.[3] On the question of Chenab river water, Pakistan has threatened to go for third party arbitration.

Maj. Gen. (Retd.) MA Durrani, the National Security Advisor of Pakistan and former Pak Ambassador to USA (July 2006 to May 2008) flatly denied ISI's involvement in the bombing of Indian Embassy in Kabul on July 7, 2008 when Indian NSA. Shri M.K. Narayanan brought this incident to his notice. And the denial was emphatic inspite of the fact that US had produced intercepts of ISI's involvement in such a Bizarre incident.

The troika of Pakistan is unique. All PMs Presidents and chiefs of Army staff rush to china to pay obeisance no sooner they take over the office. President Zardari also did not prove an exception. He thundered "China is the future of the world and a strong China means a strong Pakistan". But for economic assistance they look towards America. Though Pakistan refused entry to India to help provide assistance to earthquake effected people of PoK purely on humanitarian grounds, but China has free access in PoK. It plans to build a Hydel project in Muzaffarabad costing US $ 2 billion through Sino Hydro corporation. Strategic transport corridor through Karakoram, building trans-border road link, laying railway line connecting China with PoK (Pakistan) are a few other examples of Pak-Sino cooperation.

Pumping, Fake currency to disturb Indian economy, sending drugs into India are other 'important' jobs ISI has taken up against India. Remember, Asad Durranis, former ISI Chief, dictum "break India from within". Still there is time to wake up and put counter measures whole heartedly against these strategies of our good neighbour Pakistan.

Any amount of generosity, accommodation and forgiveness shown by India would, perhaps, go in vain. Take for example India-Pakistan peoples Forum for peace and Democracy". It was headed by Shri I.A. Rehman for Pakistan and Admiral Ram Dass represented India and was aimed at people to people contact to bring the people of the two countries together. Its 1st convention was held in New Delhi in February 1995 where in the action plan to restore dispute and a no-war pact between the two countries was discussed. In its second convention at

Lahore in November 1995 a committee was proposed comprising Kashmiri leaders from both sides of LoC to solve the problem with the wishes of Kashmiris. Its third convention was held at Calcutta in December 1996 wherein the proposal of 2nd convention were made once again. Peshawar was choosen for holding fourth convention of this Forum in November 1998 which was attended by about 450 delegates including 250 from India. It strongly condemned the Indian security forces for the atrocities committed on the innocent Kashmiris and demanded India withdraw its forces and end brutalities, rapes, arrests etc. in Kashmir. The Fifth Convention was held in Bangalore in April 2000 in which India was called upon to immediately and repression and genocide in Kashmir. Throughout the life of this peoples Forum there were always demands from Pakistan and criticism of India which ultimately ended in fiasco. In the end a tough stand against Pakistan is required to be taken as suggested by NSA recently.

Pakistani nation is firmly under the clutches of Army and it can never come out of it. Its conventional military might stands as follows in the year 2008.

Pak Army in the year 2008

Land Forces—6,19,000

Reserves—5,28,000

Para Military—3,02,000

Main Battle Tank—1 Khalid (600). Total 2620 Tanks including Alkhalid.

Special Services Group (SSG)—2100

Pak Air Force (2008)

Personnel—65,000

Reserves—10,000

Combat Air Craft—530 (more than 400 active)

Fighter Planes:
(i) F-16 Fighter Falcon
(ii) JAF-17 Thunder Air Craft (10)
(iii) Sab 2000 AWACS Air Craft (5)

(iv) JF-17 fighted (6)

(v) multi Role Aircraft (72)

Warning & Control System—

KJ 2000 (5)

Intercepts 8 Ground support (283)

F-7 PG Sky Bolt-Miraz Rose-1

Naval Support

Dessault Miraz VBA-3 (12)

Main Helictoper

Elliot MI-17.

Pak Navy (2008)

Personnel—24,000

Coast Guards—5,28,000

Reserves—5,000

Pak Navys Air Wing exists separately

Marine Commandos—1000

Warships—27

Sub Marines

(i) Active electrical Diesel Sub marine (5)

(ii) Mid-gate sub marine (3)

Combat Power—

(i) Zalalat class 200 Ton Missile boat (4)
(each less with 4 Anti-ship Missiles)

(ii) West land Links Anti-ship
Anti Sub Marine Transport Helictoper (3)

(iii) Herbine Z-9 EC Helicopter 1B

(iv) Maritime surveillance and Anti Sub Marine Warfare Aircraft Brigade Atlantic-I (2 or 3).

Missiles

Hatlf IA

Hatlf II, Abdali

Hatlf III, Ghaznavi

Hatlf IV, Shaheen

Hatlf V, Ghauri-1

Hatlf VIA, Ghauri-2

Hatlf VI, Shaheen 2

Hatlf VII, Babur Cruiz

Shaheen 3

Ghauri 3

Pakistan's army was 7th largest in the world and the military spending was $4.26 billion. Of late, it has started hiding its defence expenditure. For example the pension of retired defence employers was switched over to different head of account in order to show reduced expenditure or reduced budgetary allocation to the world. Pakistan has 110 veapons*. It is engaged in 'preparation for war against India with the facilities given by the united states to fight Taliban and Al Qaeda militants as said by President elect Mr. Barack Obama. All this is done inspite of its proclamation that it (Pakistan) is facing imminent bankruptcy. It has sought $ 10 billion from Washington, London and other countries which can be called "Friends of Pakistan". IMF has already come to its rescue by granting a package of $7.6 billions. Pakistan's economy is showing inflation @25% according to Federal Bureau of statistics & State Bank of Pakistan. Per Capita income in dollars is 1085 in 2007-08. GDP growth is 5.8, Agricultural growth is 1.5 and Fiscal deficit (percentage of GDP is 7. Islamabad's Forex reserves are rapidly plummeting and it is estimated around $ 3 billion as on October 2008. Pakistani rupee is around 78 per US dollar. The once again good old days of Pakistan after 9/11 when it started receiving foreign aid once again after joining US's 'war on terror' seem to be over. India which wants a more stable Pakistan economy has supported

* Repnt on washington poot on jan 1, 2011

multilateral assistance to it. Pakistan's behaviour with India has always been enimical whereas India has always wished it well and overlooked all the mischiefs played by it. Former US secretary of state Henry Kissinger has stated that India's neighbourhood would pose one of the toughest challenges to the new regime. On Nov. 16, 2008 Kissinger stated "Pakistan would have to be prevented from becoming a failed state, because to have a failed state with nuclear weapons will be an extraordinary case and that is a challenge to the international society". CIA and US National Intelligence Council have predicted that Pakistan would be a failed state by 2015. That status of Pakistan would pose a danger to the very existence of India because is that situation Pakistan in all probability would like to use its nuclear arsenal against India irrespective of India's friendly gestures and helpful attitude towards Pakistan. On May 9, 2008 Hafiz Mohammad Saeed during a sermon at the Jamia Masjid al-Qudsia in Lahore charged India with planning to destroy Pakistan. He said 'India is building dams on rivers flowering into the country. On the other hand, it is establishing training centres in Afghanistan where it is teaching its agents how to carry out terrorist acts in Pakistan. While our rulers insist that we should have good relations with the Afghan government, India is imposing wars upon us. Still, our rulers, pursuing a policy of unilateral Friendship under foreign pressure, have promised the world we will not fight with India." In May 2008 Jamaat-e-Islami spokesperson told Aaj Television that Pakistan authorities had erred in allowing the distribution of Indian films containing material objectionable and offensive to Islam. He said "India is our enemy and has been at the forefront of efforts to destabilise and damage Pakistan. The Indian Army is massacring Muslims in Kashmir, while India is constructing dams on our rivers in violation of treaties, in order to turn Pakistan into a desert. Besides, Indian consulates in Afghanistan are busy in conspiracies to undermine Pakistan's security. Still, we are providing India billions of dollars by importing its movies." In February 2008 former ISI Chief Hameed Gul wrote an article in the Nawa-i-Waqt (urdu daily of Pakistan) which asserted that the key to Kashmir is in Afghanistan and argued that until the United States was defeated in Afghanistan, Kashmir would not be free. But General Gul prophesised" I, being a professional soldier say with full confidence that the US can never win the war against terror in Afghanistan or Iraq. Following a withdrawal from Afghanistan in late-2009', he arrested 'the United States will disintegrate like the former USSR and this disintegration will result in the freedom of Kashmir".[4] Explaining the Pakistani establishment's perception of India in a recent interview, Ayesha Siddiq, author of Military Inc. Inside Pakistan's military economy, said "India is an enemy, it is about to eat us up. We have to challenge it."[5] She has also exposed the extent of the Army's control over the country's economy in the same book. Army has 11.58 per cent of the state land and its share is more than Rs. 200 billion. Fauji Foundation itself is a big economy. Yet the nation rushes to IMF and 'Friends of Pakistan' for economic assistance. Since Pakistan Army, has made economic provisions for itself it simply cant loosen its grip on political power of the country. Pakistan's Defence exports itself are worth more than US $ 300 millions and there is overgrowing demand for Pakistan made arms and ammunition. Moreover US would never let Pakistan fail—neither on economic front nor on political. Pakistan in turn is encircling India and openly sending ISI aided and abetted persons into India. One of the example to take a note is the fatwa issued by Maulana Mabibur Rehman Shahi Imam, Jama Masjid of Ludhiyana about a Pakistani lady who was earlier working as a journalist with the Pak newspaper 'the Muslim'. She had always been writing against India and now shows interest in friendship. The ISI agent is indeed a grave threat to India's internal security. Jaish-e-Mohammad Chief Masood Azhar in one of its rallies in Bahawalpur on April 11,2008 openly criticised Gen.. Pervez Musharraf and demanded that they be allowed to wage Jihad if they want to save Pakistan from Obliteration. Radical Islamaisation with starving economy, rudderless and directionless militants would pose a danger to India in times to come.

Of course, Pakistan Parliament for the first time in its history condemned' tourism on Oct. 22, 2008 after a debate and passed a resolution in its joint session stating "Extremism, militancy and terrorism in all forms and manifestations' pose a grave danger to the stability and integrity of the nation-state" but unless it is put to action like Resolution would prove to be redundant.

Pakistan's import of weapons and military related items from US alone exceeds $4.5 billion. The purchases of military hardware has nothing to do with fighting war on terror. Maritime patrol Aircraft, anti-tank missiles, surveillance Radars, transport aircraft, military radio sets are items that Pakistan simply does not require and it is importing these items to be specifically used against India should the need arise.

'Economist' had declared, Gen. (Retd.) Musharraf's Pakistan the world's most dangerous place. Interior Ministry's Chief advisor Rehman Malik stated in a seminar on Oct. 11, 2008 in Lahore that was organised by Jang group of newspapers that their own people are behind terror attacks, not Indians. Pakistan acknowledges that India is not doing any activity against their nation yet there is so much of arms and equipment import from US which is indeed intrigueing.

India has to find a responsive action. US report on terrorism 2007 has also cautioned India that its counter-terror operations are outdated and its system overburdened. New York Times reported on Jan. 15, 2008 that former senior Intelligence Officials and other officials close to CIA have admitted that ISI had supported militants in Kashmir and backed them but now lost control of them. Dr. Henry Kissinger has warned on Nov. 16, 2008 that nuclear weapons possessed by a likely failed state would be a big problem and as such Pakistan would have to be saved/prevented from becoming a failed state. US Military Commander General David Petraeus has warned Pakistan that militants in Pakistan pose a threat to the country's existence.[6]

Benazir Bhutto had opined that the 'perception in Pakistan is that the military is responsible for the rise of militancy and all the horrific consequences that it entails for Pakistan and its people. She explained how militancy started with General Zia's dictatorship and how the present Musharraf dictatorship has presided over the mushrooming growth of militant groups.'[7] Religion-political-militant outfits particularly JeM had dared to attack our Parliament. The terror organisation JeM had done hijacking of Indian Airlines flight 814 and ISI took its chief on a victory tour through Pakistan to raise money to create the JeM as reported by Bruce Riedel in his latest book "The search for AlQaeda, its leadership, ideology and Future". Incidently, the former head of ISI Gen. Javed Ashraf Qazi later on March 6, 2004 admitted in Parliament that the JeM was responsible for the attack through at that time the Pakistani spokesman suggested it was all a put-up Job by India. (The Hindustan Times dtd. September 11, 2008). Pakistan always denies the mischief done by. It through ISI. In fact, it first readies itself to issue a denial and then only mounts the 'operation-mischief'. The co-founder of Afghanistan's Centre for Research and Policy Studies, Mr. Haroun Mir, openly blaming Pakistan said recently that 'Pakistan is a problem, not the solution. Mr. Pervez Hoodbhoy who teaches at Qaid-e-Azam University in an article that was published in the times of India of March 13, 2008 writes: Quote "Many believe that suicide attacks will disappear if Pakistan withdraws from a war against terror that is not Pakistan's but America's. But most of the dead and wounded are perfectly ordinary people. They had nothing to do with American or Pakistani forces. Even if America retreats—which is unlikely—Pakistan is now unable to escape the terrible consequences of a weapon developed to bleed India and to secure Afghanistan for 'strategic depth". unquote.

When shall we prepare and stand up? On April 12, 1999 Gen. Musharraf had asserted that the low intensity conflict with India would continue even 'if the Kashmir problem is resolved". In February 2008 Deputy head of Lal Masjid in Islamabad asserted that a 'huge majority of Pakistan's army does not want to Fight us. Had Musharraf (Gen. Musharraf) continued to support the Jihad in Kashmir, the Mujahideen, would have broken India apart. Musharraf's biggest crime is abandoning Jihad in Kashmir. Now we have a new army chief. I appeal to him to adopt the old policy of Jihad".

Gen. Musharraf is no more in the saddle to take the Jihadi outfits. Soon 'Zia-Bharti' Army officers are to take over the reins of Pakistan Army who have been administered oath to take revenge from India. In order to counter these wishes,

India simply can not sit and relax.

The feelings of one ofthe Pakistani elite, Editor-in-Chief of "The Nation" and chairman of the Nazria Pakistan Trust (NPT) Majid Nizami towards Hindus and India are described hereunder as published by him in the said daily of March 10, 2010 : "Freedom is the greatest blessings of the Almighty, who may save us from dominance of Hindus, as our sworn enemy in bent destroying Pakistani. However, if it did not refrain from committing aggression against us, then Pakistan is destined to defeat India because our horses in the form of atomic bombs and missiles are far better than Indian donkeys"! "If one wants to have an idea of what would have been our condition had Pakistan not come into existence, he should visit India to apprise himself about untold pathetic living conditions of the Muslims there at this point of time. The day was not far off when we would once again conquer India. Pakistan had to play a key role in liberating enslaved minorities from the clutches of Hindu majority."

REFERENCES

1. The Indian Express Nov. 27, 2007 Report by Zulfiqar Ali and Laura King from Peshawar.
2. The Indian Express October 13, 2008 Slain Taliban Commander was Pak Army Officer: Report.
3. The IE Oct. 15, 2008.
4. The Hindu Ddl July 9, 2008 Jihadists polemic holds clues to mission bombing—Report by Praveen Swami.
5. The Times of India March 9, 2008 report Joy Shobhan Saxena: Friend to Foe: Pak Forces factor under Jihadi Fire.
6. The Pioneer, Oct. 1, 2008 report by Nandini Jawli from London 'Pak militants' a threat to its existence, says US military chief.
7. Report by Nandini Jawli from London 'Benezir faced dual threats to life in Pak' published in the Pioneer.

16
India-Pak Ties

After Simla agreement that was signed on July 2, 1972 between Mrs. Indira Gandhi and Zulfikar Ali Bhutto to resolve conflict and confrontation between Pakistan and India, it was Rajiv Gandhi who visited Islamabad in July 1989 as a goodwill gesture and purely a bilateral visit. In December 1988 Rajiv Gandhi alongwith his wife Sonia had gone to Islamabad on a 3-day visit to attend 4th regional summit of South Asian countries. They were welcomed by Pakistan Prime Minister Mrs. Benazir Bhutto. Both the prime ministers reached an agreement on Intelligence sharing with the specific aim of rooting out Sikh terrorism in India. The two visits by Indian PM led to a series of mutual confidence building measures (CBMs) including force reduction along the borders and an agreement that India and Pakistan would not attack each others nuclear installations. Benazir, many years later i.e. shortly before she was assassinated, revealed that she choked off assistance to militant Indian Sikhs who had been offered refuge in Pakistan by Gen. Zia. It was the termination of this support, she implied that finished off militant Sikhs who had been demanding independent homeland out of India's Punjab State.[1] Terrorism analyst Mr. B. Raman remembers Indian and Pakistani Intelligence outfits did have some kind of outreach between 1988 and 1991 with the Pakistani returning two Khalistani terrorists.[2] On Kashmir, during a joint press conference Mrs. Benazir Bhutto said on December 31, 1988 "We will move step by step towards more intractable issues before us by resolving the less intractable issues first."

1989 onwards ISI unleashed militancy, in Jammu and

Kashmir through various Pak-trained 'Jihadi Tanzeens (militant outfits). Militancy picked up in the valley at a high speed and the meetings of the then Prime Ministers Chandrashekhar and Narsimha Rao with Pak PM Nawaz Sharif proved futile. Todays May 1997 I.K. Gujral came out with a new idea known as Gujral Doctrine which required reactivating hot line between New Delhi and Islamabad and forming a Joint Working Group to work towards an integrated approach. Then appeared Mr. Atal Behari Vajpayee on the 'takht' of New Delhi who took initiative to rush to Lahore with 'Peace Bus' on February 20, 1999 to meet the Pakistan Prime Minister Nawaz Sharif. The then chief of Army staff Gen. Pervez Musharraf kept himself along from this meet and did not consider it, fit to salute the visiting Indian prime minister. Though 'Lahore Declaration' was signed by both sides but it did not mention Kashmir as the central issue which was not liked by Pakistan Army. A such it never ended mistrust between the two countries.

Vajpayee's gesture was answered by intrusions in Kargil, planned and executed by Gen. Musharaf. There is a dispute between Nawaz Sharif and Musharraf regarding keeping the latter on board and informal of Kargil mischief. Musharraf says Nawaz Sharif was informed of it but Nawaz denies it. Anyway, India discovered the intrusions and occupation of Kargil, Dran etc. in May 1999 only. Indian Army, for the first time used Bofors guns to dislodge the Pakistan Army personnel from these areas. However US President Mr. Bill Clinton played as assertive role and ordered Pak Army to vacate the aggression forthwith. Indian estimate of Pak soldiers infiltrated in Kargil is, 1100 plus who were killed. Gen. Pervez Musharraf's figure for this episode is 357 but Nawaz Sharif opines that 2700 Pakistani soldiers infiltrators were killed in Kargil.[3]

ISI enacted another drama on December 24, 1999 when an Indian Air Lines Aircraft IC-814 from Kathmandu to Delhi was hijacked by Pak militants to seek release of three jailed hardcore militants who had to be taken to Kandahar (Afghanistan) to be swapped to free the passengers of the hijacked aircraft. NDA government minister for external affairs alongwith certain senior government officials escorted these 3 militants to Kandahar. This was perhaps a saddest moment for India after our humiliating defeat to the hands of chinese Army in 1962. Pak foreign minister had sent a note verbal to Indian Mission in Islamabad to seek release of these militants from Indian Jail before the enactment of the hijacking incident.

Indian Prime Minister Atal Bihari Vajpayee, inspite of Kargil and IC-814 incidents, invited Gen. Pervez Musharraf to Agra for a summit on July 15, 2001. Agra talks broke down because of differences over Kashmir. Pakistan insisted on Kashmir as the central issue between Pakistan and India to which India did not agree and resultantly the talks failed. Even a joint statement could not be issued. Gen. Musharraf returned to Pakistan without attending to many other scheduled programme including the one to pay a visit to Ajmer Sharif.

Then came December 13, 2001 when Pak militants attacked Indian Parliament resulting in death of 14 terrorists and security personnel. (5 assailants). LeT and JeM were involved. Terrorists from Pakistan were actively helped by local contacts. Involvement of Jaish-e-Mohammed led by Maulana Masood Azhar came to notice during investigations by India. On March 6, 2004, Lt. Gen. (Retd.) Javed Ashraf Qazi, a former DG ISI and then Minister for Railways told Pakistan's Parliament "We must not be afraid to admit that the JeM was involved in the death of thousands of innocent Kashmiris, the bombing of Indian Parliament, (American Journalist) Daniel Pearl's murder and an attempt to assassinate President Musharraf".[4] India mobilised its forces and there came an eminent danger of war-which was averted because of an active involvement and role played by the United States of America. India gave a list of twenty (20) wanted men to Pakistan so that it could hand them over to India for trial. But till today no action is taken by Pakistan an the list of 20.

In, April 2003 Vajpayee again extended 'hand of peace' to Pakistan. Pakistan dropped demanding plebescite in J&K

according to UN resolution—a demand on which till then Pakistan was always harping upon. Back channel diplomacy was put in place which turned out to be meaningful and ultimately fruitful that led to resumption of talks. On Jan. 6, 2004 when Vajpayee visited Islamabad to attend SAARC submit, the back channel work of Brijesh Mishra, Yashwant Sinha, Hamid Javed and Tariq Aziz was appreciated by Gen. Musharraf. Both India and Pakistan agreed to 'commence' 'composite dialogue' in February. Pak President reassured India that *"he will not permit any territory under Pakistan's control to be used to support terrorism in any manner"*. A win-win situation was created with both sides stressing that there were no winners or loosers. Gen Musharraf praised Vajpayee's 'Vision and Salesmanship'.

A joint statement, text of which was drafted by the national security advisor of India Brijesh Mishra who had reached Islamabad on Jan. 1, 2004 itself and who exchanged several drafts between the two sides for their final approval and agreement on the wordings' was issued.

"The President of Pakistan and the Prime Minister of India met during the SAARC summit in Islamabad."

The Indian Prime Minister while expressing satisfaction over the successful conclusion of the Saarc summit, appreciated the excellent arrangements made by the host country.

Both leaders welcomed the recent steps towards normalisation of relation between the two countries and expressed the hope that the positive trends set by the CBMs would be consolidated.

Prime Minister Vajpayee said that in order to take forward and sustain the dialogue process, violence, hostility and terrorism must be prevented president Musharraf reassured Prime Minister Vajpayee that he would not permit any territory under Pakistan's control to be used to support terrorism in any manner. President Musharraf emphasised that a sustained and productive dialogue addressing all issues would lead to positive results.

To carry the process of normalisation forward, the President of Pakistan and the Prime Minister of India agreed to commence the process of the composit dialogue in February 2004. The two leaders are confident that the resumption of the composit dialogue would lead to peaceful settlement of all bilateral issues, including Jammu and Kashmir, to the satisfaction of both sides.

The two leaders agreed that a constructive dialogue would promote program towards the common objective of peace, security and economic development for our peoples and for future generations.[5]"

While addressing the UN General Assembly, on September 22, 2004 President Musharraf said "After several aborted attempts, Pakistan and India have been able to initiate confidence-building measures (CBMs) and a composite dialogue this year to address all outstanding issues. Pakistan has pursued this process with complete sincerity, giving bilateralism a final chance." ... "We feel that the dual channels of CBMs and the dialogue process must proceed in tendem. We are also firmly committed to resolving all disputes with India peacefully, including the Kashmir dispute. This cannot be ignored. It resolution can not be in ordinately delayed. We desire a resolution of Kashmir which is just and acceptable to India, Pakistan and people of Kashmir.[6] On the sidelines of UN General Assembly session, President Musharraf and PM Manmohan Singh met each other on September 24, 2004 in New York where the discussed and strived "to restore normaley and cooperation". They also decided to address the issue of J&K with a view to explore 'possible options' for a peaceful, negotiated settlement in a sincere spirit and purposeful manner'. After the detent a statement was issued, the operation part of which was as follows.

"They [the two principals] agreed that confidence-building measures [CBMs] of all categories under discussion between the two Governments should be implemented keeping in mind practical possibilities. They also addressed the issue of Jammu and Kashmir and agreed that possible options for a peaceful, negotiated settlement of the issue should be explored in a sincere spirit and purposeful manner. In the spirit of the Islamabad joint press statement of January 6, 2004, they agreed that CBMs will contribute to generating an atmosphere of trust and mutual understanding so necessary for the well-being of the peoples of both countries."[7]

As a first bilateral visit in seventeen years of an Indian foreign minister after P.V. Narsimha Rao's in 1988, K. Natwar Singh visited Islamabad on February 15, 2005 to review the progress in the ongoing composit dialogue with Pakistan foreign minister Khurshid M. Kasuri. In a major breakthrough on February 16, India and Pakistan agreed to start Srinagar-Muzaffarabad Bus Service from April 7 making LoC a 'soft border', expedite the process to resume train services between Khokrapar and Munabao, reducing risk of nuclear accident or unauthorised use of nuclear weapons and preventing incidents at sea etc. In fact, Indian external affairs minister wanted to bridge 'Trust deficit'.

President Gen. Pervez Musharraf visited Delhi under the guise of cheering up his cricket team from April 16 to 18, 2005 but admitted that 'cricket is not important, Kashmir is.' A huge team of forty five (45) members of his government accompanied him which included foreign minister Khurshid Mehamood Khan, Commerce minister Humayun Akhtar Khan, information minister Sheikh Rashid Ahmed, minister of state for religious affairs Amir Liyaqat and minister of state for youth affairs Mohammed Ali Durrani. Among senior government officials were National Security Advisor Tariq Aziz, Lt. Gen. Tariq Wasim Ghazi, foreign secretary Riaz Mohammed Khan and Commerce secretary Tasnim Noorani. National Security Advisor of India M.K. Narayanan informed (April 14, 2005) that a series of new CBMs to promote people to people contacts, introducing two new Bus services were to be discussed. Gen. Musharraf declared (April 14 in Rawalpindi) that he favoured converting the line of control into a 'soft border' but would not accept it as a permanent border for final solution to the Kashmir problem. He wanted bus service to start across LoC and more routes across the territory opened which he though was 'the real first step towards converting it into a soft border".

Musharraf said he was 'fairly optimistic' the Kashmir issue to be resolved and the peace process 'fairly irreversible'. On April 17, 2005 India and Pakistan decided to set up a Joint Business Council (JBC) to facilitate interaction among business and to strengthen economic ties and promote trade. A Joint Study Group (JSG) that was already set up between the two countries was to sort out any problem in June 2005. Increase in frequency of bus service between Srinagar-Muzaffarabad and permission to trucks to ply in the route to promote trade was decided. To operationalise additional routes including that between Poonch and Rawalkot, early start of bus service between Amritsar and Lahore and religious places such as Nankana Sahib, re-establish Khokrapar Munabao route by January 2006, opening of Consulate Generals of the two countries in Karachi and Mumbai, accomplish commitment made in the Joint press statement of January 6, 2004 (Peaceful settlement of all bilateral issues including Jammu & Kashmir to the satisfaction of both sides) and September 24, 2004 statement (possible options for a peaceful, negotiated settlement of issues) issued at New York, to endorse the decisions taken by the foreign secretaries on December 27-28, 2004 and foreign ministers on February 15-17, 2005 at Islamabad etc. were either agreed upon or endorsed.

For the first time trade was to take place through LoC. Rail Link between Khokrapar (Pakistan) and Munabao (India) which was stopped in the wake of 1965 war was to be restarted. Karachi consulate of India which was functional from 1978 was ordered shut down by Benazir in December 1994. Both the foreign ministers—Natwar Singh of India and Khurshid Mehmood Kasuri of Pakistan agreed to re-start consulate is Karachi and Bombay in June 2004.

Sir Creek and Siachen issue were also discussed in the composit dialogue. Four rounds of talks on the Siachen issue had already taken place between 1989 and 1992 between India and Pakistan.

On Sept. 24, 2004 Dr. Manmohan Singh and Gen. Musharraf met in New York where, besides other points, discussed a gas pipeline from Pakistan to India. Pakistan prime minister Shaukat Aziz also visited New Delhi in November 2004 discuss energy resources.'

On April 18, 2005 President Musharraf said while no rigid time frame could be set for resolving the Kashmir issue, there should be a reasonable limit and that India and Pakistan had to move towards resolving Kashmir issue and wondered of this issue was left un-addressed he did not know what might happen in the next 10-15 years. On Siachen issue, Musharraf desired correction of maps on both sides. On the question of Iran-Pakistan-India gas pipeline, Gen. Musharraf said where Pakistani and Indian national interests were involved, we should go ahead for it. He meant that even if America is opposing India and Pakistan to go for this pipeline from Iran, we should not obey it giving a vent, of course, inadvertently, that whenever interests of Pakistan would be involved, they would not, bother for USA and would act inspite of America's advise against such an act. Musharraf said "When America Sneezes, we get cold. I know that America does not sneez so much'.[8] He criticised the attack on Srinagar-Muzafarabad bus passengers on April 6, 2005 and branded the attackers as terrorists.

Excerpts from the joint statement issued by President Pervez Musharraf and Prime Minister Manmohan Singh in Delhi on Monday April 18, 2005 were as follows:

'The President of Pakistan and the Prime Minister of India used the opportunity provided by the (President Musharraf's) visit to review progress in Pakistan-India relations. They assessed positively the progress and determined to build on the momentum already achieved.

They reaffirmed the commitments made in the joint press statement of Jan. 6, 2004 and the joint statement issued after their meeting in New York on Sept. 24, 2004 and expressed satisfaction on the progress in the peace process between the two countries that has since been realised.

Conscious of the historic opportunity created by the improved environment in relations, the two leaders had substantive talks on all issues. They determined that the peace process was now irreversible.

The two leaders addressed the issue of J&K and agreed to continue these discussions in a sincere and forward-looking manner for a final settlement. They were satisfied with the discussion and expressed their determination to work together to carry forward the process and to bring the benefit of peace of their people.

They also agreed to pursue measures to enhance interaction and cooperation across the LOC including agreed meeting points for divided families, trade, pilgrimages and cultural interaction.

They condemned attempts to disrupt the Srinagar-Muzaffarabad bus service and welcomed its successful run. The two leaders pledged that they would not allow terrorism to impede the peace process.

They decided to increase the frequency of the bus service and also decided that trucks would be allowed to use this route to promote trade. They also agreed to operationalise additional routes, including that between Poonch and Rawalakot. They also look forward to early start of the bus service between Amritsar and Lahore and to religious places such as Nankana Sahib. They agreed to re-establish to Khokhrapar-Munnabao route by Jan. 1, 2006.

They agreed that the Consulates General of the two countries in Mumbai and Karachi would be opened before the year end.

On the issues of the Sir Creek and Siachen, they instructed that the existing institutional mechanism should convene discussions immediately with a view of finding mutually acceptable solution to both issue expeditiously.

It was agreed that the ministers of petroleum and natural gas would meet in May to explore cooperation in the sector including on the issue of pipelines.

Both leaders agreed that enhanced economic and commercial co-operation would contribute to the well-being of the peoples of the two countries and bring a higher level of prosperity for the region. The two leading economies of South Asia should work together for the greater prosperity of the region.

The leaders decided to reactivate the Joint economic commission. They also agreed, that the joint business council should meet soon.'[9]

One of the mistaken notion most of us have about Pakistan being a stooge of America who obeys all dictates commanded by USA needs to modified. It is wrong to think that Pakistan acts according whims and fancies of America all the times. Where its national interests are involved, Pakistan defies America outright. For example, when Nawaz Sharif decided to explode nuclear device, America advised it against but Pakistan defied and exploded bomb in Chagai hills. Similarly, Musharraf had given much advance warning when he said on April 18, 2005 that India and Pakistan had to move towards resolving Kashmir and wondered if this issue was left unaddressed he did not know what might happen in the next 10-15 years.... Readers may remember that 26/11 happened within this period only i.e. the next 10-15 years beginning from the date of his statement on April 18, 2005. Readers may also kindly recall that Gen. Musharraf has also said "many more Kargils will take place..." Now it is for us to take the cue and prepare the country.

Two brilliant personalities Mr. Kanchan Gupta of the Pioneer newspapers and Mr. Brahma Chellaney, professor of strategic studies at the centre for Policy Research in New Delhi have expressed their opinion in the following manner.

Mr. Kanchan Gupta says "A comparison of the Islamabad and New York statements will show marked divergence on three crucial points, each one of which reflects how much has been conceded to the advantage of Gen. Musharraf and Pakistan, First, while the January 6 statement drew a clear distinction between CBMs and the proposed bilateral composit dialogue, in the September 24 statement the two issues have been mixed up. Second while the Islamabad statement laid equal emphasis on all the issues to be addressed in the composit dialogue, in the New York statement the issue of Jammu & Kashmir has been singled out for special emphasis. And, third, whereas the earlier statement clearly linked the sustenance of the composit dialogue to Pakistan's export of terror to India, and to Gen. Musharraf's assurance to Mr. Vajpayee that, he will "not permit any territory under Pakistan's control to be used to support terrorism in any manner", in the New York statement there is no reference to cross-border terrorism. Yes, the January 6 statement does find mention, but in the context of CBMs rather than the sustenance of the composit dialogue.' 'Did the new dispensation in South Block at any stage consider offering to re-draw the LOC by shifting it eastward as part of India's peace-making proposals at the New York meeting? The report in 'Time' magazine is categorical and it quotes an unnamed 'senior official'. Notwithstanding the vehement denial issued by the Prime Minister's men, 'Time' has stood by its report. All media encounters, including deep throat sessions, are officially recorded. The encounter did take place and obviously the option of read justing the LOC is being seriously considered...'[10] Prof. Brahma Challaney writes ...'Since he became Prime Minister, Manmohan Singh has made it a point to meet Pakistani dictator Pervez Musharraf every autumn on foreign soil. While the 2004 and 2005 meetings were held in New York, the discussions this September were cleverly held in revolutionary Havana to camouflage the US angle to a decision Dr. Singh took without consulting his own Cabinet Committee on Security—to accept a US Intelligence proposal dating back to 1991 that India set up a Joint Counter-terrorism institutional mechanism with Pakistan. In a profound doctrinal shift in policy, India has publicly embraced as a partner and fellow victim the sponsor of cross-border terrorism.The decision to establish a joint mechanism was taken even before PM met with Musharraf. In fact, no sooner had the prime ministerial plane taken off from New Delhi that Dr. Singh surprised the accompanying media by calling Pakistan "a victim of terror" and claiming groups like the Lashkar-e-Toiba and Jaish-e-Mohammad—"act autonomously also". His message turned Indian counter-terror policy on its head: "terrorism constitutes a threat for both countries" and "It is incumbent on us to work together."[11]

Mr. B. Raman has come out with a correct analysis of the situation. He says: India is a victim of ISI-sponsored terror, and they (Pakistan) are a victim of their own creation? Mr. G. Parthasarthy, the former Indian High Commissioner to Pakistan is of the opinion that "Pakistan is a victim of sectarian and extremist terrorism sponsored by the ISI. India is a victim of terrorism sponsored by Musharraf and the ISI. There can be no question of equating the two".

Reverting to Indo-Pak relations, 7/11 (Mumbai train blasts) saw the secretary level talks suspended. Deadly attack on Indian Embassy in Kabul on July 7, 2008 and Mumbai attacks of November 26, 2008 all lowered the graph. The Mumbai attack by sea-borne Pakistan ISI aided terrorists was admitted by Pakistan on February 12, 2009 to have hatched on its soil after vehement initial denials by Pak PM and foreign minister as well as its interior minister Rehman Malik.

Lahore Police Chief Pervaiz Rathore pointed finger towards India for its involvement in the terror attack on Sri Lankan Cricket Team on March 3, 2009 and on Police Training Academy on March 30, 2009 (both in Lahore). However, on April 11, 2009 Interior Ministry Chief Rehman Malik told Journalists that Pakistan did not find any conclusive evidence to suggest that India was involved in the terror strikes on the Sri Lankan cricket team and a police training centre near Lahore.[12]

Now Pakistan desires to portray itself as a victim of terrorism, a cue given to it by P.M. Manmohan Singh. While the draft ministerial document put out a condemnation of the Mumbai attacks in November 2008, Pakistan was keen to put in the Lahore attack on Sri Lankan cricket team in the same mention in a recent meeting of NAM officials in the run-up to a ministerial meeting in Havana scheduled for April 27, 2009. However, now India is keen to walk backfrom its stand made in Havana three years ago where India went an extra mile to declare that Pakistan too was a victim of terrorism. Since India, Pak clashed over terror at NAM meet, there is currently no reference to these terror attacks.[13] Inspite of playing so much mischief through and through, which has became known to all the world over, Pakistan wants India come to talks. Making a strong pitch for resumption of composit dialogue stalled after November, 2008 Mumbai attacks, Pakistan has said that India's concerns could be addressed only by cooperating with it and not by accusing it.[14] Yusuf Raza Gilani opined on April 19, 2009 that the resumption of confidence-building measures between Pakistan and India will take sometime as bilateral ties have been affected after Mumbai terror attack.[15] On November 26, 2008. The point is Pakistan is so sure that whatever mischief Pakistan does against India, at still returns to the negotiating table soon. Pakistan known this weakness of India and exploits it.

Pakistan refused to accept India's nominee Mr. Sudhi Vyas as next High Commissioner to Pakistan in the first week of March 2009 on the plea that while Vyas was acting HC, he was declared PNG and expelled from Islamabad on February 8, 2003 following the December 2001 attack on Indian Parliament when India expelled Pak acting HC Jalil Abbas Jilani in Feb. 2003 and registered a case of funding Kashmiri separatists against him. The stand off was avoided by India withdrawing the name of Sudhir Vyas and proposing that of Sharat Sabharwal as new envoy.

1947 Britain decides its Indian empire into secular but mainly Hindu India and Muslim Pakistan, triggering one of the greatest and bloodiest migrations of modern history.

1947-48 India and Pakistan go to their first war over the disputed Himalayan region of Kashmir. The war ended with a UN-ordered ceasefire and resolution, seeking a plebiscite for the people of Jammu and Kashmir to decide whether to become part of India or Pakistan.

1965 India and Pakistan go to war over Kashmir. Fighting ends after United Nations call for ceasefire.

1971 Pakistan and India go to war a third time over East Pakistan, which became independent Bangladesh.

1972 Pakistan Prime Minister Zulfiqar Ali Bhutto and Indian Prime Minister Mrs. Indira Gandhi sign agreement in Simla to Ray principles meant to govern relations.

1974 India detonates its first nuclear device.

1990 Indian Army opens fire in Kashmir's summer capital Srinagar during protest against Crackdown on separatism, killing 38 and spurring a revolt. India accuses Pakistan of arming and sending Islamists militants into Indian Kashmir.

1998 May-India carries out fire underground nuclear tests and announces plans to build a nuclear arsenel; Pakistan conducts Six tests of the own in response on May 28, 1998.

1999 February—Indian Prime Minister Atal Behari vajpayee makes a historic Bus ride to Pakistan for summit with Pakistani counterpart Nawaz Sharif.

1999 May—The two countries stand on the brink of their fourth war after India launches major counter-strike against Pakistani intruders dug in on mountains in Kargil in Indian Kashmir.

2001 July—Summit between General Pervez Musharraf and Vajpayee in the Indian city of Agra ends in failure.

2001 December—Militants attack Indian Parliament. Fourteen people including the fire assailents are killed. India blames Pakistan—based Kashmiri separatists groups Lashkar-e-Toiba and Jaish-e-Mohammad and demands action against them.

2003 Pakistan announces ceasefire along the line of control, the defector border in Kashmir. India welcomes the move.

2004 The two countries launch a peace process that brings an improvement in diplomatic, sporting and trade links but no progress on Kashmir. Peace process comes under strain from occasional bomb attacks in India.

2008 July 7, India says Pakistan's ISI was behind a bomb attack on the Indian Embassy in Kabul that killed 58 people.

2008 Nov. 26—Mumbai attacks bring tension to the highest level since the weeks following the December 2001 attack on India's Parliament. Tensions are running high between India and Pakistan after Pakistani militants attacked Mumbai.[16]

Former Pakistan foreign minister Capt. Gohar Ayub Khan son of Late Field Marshal Ayub Khan says that Pakistan would have launched a full-fledged air attack on India had it attempted to prevent its 1998 nuclear tests. He mentions this fact in his new book "Testing Times as Foreign Minister".

Pakistan has requested India to allow it to open a consulate in Amritsar to facilitate Sikh pilgrims who want to visit their gurudwaras in Pakistan. Chairman of the Evacuee trust property board Asif Hashmi made this disclosure on April 20, 2009.[17] If the government of India grants such a requests, in all its wisdom it will not, it would make another blunder. Pakistan's denials, lies, white lies, blatant lies, willful ignorance, deliberate falsehood and Islamic fundamentalism resulting in generating more and more militants and terrorists have attracted the concern of world polity. Pakistan's denial mode on 26/11 Mumbai carnage is known world over. Now Pakistan makes a hue and cry with US special representative Richard Holbrook saying "New Delhi was using Kabul to destabilise Pakistan'. Us rubbished Islamabad's allegation and directed it to worry about its own terrorists rather than Indian presence in Afghanistan. Mr. Holbrook narrates an incident "Quote Pakistan has told me India has hundred of people in (the consulate) at Kandhar. I asked people asked Americans and the UN how big is the Indian Consulate in Kandhar ... and they said six to eight people. unquote."[18] During his recent visit to New Delhi, even Gen. (Retd.) Musharraf harped on India's two consulates in Afghanistan and conveniently forgot ISI's role in bombing Indian Mission in Kabul. Such are the ways of Pakistan vis-a-vis India, which is considered as enemy No. 1 by Pakistan and yet it wants India to come to the negotiating table for talks for it is sure India will.

US Vice-President Joe Bidden impressed upon Pakistan stating "there got to be an overall culturally difficult thing to happen, a realization that India in not the enemy ..... It is FATA, it is Mehsul, it's the al Aqeda influence, it's the Taliban." Biden, a known authority on Pakistan and AFghanistan further stated "it (Pakistan) is a badly fractured country" and Pakistan needs to move away from its India enemy mentality. Biden stated this opinion on April 29, 2009 while answering a question at Fundrainer meeting in Housten.[19]

World personalities and authorities have, time and again, given caution to Pakistani authorities even warning it on its very existence. Mr. David Kilcullen, a former Lt. Col. in the Australian Army turned Reservist turned US state Department strategic advisor to Gen. David H. Petraeus of the Iraq theatre warned Pakistan on March 22, 2009 predicting in the 'Washington Post' that 'We are now reaching a point within one to six months we could see the collapse of the Pakistani state, also because of the global financial crisis, which just exacerbates all these problems.... the collapse of Pakistan, Al Qaeda acquiring nuclear weapons, an, extremist takeover—that would dear everything we've seen in the war on terror today."[29] British Prime Minister Gordon Brown, who war on a visit to Islamabad described Pakistan's tribal belt near Afghan border as a 'crucible of terror" on April 27, 2009. He further said "Al Qaeda continues to find safe heavens in border areas and from there they continue to plot deadly attacks not only on your country but on ours".[21] On April 27th itself Gordon announced a 10-million pound package to boost the Islamic nations center-terrorism capabilities." President Zardari pulled out of the Press Conference with Brown for his remarks branding Pakistan the 'crucible of terrorism'.[23] Pakistan had disliked Obamas action in cutting aid and asking for accountability. A free hand to Taliban to come towards urban cities was allowed as a reply to reduction in aid and asking for accountability. But the moment US prepared to announced $1 billion gift to Pak during Zardari's trip to Washington made Pak Army to show action against Taliban. All these are tactics played by Pak Army toe extract billions of dollars and pounds. But many feel it is windo-dressing to extract aid during the Zardari visit. Ms. Fatima Bhutto, piece of Benazir, wrote a scathing op-ed in an online journal. She wrote "It is phenomenally silly to give that kind of money to a President who was facing corruption charges. It is also dangerous."[24] Many other critics warned that Pakistan's offensive against militant could be just a ploy to shaw its commitment to the war on terror.[25] President Barak Obama expressed 'grave concerns' on April 29, 2009 about the prevailing situation in militancy-hit Pakistan but was confident that the US "can make sure that Pakistan's nuclear arsenel is secure.". Obama also commented that Islamabad had begun to recognise its 'misguided' obsession with India and branded the Pakistan civilian government is 'very tragile' that did not seem to have the capacity of deliver basic services to the people.[26] But prime minister Yusuf Raza, Gilani dismissed (May 1) Barak Obama's unusual censure of the Pak government saying that his remarks of 'very tragile' was President's personal opinion.[27] Meanwhile, French Law maker, lawyer and foreign policy expert Pierre Lellouche fold Reporters in New Delhi on April 30, 2009 after a fact-finding visit of Islamabad that 'Pakistan has a "fire inside its won Rouse." There is 'not a lot of time in the light of gravity of situation.[28]

Indo-Pak relations touched another law when Taliban Commander Hakeemullah Mehsud, the head of the militants in Aurakzai Agency and a deeply of Tehrik-e-Taliban chief Baitullah Mehsud demolished eleven homes of members of Sikh Community in Aurakzai tribal region after they failed to pay 'Jaziya' (a tax levied on non-muslims)[29]. Taliban forced a cloth merchants family of Kalyan Singh out of their houses and shops and occupied his properties when he failed. Pay 13 million rupees demanded by Taliban. All the 24 members of his family were ousted. He himself was kidnapped and was released only after he paid Rs. 3.5 million out of $13 million.[30] Targeted by Taliban, 35 Sikh families began migrating from Orakazai area when they were unable to pay Jamia (protection money). A local Jirga ruled that Sikh Community should annually pay Rs. 15 million ($ 787000) as Jazia. Earlier the demand was for Rs. 50 million but later on it was reduced to 15 million rupees.[31] The militants acted after a deadline set by them for payment of 'Jaziya' by Sikh expired on April 29, 2009.[32] More than 400 Sikh families from Orakzai Agency in FATA moved away and sought refuge in Gurdwara Punga Sahib in Hasan Abdal.[33]

Government of India lodged official protest on May 1, 2009 expressing concern about the treatment meted out to minorities specially Sikhs in Swat Valley by Taliban. Pak foreign office spokesperson Mr. Abdul Basit said his country had responded to India's 'verbal demarche' on the issue by making it clear that the Sikhs were Pakistan's citizens; PM Manmohan Singh too personally voiced Indias concern on May 2 saying that it was the duty of Pakistan government to protect the interests of its minorities. "Jaziya is uncalled for. We have protested to them that the Sikhs there are not being treated properly.'[34] Meanwhile US Commission on International Religious Freedom, an independent body set up under a mandate of US Congress blamed Islamabad for 'ending effective control of more of the country to the Taliban associated extremists groups. Particularly acute are violations against Shia, Muslims, Ahmadis, Christians, Hindus and Sikhs.[35] Later on Richard Holbrook the US special envoy for Afghanistan and Pakistan stepped in to control the hurt feelings on Zardari-Gilani government stating that "President Obama has very deep personal feelings for Pakistan. As a young man he visited Pakistan. His mother worked there, she loved Pakistan." And that the government in Islamabad in capable of running the country. They are democratically elected, a five group of people."

By and large, President Gen. Musharraf's last three years rule i.e. between 2004 and 2007 can be termed as the period when Indo-Pak relations were tension-free. But the Bombay carnage of November 26, 2008 again worked as a damper and put a spoke into it. On Jan. 6, 2004 President Gen. Musharraf assured India that he will not permit any territory under Pakistan control to be used to support terrorism in any manner on April 18, 2005 when Gen. Musharraf and Prime Minister Manmohan Singh met in New Delhi, they reaffirmed the commitment of the two countries for durable peace declaring that "the peace process was nor irreversible". Soon after both of them met in New York on September 14, 2005 during United Nations meeting and issued a joint statement reiterating their pledge not to allow terrorism to impede the peace process. On September 16, 2006 both Gen. Musharraf and PM Manmohan Singh met in Havana where they agreed that terrorism is a courage that needs to be effectively dealt with and decide to put in place a joint institutional mechanism to combat terrorism, Gen. Musharraf had confessed that Pakistan and India were tantalisingly close to an agreement on Kashmir and two other contentious issues during his rule—Kashmir, Siachen and Sir Creek. Potential agreement on Kashmir was based on (i) demilitarisation (ii) self-governance and (iii) a joint mechanism. He wanted demilitanisation on the line of control and also within Kashmir and suggested Indian military to move out of Srinagar, Baramulla and one more city. On the point of self governance, Gen. Musharraf desired to give maximum governance to people of Kashmir on both the sides. His idea was to make the LoC irrelevant.

By the way, one of the ISI agents Amir Ahmed @Bhura, arrested in Meerut on Jan. 10, 2009 during his interrogation has disclosed that Pakistan is preparing for a final war with India in the year 2012.

(August 24, 2011) which are reproduced below:

(i) Payment of Rs. 75 crores to Pakistan on account of division of assets of undivided, Rs. 20 crores were paid in August 1947 and balance of Rs. 55 crore in January 1948 even as Pakistan was attacking India.

(ii) Non pursuit of its claims vis-a-vis Pakistan for non-payment of the letters Partitioned debt of Rs. 300 crores.

(iii) Conclusion in 1960 of the Indus Water Treaty under which India, though it had 40 per cent of the catchment area, agreed to an allocation of only 20 per cent of the flows of the Indus Waters. In addition, it agreed to pay Pakistan over 62 million pounds sterling for building replacement canals, reservoirs etc.

(iv) Following Pakistan's defeat in 1971 India, rather than imposing a settlement upon it. choose to negotiate an agreement with it at Simla in 1972 for across the board normalisation of relations. In the process India returned the 5386 square miles of Pakistani territory captured by it in Sind (5000 square miles) and Punjab (386 square miles) without expecting any guide pro quo.

(v) India obtained 'the concurrence of Bangladesh" for the return of nearly 92000 Pakistani prisoners of war held by it under the Joint India-Bangladesh Command without asking for anything in return.

(vi) India facilitated Pakistan's entry into NAM in 1979 and re-entry into the commonwealth in 1989.

(vii) India has for years, been unilaterally according Pakistan most favoured nation's treatment. Unquote.

LoC & Recent attempts to infiltrate into Kashmir (743 Km. LoC)

The present line of control (LOC) came into being in July 1972 after Shimla Agreement between Z.A. Bhutto and Indira Gandhi. Representatives of Army Chief of both the countries held a series of nine meeting in suchetgarh (India) and Wagha (Pakistan) between August and December 1972. Indian side was led by Lt. Gen. P.S. Bhagat whereas Pakistan was represented by Lt. Gen. Abdul Hameed Khan. LoC was meticulously delineated on two sets of map prepared for each other, each set consisted of 27 maps.

From July, 2001 onwards Gen. Pervez Musharraf had been harping on making the LoC irrelevant. Pakistan, of late, has been trying hard to breach LoC with India in J&K sector.

Number of Infiltration[36]

In the year	2002	1504
	2003	1374
	2004	537
	2005	597
	2006	573
	207	499

War casualties[37]

	India	Pakistan
1947-48	1104	1500
1965 war	3264	3800
1971 war	3843	7900
Kargil	522	696

Indian estimate of Pak soldiers/infiltrators killed in Kargil is 1100 plus, Gen. Musharraf's figure in 357, Nawaz Sharif's figure in 2700.[38]

2008

July 2	In Karnah sector about 15 heavily armed militants tried to infiltrate. A night-long battle ensued in which 6 militants were killed by Indian Army.
July 28	Pak troops intrude in Nowgam sector in Kupwara, kill an Indian soldier.
Aug. 22-24	3-day long encounter with militants in Machil sector in Kupwara. 14 militants killed.
Sept. 26-27	Laanz area of the Kangan-Bandipore belt in an encounter Indian Army killed 7 militants.
Nov. 8	6 militants trying to cross the LoC in Poonch district. 4 were killed by Indian Army whereas 2 escaped.

2009

Jan. 1	Militants/terrorists spotted in Mandhar in Poonch where in a 9-day encounter only 2 terrorists could be killed. Rest escaped.
March 21-25	More infiltration on March 21 in Uri sector in comparison of last year. In fact 3-told increase in infiltration in March 2009 was noticed. 5-day long operation-encounter in Kupwara area. 18 terrorists were killed.
March 23	Encounter in Kupwara, 17 militants killed
March 25-26	Yet another batch of 15-20 militants was intercepted by our Army in Gurer sector. Some of the militants escaped.
April 2	A group of militant infiltrators encountered by Indian army. 2 infiltrators killed while others escaped from Gurez area to Lolab forests. 1 militant infiltrate caught by Army.

April 6 In gun-battle that lasted for 3 days in Midnapore village in Lolab valley of Kupwara district. 2 top commanders of LeT killed. Encounter called off on April 7, 2009.

Security agencies have detected that in the first two weeks of March (2009) militants infiltrated in three groups—One comprised 10 Huji militants, the second was a large contingent of 120 men mostly Pashtum from a new group and the third a batch of 28 militants. Army intercepted the third group while the other two groups sneaked in unnoticed. The used LoC in Gurez Sector.[39] A Pakistani militant Sahib Moimullah Shah, a resident of Katanpayeer village of Dir district in NWFP, a first infiltrator to be caught alive from Shansabari forests after sneaking into Gurez valley around March 21, 2009 was presented by the Army before the media on April 25 confessed "In all 120 of us infiltrated into Kashmir, 31 were terrorists from Hizbul Mujahideen Lashkar-e-Tayyeba, Jaish-e-Mohammaed and Pir Payal Rangers to take part in Jehad. Rest were porters and guides and snow cutters. Before coming to Kashmir alongwith other militants we were given weapons training at Manshera forests in Pak for one month."[40] J&K Police had arrested Ashiya Begum (25 years) from the Sundarban area of Rajouri district while she was trying to infiltrate in November last year (2008). She disclosed that "700 women were being trained in ISI-run camps at Bhimbar, Kotli, Sinsa where they were being shown video footage of the tensing on the LoC and taught hair to breach it."[41]

July 27 Three militants trying to infiltrate near Eagle post in Northern Tangdhar sector of Kupwara district were killed by Indian Security Forces in an esnuing fierce gun battle. The heavily armed militants were trapped and asked to surrender but they opened fire and got killed.

Ministry of Home Affairs of Govt. of India states that till June 30, 2011, 1283 Pakistani nationals who entered India were untraced/missing. After entering India they had not returned to Pakistan.

August 5 Two infiltrators killed along LoC in Karen sector two militants billed at Tregham. Gunbatte was on at Didan Gate in Pir Paryal range but no casualty. In total, eight militants were killed along LoC while speaking into Indian territory.

In June, July and August 2009 about 20 infiltration attempts were foiled and 25 terrorist killed. The corresponding period last year in 2008 saw eight infiltration attempts in the valley. A peculiar feature of the infiltrators sneaking into Kashmir from across the LoC was that they were diehard fighters in the age group of 18 to 30 (The Pioneer August 26, 2009).

August 10 Two militant killed in Gurez and Karen sectors during infiltration bid by them.

August 20 Terrorist sneak in across LoC in Kupwara. One terrorist killed GPS and ammunition recovered.

August 23 Infiltration bid foiled along LoC in Macchil sector of Kupwara. 2 militants killed.

September 2 Five militants killed in cross over bid in Gurez Sector.

September 9 In Mendhar sector of Poonch district Army gunned down three militant infiltrators. Major Akash Singh Sambayal of 5 Maratha Light Infantry sacrificed his life for the nation in this action.

2010 25 infiltration attempts were made by terrorist across LoC in August and September and 40 terrorist killed by our security forces in the same period.

Terorrism in J&K continues to be dominated by foreigners of the 398 terrorist killed in 2008-09. 304 (76%) were foreign nationals. In 2008 of the 237 militants killed 171 were foreigners and in 2009 of the 161 militants killed, 131 were foreigners. (The Pioneer, October 18, 2010 article by Joginder Singh "Callow and Unreliable")

Aug. 29-30	Army killed nine terrorist in a failed infiltration attempt near the LoC in the sector. The infiltrating militants were numbering about 15.
October 23, 2010	Three terrorists were killed as the Army foiled an infiltration bid near the LoC in the Uri sector.

Recent Drone Attacks by US an Militants in Pakistan (since June 2004)

Though very late, US realised the fact that Pakistan would not fight the Al Qaeda and Taliban militants in the tribal areas where Al Qaeda Chief Osama bin Laden and its second-in-command Al Jawahiri are believed to be hiding. At last America concluded that if has to be effective in its 'war on terror', it has to swung into action using their drones in militant areas to destroy them. There was vehement objection to the use of drones in Pakistan terrirtory by Pakistan's foreign minister and the President of the Islamic Republic of Pakistan. The objections were lodged before the US special envoy Richard (Holbrook and Joint Chiefs of Staff Adm. Mike Mullen during their visit to Kabul and Pakistan in the second week of April 2009. (April 6, 2009) Pak foreign minister Shah Mehmood Qureshi told the above referred US personalities on April 7, 2009 that drone attacks fulled extremism in the nuclear-armed nation and that the drone attacks to which Pakistan is opposed—work to the advantage of the extremists and Hagged up "red lines' in Pakistan's cooperation with Washington.[1] Taliban leader Baitullah Mehsud vowed on April 5 to unleash two suicide attacks a week unless the CIA stopped firing missiles at militants. Despite threats of retaliation from Pakistani militants, senior administrative officials retorted on April 6, 2009 that the US intended to step up its use of drones to strik militants in Pakistan's tribal areas and might extend them to a different sanctuary deeper inside the country.[43]

Alarmed with the effectiveness of unexpected so many attacks by drones, militants have really shattered. Drone attacks have become a cause of concern for ISI Pakistan Army and militants of Al Qaeda and Taliban outfits. Nine out of twenty senior al Qaeda operatives have been killed last year in Drones attacks[44]. More than 35 missile strikes in the region have killed over 350 people, most of them terrorists since August 2008.[45] Pakistan has asked US to shift the drone technology and authority to Pakistan Army.[46] Make no mistake, America must never agree to such a suggestion of Pak Army least one day Pakistan uses the same technology against US itself. America, under no circumstances allow Pakistan to have any inkling of drone technology what to talk of allowing its use by Pak Army & ISI. Pakistan may try to steal it as its nuclear scientist A Q Khan did while developing nuclear technology for Pakistan.

ISI is concerned about safety and security of its protege Baitullah Mehsood. Had Pakistan Army been sincere in carrying out operations against militants, it would not have reflected US offer for joint ground operations in Pakistan to hunt down al Qaeda and Taliban leadership.[46] It seems non America has realised the double-dealings of Pakistan and it has started demanding results of the billions and billions of dollars it has been giving to Pakistan to fight terror. Believe it or not, Pakistan has always been snubbing America, particularly its ISI Chief.

Recall ISI Chief Lt. Gen. Mehmood Ahmad's behaviour and double dealing. He was in America on the sad day when 9/11 was done. He promised 'moon' to Richard Armitage but when he was sent to Kandahar by his Army Chief Gen. Musharraf to ask Mullah Mohammad Omar to hand over Osama bin Laden, he instead, asked him to resist any such move to hand over Osama. Incidently, the perfidy came to the knowledge of Gen. Musharraf and he removed Gen. Ahmed, the then ISI chief on October 7, 2001 itself. Pakistan plays double game, deceit and lies. World realised Pakistans behaviour after the Mumbai attacks on November 26, 2008. It persisted on denying that any of the participant militants were Pakistani national or the 'operation' was launched from Pakistani soil or any state actors of Pakistan were involved. It kept on denying all this inspite of the fact that FBI had investigated and found solid proof of participation of Pakistani nationals. So much so, Pakistan denied that one of the perpetrators of 26/11 was a Pakistani national inspite of FBI visiting his village and collecting all details. Way back in nineties one of the Pakistanis has in the presence and full hearing of ISI man (men) stated that Pakistan's foundation was laid on lies. What ISI fellows did to that Pak national, one can guess. Take another example of Kargil war. Pakistan denied infiltration by its Army personnel, when they died in firing by Indian security forces, Pakistan flatly and straightaway denied that those killed in action were Pak Army personnel and refused to accept their bodies. It was only after US President Bill Clinton gave them a stern warning. Pakistan withdrew the Army personnel (from NLI) from Kargil area. Now they are playing another clever game of asking US to give them drones for their use. In fact, Pakistan think they are the only clever people in the world. But President Obama, David E. Sanger, Bruce Riedel etc. have started realising the game played by Pakistan so far the main aim of Pakistan was to extract as much dollars as possible from America whereas their real friend in China. Let America stop giving them money and then see all the hardware of military concerns, America has given them, turn against America itself. The policy of Pakistan is "Agle ko Zirkao, agar na zirke to aappe Zirak Zao" (bully and terrify the opposite party, if it refuses or does not feel bullied or terrified then you yourself withdraw). Pakistanis creating panic among the civilised world on the name of Taliban. In reality, Pakistan Army does not want to fight muslims in muslim land. Even to Ajmal Kasab, there were instructions to spare muslim from killing in mumbai in the wake of 26/11. Did Pak Army not fight the taliban militants in 'Lal Masjid' in the heart of Islamabad and silence them? Now what holds them to replay the who action in Swat Mingova etc.? The hard line derik Abdul Aziz who was trying to escape wearing a 'Burka' veil of ladies and was captured on July 10, 2007 has been granted bail by Supreme Court on April 15, 2009 and is back in the Lal Masjid. Pakistan demands aid without strings from the United States which has been rejected by Obama administration and for the first time in US Pak relationship, Pak has become stunned. Pakistani elite is making so much hulla-ballu simply because they are afraid that once Taliban rule comes in force, their lavish life style would be curtailed. Yet Pakistan Army would not fight taliban even if they take over the administration of whole of Pakistan. It could be a temporary set back for Pakistan, but it would emerge victorious, more robust and vibrant once America again hands them over billions and billions of dollars. Pakistan alone is highly capable of coping up with Islamic insurgency and it would emerge stronger and stronger. David Kilcullen's assessment that Pakistan could be facing internal collapse within six month is right in the sense that Taliban militants, may take control all over Pakistan and the makes might fall in the hands of these militants. Now here meica Israel and India has to ensure that it does not happen. More and more drone attacks would desprive militants fr os preading their tantacleo all over Pakistan.

Drone Attacks on Pakistan by the US

1. June 18, 2004	5 killed in a strike near Wana (Pak).
2. May 14 2005	Haitham al-Yemeni an Al Qaeda explosive expert from Yeman, killed.
3. Nov. 30, 2005	Al Qaeda 3 Abdul Haza Tabia & killed.
4. Jan. 13, 2006	Damdola strikes (air) by US drones killes 18 in Bajaur but misses Ayman Al Zawahiri, Al Qaeda N.2.
5 April 26, 2008	4 killed in village saidgi in North Waziristan.

6 June 19, 2007	20 killed in Mami Rozha in North Waziristan.
7 Nov. 2, 2007	5 killed in an attack on a madarsa in North Waziristan.
8 Jan. 29, 2008	Abu Laith al-Libi, a senior Al Qaeda leader killed in North Waziristan.
9 Feb. 27, 2008	12 people killed in a strike near Kalosha village in South Waziristan.
10 March 18, 2008	16 killed in a strike in South Waziristan
11 May 14, 2008	12 including Abu Salayman Al-Jazairi killed near village of Damdola.
12 July 28, 2008	Midhat Mursi and 5 other Al Qaeda operatives killed in South Waziristan
13 Sept. 8, 2008	23 killed in Daande Daropkhel airstrike
14 Sept. 30, 2008	6 killed in a strike near Mir Ali, Pakistan
15 Oct. 16, 2008	Senior Al Qaeda leader Khalid Habib killed.
16 Oct. 22, 2008	4 killed in a village near Miranshah by missiles fired from suspected US drone
17 Oct. 26, 2008	20 killed in a strike in South Waziristan
18 Oct. 31, 2008	20 killed including Al Qaeda operative Abu Akash after 4 missile hit Waziristan.
19 Nov. 14, 2008	12 killed in a strike near Miranshah
20 Nov. 22, 2008	British Al Qaeda operative Rashid Rauf and 4 others including Abu Zubair al-Masri killed in a strike in North Waziristan. (Rashid Rauf killing in doubtful).
21 Dec. 22, 2008	At least 8 killed in South Waziristan by suspected US drone strike.
22 Jan. 1, 2009	2 senior Al Qaeda leaders Usama al-Kini and Sheikh Ahmed Salim Swedan killed in a missile strike by US drones

23 Jan. 23, 2009	In the first attacks since Barack Obama became President, at least 14 killed in Waziristan in 2 separate attacks by 5 missiles fired from drones.
24 Feb. 14,2009	More than 30 killed when two missiles are launched by drones into Pakistan near the town of Makeen in South Waziristan.
25 Feb. 16, 2009	Strike in Kurram valley kills 30.
26 March 1, 2009	Strike in Sargodha village in South Waziristan kills seven suspected militants.
27 March 12, 2009	Twenty-four killed in attack in Berju in Khurram Agency[48] A militant camp and a hide out was destroyed.
28 March 16, 2009	US missiles hit a house in Chota Janikhed.
29 March 25, 2009	8 foreign al Qaeda militants killed in Makeen area of South Waziristan.
30 March 26, 2009	Killed 4 in north Waziristan. Same day hours after in another drone attack in Mir Ali in north Waziristan two vehicles were forgetted.
31 April 1, 2009	A pilotless US drone aircraft fired missiles at a Taliban compound in Orakzai region and killing 12 people.
32 April 4, 2009	US drones fired 3 missiles in northwestern tribal area killing 13 people.
April 8, 2009	4 militants killed in South Maziristan tribal area in missiles strike by US.
April 19, 2009	People killed in 2 missile attacks in South Waziristan-a stronghold of Baitullah Mehsud.

What one has to read behind the lines is that whereas the whole world is worried about Taliban spreading all over Pakistan, its prime minister Yusuf Raza Gilani comes out with a strange statement on April 20, 2009 rejecting American concern about the peace deal with the Talibanin Swat, saying Pakistan knew better about the policies it should adopt to tackle the problems of terrorism and extremism. Reacting to concerns expressed by US special envoy to Pakistan and AFghanistan. Richard Holbrooke, Gilani said: "He (Holbrooke) does not need to worry much about it. This is our country. We know the ground realities better than him. We know much better what kind of strategy should be evolved (to tackle insurgency)". Gilani said in an interior with Geo News channel.[8] Gilanis statement gives an impression that Pakistanis capable to control Taliban as and when it wants. It is not doing so presently simply to make the whole world in general and American in Particular concern so that they keep on showering dollars on Pakistan in the name of fighting terror or America's war on terror, without holding Pakistan responsible for accountability of the dollars so received. In contrast, President Obama made it clear on March 27, 2009 that if they had actionable intelligence about significant, high value terrorists, they will do whatever is necessary to take care of that threat.

On April 10, 2009 "The News", a Pakistan Daily newspaper reported as follows: "Of the 60 cross-border predator strikes carried out by the Afghanistan-based American droner in Pakistan between January 14, 2006 and April 8, 2009 only 10 were able to hit their actual targets, killing 14 wanted al-Qaeda leaders besides perishing 687 innocent Pakistani civilians. The success percentage of the US predator strikes thus comes to not more than six percent. Figures compiled by the Pakistani authorities show that a total of 701 people, including 14 al-Qaeda leaders have been killed since January 2006 in 60 American predator attacks targeting the tribal areas of Pakistan. Two strikes carried out in 2006 had killed 98 civilians while three attacks conducted in 2007 had slain 66 Pakistanis, yet none of the wanted al-Qaeda or Taliban leaders could be hit by the Americans right on target. However, of the 50 drone attacks carried out between January 29, 2008 and April 8, 2009, 10 hit their targets and killed 14 wanted al-Qaeda operatives. Most of these attacks were carried out on the basis of intelligence believed to have been provided by the Pakistani and Afghan tribesmen who had been spying for the US-led allied forces stationed in Afghanistan. The remaining 50 drone attacks went wrong due to faulty intelligence information, killing hundreds of innocent civilians, including women and children. The number of the Pakistani civilians killed in those 50 attacks stood at 537 in which 385 people lost their lives in 2008 and 152 people were slain in the first 99 days of 2009 (between January 1 and April 8)."

President Asif Ali Zardari, during his visit to Washington (May 7, 2009) renewed the demand for 'ownership' of Drones with President Barak Obama. US, so far, was wise to deny this facility to Pakistan. No wonder, Pakistan thinks of using these very drones against American targets. Regarding success of these drone attacks in Pakistan's tribal and troubled areas, Washington Post-quoting US Counter-terrorism officials claimed (June 1, 2009) to have killed about half of the 20 US designated high value al Qaeda and other targets. Meanwhile, Pak interior minister Rehman Malik also made a hue and cry against drone attacks. Pak newspaper 'Dawn' reported the Chairman of the Senate Armed Services Committee Mr. Car Levin as having stated force a congressional hearing that the attacks would not have taken place without the 'tacit approval' of the Pakistani leadership, so it was wrong on Islamabad's part to unilaterally blame the US for the missile hits. "Pakistan government is being dissigenuous claiming to oppose the drone attacks to win domestic support while being quiet happy to benefit from them". US official in Islamabad were reported saying. Pakistan, which was dubbed as "Denialistan"[9] by one of Pakistan's own commentators, is a past master of saying one thing, doing completely opposite and thin denying it. It is very taste in denying the even done by it.

April 29, 2009	US drone fired a missile into Pakistan's South Waziristan—a major sanctuary for al Qaeda and Taliban killing 6 militants.
May 9	5 persons killed 10 injured in a missile attack by US drone in South Waziristan. 4 missiles were fired at a home and adjacent seminary in Sararogha area of South Waziristan.
May 12	Missile fired by drone flattened a house in Sarakhwara in South Waziristan.
May 16	US drone fired missiles killed 27 and injured 6 in North Waziristan troubled area.
June 14	US Missile strike killed 5 people in Ladha area of South Waziristan targeting a militant vehicle. Uzbek and Arab militants were killed in the strike.
June 18	US drone fired at insurgent training camp killing 9 militants in Waziristan.
June 23	Drone hit with 3 missiles at Taliban position of South Waziristan killing 45 persons when it struck after a funeral of an insurgent commander killed earlier in the day.
July 3	Three missiles attacked a close ally of Mehsud by US drone and hit his hideout of Taliban Commander Noor Wali. Seven militant killed in Kohat Khel.
July 7	13 militants killed when the drone struck in Ladha an area in South Waziristan agency. Drone tired two missiles.
July 8	28 militants killed in two missile attacks by US drone in South Waziristan tribal region. One of US drones fired several missiles at a convoy of vehicle in Makeen area of South Waziristan tribal agency destroying five cars from which bodies of 18 militants were pulled out.

July 10 Two missiles fired from a drone destroyed a communication centre belonging to Baitullah Mehsud in South Waziristan.

August 5 Two missiles hit a sprawling high-walled compound of Ikramuddin Mehsud, a cleric whose daughter married Baitullah Mehsud in November 2008 in Makeen village of South Waziristan. Two militants and Baitullah Mehsud's wife were killed. Ikramuddin's daughter is second wife of Baitullah Mehsud. Late on it was reported by media that Baitullah Mehsud was also killed in this drone attack.

Aug. 11 US drone struck a militant training camp 7 km, from Ladda where Mehsood was said to have been killed. 10 suspected militants killed. Militants training camp was in Kanniguram where Baitullah was reported to have been killed on August 5, 2009.

PM Gilani, on August 17, 2009 again gave vent to his opposition to drone attacks by US in Pakistan. He said the continued drone attacks in the tribal areas were "counter productive" as the collateral damage of such strikes were exploited by the militants for fuelling anti-American sentiments in Pakistan. Yet it once again called upon the US to provide drone technology to Pakistan and demanded an end to predator strikes within its territory. The demand was made when US special envoy to Pak & Afghanistan Richard Holbrook met with PM Gilani where interior minister and state finance minister and US Ambassador to Pak Ann W. Patterson was also present.

August 27 Yet another strike by US dron in tribal area of Pakistan.

According to the website www.longwarjournal.com attacks on tribal area of Pakistan have killed more than 1900 insurgents since 2006 (till May 2011).

Newspapers & Periodicals referred

1. The Nation Pakistan
2. The Frontier Post Pakistan
3. Herold Pakistan
4. Newsline Pakistan
5. The Times of India
6. The Hindustan Times
7. The Pioneer
8. The Hindu
9. India Today
10. The Outlooks
11. The News Pakistan
12. The Statesman
13. The Indian Express

REFERENCES

1. Goodbye Shehzadi page 61 by Shyam Bhatia.
2. The Sunday Times of India Sept. 24, 2006 article will be the than last" by Indrani Bagchi.
3. The Indian Express March 29, 2009.
4. The Pioneer December 11, 2008 article 'Evidence? It is with Pakistan' by G. Parthasarthy.
5. PTI report on the text of the joint press statement. Appeared in the Hindustan Times January 7, 2004.
6. The Hindu Sept. 23, 2004 Report by Sridhar Krishnaswamy from UN.
7. The Hindu Sept. 25, 2004 Report by Harish Khare "India, Pakistan to explore possible options on Kashmir issue.
8. The Hindu April 19, 2005 Report by Amit Baruah.
9. The Hindustan Times April 19, 2005 PTI Report.
10. The Pioneer September 29, 2004 article Business at what cost by Kanchan Gupta.

11. The Pioneer Sept. 24, 2006 article "Shifty Policy". by Brahma Chellaney.
12. The Hindu April 13, 2009 PTI report 'No evidence to prove India's link.
13. Times of India, April 2009.
14. The Hindu April 13, 2009 PTI report "Resume talks, says Pakistan Minister.
15. The Indian Express, April 20, 2009.
16. Compilation by the Indian Express that appeared on December 1, 2008.
17. The Indian Express April 21, 2009 PTI report.
18. The Times of India April 27, 2009 'US endorses India's leading role in S Asia' by Chidanand Rajghatta from Washington.
19. The Times of India, April 30, 2009. PTI report & The Hindustan Times April 30, 2009 PTI report.
20. The Pioneer April 30, 2009 article by Gautam Mukherjee "Naive America, Silly policy.
21. The Indian Express April 28, 2009. PTI Report from Islamabad.
22. Ibid.
23. The Times of India dt. April 29, 2009 PM Report.
24. The Times of India dt. April 29, 2009 Report by Chidanand Raj & hatton. "US readies $ 1 BN gift for Pak."
25. The Times of India dt. April 29, 2009 Report by Omer Farooq Khan TNN.
26. The Pioneer May 1, 2009 Report by S. Rajgopalan from Washington: 'Obama gravely cultured.
27. The Times of India May 2, 2009 PTI Report.
28. The Indian Express May 2, 2009 PTI Report from Washington.
29. The Hindustan Times May 1, 2009. PTI Report.
30. The Times of India May 1, 2009. ANI Report.
31. The Pioneer at May 2, 2009.
32. The Times of India May 2, 2009.
33. The Times of India May 3, 2009 report by Yudhvir Rana of TNN.
34. The Times of India May 2 & 3, 2009 Times News Network.
35. The Pioneer May 3, 2009 Report by S. Rajagopalan from Washington.

36. Compilation taken from the Indian Express by March 29, 2009.
37. The Times of India December 24, 2008.
38. The Indian Express May 29, 2009.
39. The Indian Express April 21, 2009 Report by Muzanil Jaleel from Srinagar "upto 158 sneaked into Gurez with arm arrested militant.
40. The Indian Express April 26, 2009 and the Times of India of April 26, 2009.
41. India Today April 27, 2009 issue: The New Terror Threat by Bhavna Vij-Arora.
42. The Hindu April 8, 2009 AFP report.
43. The Times of India April 8, 2009 report by Eric Schmitt & Christopher Drew.
44. The Hindustan Times April 17, 2009—Pak double talk on drone attack? Report appeared in the New York Times.
45. The Indian Express April 5, 2009 13 killed in US Drone Attack in Pak-PTI report.
46. The Indian express April 9, 2009 Report by Rezaul H. Laskar
47. The Times of India April 9, 2009 Report by Chidanand Rajghatta.
48. The Hindustan Times, March 19, 2009.
49. The Indian Express April 21, 2009 PTI Report "Gilani rejects US concerns on peace deal withTaliban."
50. The Times of India May 13, 2009 Report by Shri Chidanand Rajghatta.

Bibliography

1. Friends Not Masters—Mohammad Ayub Khan.
2. Ayub Khan—Altaf Gauhar.
3. Memoirs—Lt. Gen. Gul Hassan Khan .
4. Diaries of Field Marshal Mohammad Ayub Khan 1966-1972 edited by Craig Baxter.
5. Three Presidents and an aide—Ambassador Arshad Sami Khan S.
6. The way it was—inside the Pakistan Army—Brig (Retd.) Z.A. Khan.
7. Working with Zia—General K.M. Arof.
8. Raiders in Kashmir—Maj. Gen.(Retd.) Muhammad Akbar Khan.
9. Pakistan—a dream gone sour—Roeded Khan.
10. Paksitan at the cross current of History—Lawrence Ziring.
11. Pakistan between Mosque and Military—Husain Haqqani.
12. Pakistans' Drift into extremism—Hassan Abbas.
13. The Idea of Pakistan—Stephen Philip Cohen.
14. Crossed swords; law, its Army and the Wars within—Shiya Nawaz.
15. Benazir Bhutto—Reconciliation, Islam Democracy & the West.
16. Deception—Pakistan, the United States and the Global—Adrian Levy & Clatherine Scott-clerk .
17. Pakistan—Owen Bennett Jones.
18. Pakistan affairs—Past & Present—Tariq Mahmood Dogar.
19. The Forbidden Truth—by Jean Charles Bristard & Guillaume Dasquie.
20. Descent into Chaos—Ahmed Rashid.
21. A History of the Pakistan Army—Brian Cloughley.
22. Goodbye Shehzadi—Shyam Bhatia.
23. The Duel—Tariq Ali.
24. Talibanisation of Pakistan—Amir Mir.

25. Flattering Flag of Jihand—Amir Mir.
26. The Search for Al Qaeda—Bruce Riedel.
27. Deadly Embrace—Bruce Riedel.
28. My life with Taliban—Abdul Saleem Zaeef.
29. Tinder box—M.J. Akbar.
30. The Rise and Fall of the Great Powers—Paul Kennedy.
31. Inside Al Qaeda and Taliban—Syed Saleem Shehzad x.

Index

O

P

Z